The NEW ENCYCLOPEDIA *of* SOUTHERN CULTURE

VOLUME 15 : URBANIZATION

D0980435

Volumes to appear in
The New Encyclopedia of Southern Culture
are:

The NEW

ENCYCLOPEDIA *of* SOUTHERN CULTURE

CHARLES REAGAN WILSON General Editor

JAMES G. THOMAS JR. Managing Editor

ANN J. ABADIE Associate Editor

VOLUME 15

Urbanization

WANDA RUSHING   Volume Editor

Sponsored by

THE CENTER FOR THE STUDY OF SOUTHERN CULTURE

at the University of Mississippi

THE UNIVERSITY OF NORTH CAROLINA PRESS

Chapel Hill

This book was published with the
assistance of the Anniversary Endowment Fund
of the University of North Carolina Press.

Designed by Richard Hendel
Set in Minion types by Tseng Information Systems, Inc.
Manufactured in the United States of America
The paper in this book meets the guidelines for permanence and
durability of the Committee on Production Guidelines for Book
Longevity of the Council on Library Resources.
The University of North Carolina Press has been a member
of the Green Press Initiative since 2003.

Library of Congress Cataloging-in-Publication Data
Urbanization / Wanda Rushing, volume editor.
p. cm. — (The new encyclopedia of Southern culture ; v. 15)
"Sponsored by The Center for the Study of Southern Culture at the
University of Mississippi."
Includes bibliographical references and index.
ISBN 978-0-8078-3370-4 (cloth : alk. paper) —
ISBN 978-0-8078-7139-3 (pbk. : alk. paper)
1. Urbanization—Southern States—Encyclopedias. 2. Cities and
towns—Southern States—Encyclopedias. 3. Popular culture—
Southern States—Encyclopedias. 4. Southern States—Social
conditions—Encyclopedias. 5. Southern States—Social life and
customs—Encyclopedias. I. Rushing, Wanda. II. University of
Mississippi. Center for the Study of Southern Culture. III. Series.
F209 .N47 2006 vol. 15
[HT384.U52]
975.003 s—dc22
2009655117

The *Encyclopedia of Southern Culture*, sponsored by the Center for
the Study of Southern Culture at the University of Mississippi, was
published by the University of North Carolina Press in 1989.

cloth   14 13 12 11 10   5 4 3 2 1
paper   14 13 12 11 10   5 4 3 2 1

Tell about the South. What's it like there.

What do they do there. Why do they live there.

Why do they live at all.

WILLIAM FAULKNER

Absalom, Absalom!

CONTENTS

In 1989 years of planning and hard work came to fruition when the University of North Carolina Press joined the Center for the Study of Southern Culture at the University of Mississippi to publish the *Encyclopedia of Southern Culture.* While all those involved in writing, reviewing, editing, and producing the volume believed it would be received as a vital contribution to our understanding of the American South, no one could have anticipated fully the widespread acclaim it would receive from reviewers and other commentators. But the *Encyclopedia* was indeed celebrated, not only by scholars but also by popular audiences with a deep, abiding interest in the region. At a time when some people talked of the "vanishing South," the book helped remind a national audience that the region was alive and well, and it has continued to shape national perceptions of the South through the work of its many users—journalists, scholars, teachers, students, and general readers.

As the introduction to the *Encyclopedia* noted, its conceptualization and organization reflected a cultural approach to the South. It highlighted such issues as the core zones and margins of southern culture, the boundaries where "the South" overlapped with other cultures, the role of history in contemporary culture, and the centrality of regional consciousness, symbolism, and mythology. By 1989 scholars had moved beyond the idea of cultures as real, tangible entities, viewing them instead as abstractions. The *Encyclopedia*'s editors and contributors thus included a full range of social indicators, trait groupings, literary concepts, and historical evidence typically used in regional studies, carefully working to address the distinctive and characteristic traits that made the American South a particular place. The introduction to the *Encyclopedia* concluded that the fundamental uniqueness of southern culture was reflected in the volume's composite portrait of the South. We asked contributors to consider aspects that were unique to the region but also those that suggested its internal diversity. The volume was not a reference book of southern history, which explained something of the design of entries. There were fewer essays on colonial and antebellum history than on the postbellum and modern periods, befitting our conception of the volume as one trying not only to chart the cultural landscape of the South but also to illuminate the contemporary era.

When C. Vann Woodward reviewed the *Encyclopedia* in the *New York Review of Books*, he concluded his review by noting "the continued liveliness of interest in the South and its seeming inexhaustibility as a field of study." Research on the South, he wrote, furnishes "proof of the value of the *Encyclopedia* as a scholarly undertaking as well as suggesting future needs for revision or supplement to keep up with ongoing scholarship." The two decades since the publication of the *Encyclopedia of Southern Culture* have certainly suggested that Woodward was correct. The American South has undergone significant changes that make for a different context for the study of the region. The South has undergone social, economic, political, intellectual, and literary transformations, creating the need for a new edition of the *Encyclopedia* that will remain relevant to a changing region. Globalization has become a major issue, seen in the South through the appearance of Japanese automobile factories, Hispanic workers who have immigrated from Latin America or Cuba, and a new prominence for Asian and Middle Eastern religions that were hardly present in the 1980s South. The African American return migration to the South, which started in the 1970s, dramatically increased in the 1990s, as countless books simultaneously appeared asserting powerfully the claims of African Americans as formative influences on southern culture. Politically, southerners from both parties have played crucial leadership roles in national politics, and the Republican Party has dominated a near-solid South in national elections. Meanwhile, new forms of music, like hip-hop, have emerged with distinct southern expressions, and the term "dirty South" has taken on new musical meanings not thought of in 1989. New genres of writing by creative southerners, such as gay and lesbian literature and "white trash" writing, extend the southern literary tradition.

Meanwhile, as Woodward foresaw, scholars have continued their engagement with the history and culture of the South since the publication of the *Encyclopedia*, raising new scholarly issues and opening new areas of study. Historians have moved beyond their earlier preoccupation with social history to write new cultural history as well. They have used the categories of race, social class, and gender to illuminate the diversity of the South, rather than a unified "mind of the South." Previously underexplored areas within the field of southern historical studies, such as the colonial era, are now seen as formative periods of the region's character, with the South's positioning within a larger Atlantic world a productive new area of study. Cultural memory has become a major topic in the exploration of how the social construction of "the South" benefited some social groups and exploited others. Scholars in many disciplines have made the southern identity a major topic, and they have used a variety of methodologies to suggest what that identity has meant to different social groups. Literary critics have adapted cultural theories to the South and have raised the issue of postsouthern literature to a major category of concern as well as exploring the links between the literature of the American South and that of the Caribbean. Anthropologists have used different theoretical formulations from literary critics, providing models for their fieldwork in southern communities. In the past 30 years anthropologists have set increasing numbers of their ethnographic studies in the South, with many of them now exploring topics specifically linked to southern cultural issues. Scholars now place the Native American story, from prehistory to the contemporary era, as a central part of southern history. Comparative and interdisciplinary approaches to the South have encouraged scholars to look at such issues as the borders and boundaries of the South, specific places and spaces with distinct identities within the American South, and the global and transnational Souths, linking the American South with many formerly colonial societies around the world.

The first edition of the *Encyclopedia of Southern Culture* anticipated many of these approaches and indeed stimulated the growth of Southern Studies as a distinct interdisciplinary field. The Center for the Study of Southern Culture has worked for more than a quarter century to encourage research and teaching about the American South. Its academic programs have produced graduates who have gone on to write interdisciplinary studies of the South, while others have staffed the cultural institutions of the region and in turn encouraged those institutions to document and present the South's culture to broad public audiences. The center's conferences and publications have continued its long tradition of promoting understanding of the history, literature, and music of the South, with new initiatives focused on southern foodways, the future of the South, and the global Souths, expressing the center's mission to bring the best current scholarship to broad public audiences. Its documentary studies projects build oral and visual archives, and the New Directions in Southern Studies book series, published by the University of North Carolina Press, offers an important venue for innovative scholarship.

Since the *Encyclopedia of Southern Culture* appeared, the field of Southern Studies has dramatically developed, with an extensive network now of academic and research institutions whose projects focus specifically on the interdisciplinary study of the South. The Center for the Study of the American South at the University of North Carolina at Chapel Hill, led by Director Harry Watson and Associate Director and *Encyclopedia* coeditor William Ferris, publishes the lively journal *Southern Cultures* and is now at the organizational center of many other Southern Studies projects. The Institute for Southern Studies at the University of South Carolina, the Southern Intellectual History Circle, the Society for the Study of Southern Literature, the Southern Studies Forum of the European American Studies Association, Emory University's SouthernSpaces.org, and the South Atlantic Humanities Center (at the Virginia Foundation for the Humanities, the University of Virginia, and Virginia Polytechnic Institute and State University) express the recent expansion of interest in regional study.

Observers of the American South have had much to absorb, given the rapid pace of recent change. The institutional framework for studying the South is broader and deeper than ever, yet the relationship between the older verities of regional study and new realities remains unclear. Given the extent of changes in the American South and in Southern Studies since the publication of the *Encyclopedia of Southern Culture*, the need for a new edition of that work is clear. Therefore, the Center for the Study of Southern Culture has once again joined the University of North Carolina Press to produce *The New Encyclopedia of Southern Culture*. As readers of the original edition will quickly see, *The New Encyclopedia* follows many of the scholarly principles and editorial conventions established in the original, but with one key difference; rather than being published in a single hardback volume, *The New Encyclopedia* is presented in a series of shorter individual volumes that build on the 24 original subject categories used in the *Encyclopedia* and adapt them to new scholarly developments. Some earlier *Encyclopedia* categories have been reconceptualized in light of new academic interests. For example, the subject section originally titled "Women's Life" is reconceived as a new volume, *Gender*, and the original "Black Life" section is more broadly interpreted as a volume on race. These changes reflect new analytical concerns that place the study of women and blacks in broader cultural systems, reflecting the emergence of, among other topics, the study of male culture and of whiteness. Both volumes draw as well from the rich recent scholarship on women's life and black life. In addition, topics with some thematic coherence are combined in a volume, such as *Law and Politics* and *Agriculture and Industry*. One new topic, *Foodways*, is the basis of a separate volume, reflecting its new prominence in the interdisciplinary study of southern culture.

Numerous individual topical volumes together make up *The New Encyclopedia of Southern Culture* and extend the reach of the reference work to wider audiences. This approach should enhance the use of the *Encyclopedia* in academic courses and is intended to be convenient for readers with more focused interests within the larger context of southern culture. Readers will have handy access to one-volume, authoritative, and comprehensive scholarly treatments of the major areas of southern culture.

We have been fortunate that, in nearly all cases, subject consultants who offered crucial direction in shaping the topical sections for the original edition have agreed to join us in this new endeavor as volume editors. When new volume editors have been added, we have again looked for respected figures who can provide not only their own expertise but also strong networks of scholars to help develop relevant lists of topics and to serve as contributors in their areas. The reputations of all our volume editors as leading scholars in their areas encouraged the contributions of other scholars and added to *The New Encyclopedia*'s authority as a reference work.

The New Encyclopedia of Southern Culture builds on the strengths of articles in the original edition in several ways. For many existing articles, original authors agreed to update their contributions with new interpretations and theoretical perspectives, current statistics, new bibliographies, or simple factual developments that needed to be included. If the original contributor was unable to update an article, the editorial staff added new material or sent it to another scholar for assessment. In some cases, the general editor and volume editors selected a new contributor if an article seemed particularly dated and new work indicated the need for a fresh perspective. And importantly, where new developments have warranted treatment of topics not addressed in the original edition, volume editors have commissioned entirely new essays and articles that are published here for the first time.

The American South embodies a powerful historical and mythical presence, both a complex environmental and geographic landscape and a place of the imagination. Changes in the region's contemporary socioeconomic realities and new developments in scholarship have been incorporated in the conceptualization and approach of *The New Encyclopedia of Southern Culture*. Anthropologist Clifford Geertz has spoken of culture as context, and this encyclopedia looks at the American South as a complex place that has served as the context for cultural expression. This volume provides information and perspective on the diversity of cultures in a geographic and imaginative place with a long history and distinctive character.

The *Encyclopedia of Southern Culture* was produced through major grants from the Program for Research Tools and Reference Works of the National Endowment for the Humanities, the Ford Foundation, the Atlantic-Richfield Foundation, and the Mary Doyle Trust. We are grateful as well to the College of Liberal Arts at the University of Mississippi for support and to the individual donors to the Center for the Study of Southern Culture who have directly or indirectly supported work on *The New Encyclopedia of Southern Culture*. We thank the volume editors for their ideas in reimagining their subjects and the contributors of articles for their work in extending the usefulness of the book in new ways. We acknowledge the support and contributions of the faculty and staff at the Center for the Study of Southern Culture. Finally, we want especially to honor the work of William Ferris and Mary Hart on the *Encyclopedia of Southern Culture*. Bill, the founding director of the Center for the Study of Southern Culture, was coeditor, and his good work recruiting authors, editing text, selecting images, and publicizing the volume among a wide network of people was, of course, invaluable. Despite the many changes in the new encyclopedia, Bill's influence remains. Mary "Sue" Hart was also an invaluable member of the original encyclopedia team, bringing the careful and precise eye of the librarian, and an iconoclastic spirit, to our work.

Representations of the historical South often feature cotton crops in the fields, the rural crossroads store, and the country church—all reflecting the importance of rural life for most southerners. But the urban South was a significant component of southern life from early on. Coastal cities like Savannah and Charleston connected southern colonies to the Atlantic world and its trade in slaves and staple crops, which would come to define the region. Cities along the Gulf Coast reflected enduring French and Spanish influences now seen as formative in those regions of the South. Later, inland river towns like Memphis and Nashville became crucial transportation and commercial crossroads as well as home to world-class musical cultures. Birmingham and Richmond supported industrial enterprises that brought modernization to the region, and Atlanta's growth led to its iconic role as regional leader by the early 20th century. Scenes of southern history played out not just on the plantations and in the small towns of the South but in cities as well. The slave markets of Charleston and Natchez, the Confederate government in Montgomery and Richmond, Sherman's burning of Atlanta, yellow fever epidemics in Memphis and New Orleans, unemployment lines in southern cities that dramatized the impact of the Great Depression, World War II's booming urban areas like Mobile and Biloxi with their military bases and defense plants, and the litany of civil rights sites, from Montgomery's Rosa Parks, to Jackson's hostile reception to Freedom Riders, to Birmingham's dogs attacking peaceful demonstrators, to Memphis's garbage strike that led to Martin Luther King's assassination—cities were staging grounds for events that anchor the broader southern imagination.

The urban South has come to play an even larger role than earlier as the South has lived through turbulent changes in the last few decades. The *Urbanization* volume of *The New Encyclopedia of Southern Culture* responds to these changes with a special focus on contemporary cities and the processes that are making them vibrant 21st-century communities. Globalization, gentrification, immigration, population change redevelopment, suburbanization, and white flight are all thematic articles that analyze the ways that southern cities remain in the process of development. The editors give due attention to urban problems, with entries on crime and delinquency, deindustrialization, resegregation, gangs, poverty, homelessness, and the underclass. The volume explores such concrete urban institutions and spaces as banks, schools, medical centers, and megachurches. Readers can explore waterfronts and historic districts, sports arenas and farmers markets. The Urbanization section of the *Encyclopedia of Southern Culture* was modest in coverage, with only eight key thematic articles. This *New Encyclopedia* volume has expanded coverage to 41 thematic articles and 23 entries on specific cities, chosen for their historical-cultural importance and their significance in showing urbanization's processes. Topical entries also include case studies with broad meaning for the South, including the desegregation of Little Rock's Central High School, the 1996 Atlanta Olympics, the annual convocation of the Church of God in Christ (a unique ritual of the religious South), New Orleans's Mardi Gras (with its concentrated illustration of regional issues of race, social class, and gender), and theme parks, from east Tennessee's Dollywood to Florida's Busch Gardens.

The New Encyclopedia of Southern Culture appears at a time of the South's transition, full of apparent social, cultural, economic, and political changes, and change is occurring at an accelerating rate. The urban South will surely be central to any future South. This volume gives glimpses of that future.

The NEW ENCYCLOPEDIA *of* SOUTHERN CULTURE

VOLUME 15 : URBANIZATION

GROWTH AND DIVERSITY IN
THE URBAN SOUTH

Urbanization describes the growth and expansion of cities and suburbs and the transformation of surrounding rural areas. It is a global phenomenon, dating back to antiquity. In comparison to Europe and Asia, American cities are fairly young, but even in the southern United States cities have been in existence since the colonial era and have played important social, economic, and cultural roles in the nation and region. Yet many fictional and historical accounts of southern life and culture depict a rural, and a rural-minded, South. Described by Tara McPherson as "the mythic location of a vast nostalgia industry" and referenced by social scientists who measure regional convergence, the rural South with its small towns and villages still captures the national imagination. In the minds of many Americans, a rural-urban dichotomy seems parallel to a North-South dichotomy; consequently, it follows that as the South becomes more urban, southerners are expected to become less southern. Not surprisingly, some discussions of urbanization in the South narrowly focus on a perceived homogenization of culture that blurs regional distinctiveness. Others, however, consider that contemporary works on globalization, urbanization, migration, and other social processes offer new perspectives for studying the dynamics of urbanization within the region and for presenting alternative explanations of southern life and culture.

Historically, until fairly recently, the majority of Americans have not lived in urban places and southerners have been the most rural. Since World War II, however, the United States has experienced explosive metropolitan growth. The majority of the country's population has become urban or metropolitan, with the South experiencing the greatest population increase. In the first half of the 20th century, the decline of agricultural production helped push rural southerners away from rural areas and into industrializing American cities. In the latter half of the century, the appeal of warm winters, the comforts of air-conditioned summers, the prospects of lower-cost housing in suburban vistas, the absence of unions, and the profitability of lower-waged labor drew newcomers to the South and reversed historical out-migration patterns. State and regional economic development efforts intensified after World War II. The Southern Economic Council, state and local governments, and other groups offered incentives for recruiting industry and promoting growth in southern states. Consequently, in 2008, 8 of the 10 fastest-growing metropolitan areas in the nation were located in the South. Because of global economic and population shifts associated with industrialization and deindustrialization, all cities and metropolitan areas face dramatic challenges. Despite periods of growth and decline and occasional disruptions caused by economic and environmental disasters, cities in the South and the nation display remarkable resilience and adaptability.

Cities are centers of art, music, and cultural activities, as well as hubs of economic activity, civic organization, and metropolitan growth. Accompanied by the industrialization of production and information, urbanization involves the centralization and bureaucratization of many activities in cities but also permits innovation and creativity to flourish. Designing and redesigning building codes for residential and commercial purposes, enacting zoning laws, recruiting industry, and maintaining a tax base to support an infrastructure of water, sanitation, transportation, recreation, as well as education, law enforcement, and health services, are a few familiar urban activities. The ongoing processes of urbanization are associated with increasing size, density, and diversity of human populations, along with changes in land use, technology, economic activity, social composition, and cultural practices. As people are drawn to cities, their numbers and needs affect and are affected by forms of economic development and artistic expression. Urbanization is linked with disruptions to traditional forms of social life and social relations, changes in social hierarchies, and the emergence of alternative lifestyles. Families get smaller and become economically dependent on wage labor. Gender roles and aspirations change. Religious affiliations and identities adapt to new circumstances. Patterns of production and consumption change and new demands are placed on human and environmental resources.

The South has been a site of dramatic population growth and notable social diversity, especially since the middle of the 20th century. Canonical southern literature, well known for capturing the details of life in southern rural communities and small towns, sometimes presages the effects of urbanization in the region. Faulkner's fictional trilogy, *The Hamlet*, *The Town*, and *The Mansion*, portrays the deterioration of rural life and small-town manners, transportation shifts—from walking to riding horses, then taking trains, automobiles, and planes—and the restructuring of southern agrarian society. Social scientists also have identified demographic and cultural shifts. Sociologist John Shelton Reed noticed more than 25 years ago that the vast majority of all southerners were urban. "If ever a society can be said to have repudiated agrarianism," he wrote, "the South, to all appearances, is it." Despite decades of cultural and social observations, however, the evidence of urbanization and metropolitan sprawl challenges deeply held understandings about a region noted for its historical ties to agricultural production, an enduring regional identity, resistance to industrialization, and ambivalence about city life. Hence, journalists and scholars, as well as advocates of economic development, sometimes find it more useful to talk about growth in the "Sunbelt," a region with rather indeterminate boundaries spanning North Carolina to Arizona and California. Discussions about growth in the Sunbelt tend to put the emphasis on exemplars of progress and prosperity, while sites deemed less progressive and less prosperous are discounted as exceptions, shadows, or dark spots. General discussions about economic progress and population shifts in the rapidly growing Sunbelt may be compelling, but they are unsatisfying and confusing. They remain somewhat vague and imprecise because they fail to consider the importance of southern history in global flows of commerce and culture. Critics have noted that studies of the Sunbelt region tend to overstate the demise of cities in the American Rustbelt. Similarly, it can be argued that the Sunbelt framework tends to exaggerate the achievement of progress and understate the complexity of urbanization and uneven development. The term also fails to consider the South as a socially constructed "place" of meaning and value and overlooks the effects of urbanization in areas outside of all but the largest metropolitan centers in the region. This examination of urbanization in the South, however, focuses on the processes of rapid growth, return migration, regional disparity, recovery and resilience, and the dynamic impact of globalization on southern communities and culture.

The title of David Goldfield's book, *Cotton Fields and Skyscrapers*, captures the clash of Old South and New South images and offers an apt metaphor for urbanization in a regional context. The southern physical landscape, once distinguished by cotton fields, rural communities, mill villages, and small towns dotting a sparsely populated countryside and connecting agricultural commodities to regional centers and global markets, has changed. Today, casinos, automobile manufacturing plants, medical centers, shopping malls, and upscale retirement communities make up the built environment on land where cotton and tobacco grew for generations. Theme parks compete with citrus groves along interstate highways in Florida and create jobs replacing those lost when extractive industries left disadvantaged Appalachian communities. Tourist resorts and upscale gated communities infringe on coastal wetlands and threaten mountain ridges. Textile mills have moved abroad, leaving mill villages to be inhabited by urban gentrifiers or razed by suburban developers. Urban farmers markets bring locally produced foods and agricultural products to city streets, despite the presence of supermarkets and the prevalence of global agricultural production. And those icons of 20th-century urbanization—skyscrapers—rise above expanding commercial districts in downtown Atlanta, Charlotte, Dallas, Houston, Miami, and Nashville.

Urbanization, as represented in physical and symbolic landscapes, supports Goldfield's observation that southerners tend to live in multiple time zones at once—past, present, and future. This is certainly the case for southerners whose lives and histories are embedded in metropolitan development and shaped by what C. Vann Woodward described as the "burden" of southern history. In some port cities established in the colonial era, including Charleston and Savannah, downtown neighborhoods financed with antebellum wealth and constructed with slave labor have been preserved. Their architectural design differs remarkably from many interior cities, such as Memphis, Montgomery, Selma, Birmingham, Greensboro, and Atlanta, which developed later and maintain commemorative sites on the very streets where the struggle for the civil rights movement took place. In various municipalities, particularly near county courthouses with streets renamed for civil rights leaders, it is not uncommon for memorials that champion civil unrest and nonviolence to stand only blocks away from monuments to Civil War generals and Civil War mortars. A few miles away, plantation pilgrimages offer tourists from the region and all over the world a nostalgic return to "the white-pillared past." For decades, many of these tours were supported by narratives of a grand and opulent past. Today, some are contested by counternarratives of enslavement and repression presented at nearby sites.

Tourism has become a major part of the southern economy. In the Mississippi Delta, the bright lights of Tunica casinos, built in the midst of cotton fields and sweet potato farms, attract millions of visitors to the nation's third-largest gaming resort for 24-hour nonstop gaming action and entertainment. Meanwhile, driverless tractors, computerized gins, and Internet commodity trading continue the agricultural revolution that introduced mechanical harvesters, incorporated plantations into agribusiness, and converted small farms into subdivisions with genteel southern names like Tara and Foxcroft. Tourists who venture past the casinos can choose to spend the night in a rented sharecropper's shack in Clarksdale, Miss., or at a bed and breakfast located at the "big house" in Natchez, or at any number of discount motels along interstate highways. Millions of tourists in the Smoky Mountains visit Dollywood, the theme park that offers gospel music during fall harvest time and names its rides after lumberjacks and miners—former figures in the regional economy now consigned to Appalachian folklore.

On Sunday morning, in most southern states, rural and urban churches minister to local congregations ranging from Presbyterians to Pentecostals, some of whom still profess old-time religion at 11 o'clock despite dwindling flocks. At the same time, tens of thousands of suburbanites drive automobiles along interstate highways to megachurches. Some of these churches appeal to multiracial congregations; others are predominantly white or African American. Some offer motivational and nondenominational messages in several different time slots. The messages are digitally displayed on Jumbotrons, as well as broadcast and podcast to millions of worshippers around the world.

Remarkable Growth. More than 50 years ago, sociologist Rupert Vance observed the prevalence of small cities in the South and deemed them unremarkable within a national context, except for their "recent rapid growth." Growth and metropolitan development continues its astonishing pace in what has become the most populated region of the United States. More than one-third of the population of the United States lives in the South. Between 1990 and 2000, 13 of the 20 fastest-growing metropolitan areas in the nation were located in the South, a region that attracts immigrants, retirees, and entrepreneurs, as well as military installations and transnational corporations. Along with diverse population growth and economic investment, striking social and cultural transformations are taking place in southern cities embedded in global flows of people, capital, and ideas. The cultural "mind of the South," once identified with bucolic agricultural images of an idealized rural past as critiqued by W. J. Cash, is being challenged by the dissonance of diversity ushered in by the civil rights movement, racial desegregation, economic restructuring, and migration. The crucible of cultural and economic interactions in post–World War II southern cities reflects the dismantling of Jim Crow, the interregional and transnational relocation of jobs, and the population influx of people from throughout the rest of the United States and the world.

Despite popular mythology of cultural homogeneity, southern culture was never limited to Anglo influences, or to Anglo and African cultures. After all, the Spanish founded St. Augustine, Fla., and San Antonio, Tex., and the French established New Orleans, La., Biloxi, Miss., and Mobile, Ala. And many pre–World War II downtown stores and businesses were owned and operated by immigrant families, including Jews and Italians. But urban settlements shaped by the dominance of plantation agriculture, then by Civil War and Reconstruction, received significantly fewer immigrants from foreign countries during 19th-century and early 20th-century waves of immigration than did northeastern American cities. Consequently, by 1970, the Southeast contained the smallest proportion of foreign-born population in the United States. But between 1990 and 2000, when a period of new investment and rapid growth generated intensified labor demands, particularly in the construction and meatpacking industries, the South became a receiving locality for transnational migration. Since 1990, southern states have shown the greatest increase in foreign-born populations, primarily from Mexico and Latin America. Following Hurricanes Katrina and Rita and other events in the 2005 hurricane season, large numbers of immigrants responded to demands for workers to remove debris and rebuild New Orleans, Biloxi, and other Gulf Coast locations. Some southern cities, previously identified with sending migrants to cities in other states, now receive record numbers of immigrants and are sometimes described as "the New Ellis Islands."

Today, the "Nuevo" South contains Spanish-language radio stations and newspapers that not only serve immigrant communities but also may redefine urban culture and images. Nashville, the country music capital of the world, has a new sound—norteño music. Mike Davis quips that "Los Tigres del Norte compete with Garth Brooks and chipotle complements chitterlings across a vast stretch of the South." Never mind those *Grand Ole Opry* fans still wondering how Garth Brooks, or perhaps Keith Urban, displaced "authentic" country music legends such as Roy Acuff, the Carter Family, and Hank Williams. In Memphis, the city known for blues, soul, and rock and roll, Beale Street Caravan—a locally based radio program syndicated by National Public Radio—hosted a show on Latino music showcasing local and international artists. In Texas, Houston's ethnic neighborhoods include a Little Saigon, two Chinatowns, and the largest Nigerian community in the United States. Meanwhile, "Little Mexicos," East Asian neighborhoods, and mosques have appeared throughout southern metropolitan areas. Cinco de Mayo, JapanFest, and Chinese Lunar New Year celebrations have been added to the list of southern community events, which also includes barbecue, blues, and catfish festivals as well as jazz and Mardi Gras.

It remains to be seen what kind of new urban collective identity is emerging. Some studies suggest that cosmopolitan newcomers want to acquire knowledge about local cultural and symbolic resources when they move from one region to another. Because they adopt local cultural practices, especially those associated with literature, music, and the arts, newcomers help reproduce local culture and perpetuate regional distinctiveness. But newcomers develop their own organizations and affect regional culture. A Japanese Chamber of Commerce based in Atlanta offers programs for improving understandings between American and Japanese workers in Georgia's Japanese firms. Jackson, Miss., hosts the International Museum of Muslim Cultures to educate the public about the diversity of culture and religion. Confucius Institutes, designed to enhance the understanding of Chinese language and culture and improve international relations, are located in most southern states. They can be found at the University of Memphis, North Carolina State University, University of South Carolina, Emory University, University of Central Arkansas, Troy University (Alabama), the University of South Florida, Texas A&M, and George Mason University. No matter what happens in the future, however, the flow of diverse peoples through the region makes it clear that the South is not, and never was, a static, racially dichotomous, and culturally homogeneous region. And the cultural crossroads for social and cultural dynamics can be found in cities.

Return Migration. Pete Daniel, looking at rural-urban migration in the 1950s, described a cultural collision taking place between the rhythm of the land and the beat of the city. The energy produced by the urban fusion of black and white country traditions formed rock and roll, challenged southern identity, and redefined global popular music. Today, migration and the fusion of rural rhythms and urban beats occurring in southern cities can be found in the contemporary sounds of norteño music, as well as with a brand of southern hip-hop culture known as "crunk." A synthesis of black rural musical tradition and post–civil rights urban experiences and sounds, crunk music calls attention to the South as America's "third coast" in the production of hip-hop. Film, as well as music, represents black life in the urban South for 21st-century audiences. Craig Brewer's film *Hustle and Flow* (2005) has been described by its producers as the first crunk film. Similarly, Chris Robinson's *ATL* (2006) and Bryan Barber's *Idlewild* (2006) stake claims to regional cultural ties. All of these shifts in population and culture contribute to newly emerging understandings about racial formation and region and stir new interest in redefining and reexamining southern culture.

But the return of hip-hop culture to southern roots is not the only noteworthy homecoming. The South, especially in large urban and metropolitan areas, has become a return migration destination for African Americans. Southern urban communities received significant migrations of African Americans and whites from rural areas between 1870 and 1930, which increased the region's urban population from 10 percent to 30 percent. But cities outside the South received significant flows of southern migrants that dramatically changed national and regional demographics. Approximately 4 million southern-born migrants, primarily but not exclusively African American, headed for industrial centers in the North and West during the Great Migration, seeking better economic opportunities and improved life chances. Many people embarked on their journeys from towns and cities, not just from rural areas. But since the 1970s, the interregional migration flow has reversed, creating a net in-migration of blacks to the South. Joining streams of primary migrants—black and white—who relocated to the South seeking lower taxes and warmer winters, former migrants and their offspring are returning to the region. And, despite the trend of metropolitan sprawl, since the 1990s, central city lofts and condominiums have attracted young childless adults to live and work in cities. This is especially true in Memphis and Atlanta.

Regional Disparities. Atlanta, benefiting from years of sustained economic growth and migration, is considered by many to be a mecca of black culture. The city's history from the civil rights movement, the visibility of black businesses and entrepreneurialism, the strong representation of blacks in public office, and the city's consortium of historically black colleges and universities resonate with newcomers and returning migrants. But, despite impressive social and economic gains, particularly in affluent neighborhoods, Atlanta, like other American cities, continues to report high poverty rates, especially among blacks and Latinos. Atlanta, along with New Orleans, Louisville, and Miami, ranks among the nation's top 10 large cities for high rates of concentrated poverty. Poor people living in disadvantaged neighborhoods segregated by low income face greater economic and social challenges than those living in neighborhoods where poverty is more dispersed.

Southern urban areas, like their counterparts throughout the United States, show evidence of uneven development. Consequently, urban landscapes are defined by pockets of prosperity and poverty. As is the case throughout the country, the most disadvantaged populations experience higher rates of infant mortality, school disengagement, violent crime, property crime, and health consequences of environmental pollution and degradation. National comparisons, however, show that southern city dwellers fare much worse. The proportion of city dwellers living in extreme-poverty neighborhoods is far above the national average. In 2000, New Orleans ranked second nationally in percentage of poor people living in neighborhoods of concentrated poverty. As a result of Hurricane Katrina and the breaking of the levees, 38 of the city's 47 extreme-poverty census tracts were flooded. The disaster highlighted the reality of urban disparities and the consequences for the South's most marginalized and vulnerable people, especially women and minorities. Southern cities also have higher rates of violent crime and property crime. In 2007, the 10 cities with the highest crime rates in the United States included five southern cities—Memphis, Baltimore, Nashville, Houston, and Dallas. Infant mortality, associated with high rates of poverty, low rates of education, and limited access to health care, also stands out. Memphis has the highest infant mortality rate in the United States, and infant mortality in the Mid-South is often compared to that of developing nations.

The regional differential for urban problems is usually explained by a combination of cultural and structural factors. For some time, patterns of violence have been associated with a culture of interpersonal violence that was transported to the South from the British Isles and shaped by frontier experiences and that became entrenched as part of the southern way of life. Others point to the southern region's legacy of structurally embedded disadvantage, created by slavery, sharecropping, and segregation. That legacy has been complicated further by federal urban redevelopment programs, which have produced varied results. Many of them have disrupted urban cores by destroying schools, residences, churches, and businesses in low-income communities and replacing them with expressways and housing projects. Metropolitan growth and sprawl have created pockets of distress as well as areas of prosperity within cities. By the 1970s, problems in the centers of southern cities began to mirror crises in cities such as Los Angeles, Philadelphia, and Detroit—places identified with higher rates of unemployment, pollution, and crime. The spatial mismatch between metropolitan job growth and people left behind in urban cores in the South is similar to that of cities in other parts of the United States. But the region's institutional foundation of social inequality and structural shifts, resulting from uneven development, produce and reproduce patterns of inequality. Poverty in southern cities is characterized by well-established historical patterns of class, race, and gender inequality, as well as emerging trends associated with transnational labor migration. Consequently, urbanization of the region since World War II has not changed national poverty rankings. The position of southern states may vary periodically, but overall they continue to occupy the lowest standings in terms of income and educational attainment.

Rapid growth produces additional strains and stresses. Southerners embraced the automobile in the 1920s and continue to have high rates of ownership. But what began as a symbol of mobility and progress has contributed to gridlock, sprawl, and pollution. Southern cities have been slow to endorse mass transit, although some commuters in Charlotte and Atlanta now have the option of leaving their cars behind and taking light rail into the city. Throughout the South, pressures to build roads, water lines, and sewers into newly sub-divided rural communities and retail shopping centers, as well as difficulties in managing overcrowded schools, still challenge local and state governments to find solutions. The settlement of non–English-speaking workers and families in communities having little or no experience in receiving immigrants further strains local governmental and educational resources and exacerbates commu-nity tensions in the "Nuevo South," reproducing Old South divisions.

Recruitment. Growth was the mantra of the New South era and has been the pride of the civic and commercial elite for more than a century. Business and property owners, especially members of religious institutions, civic clubs, and voluntary organizations who formed the leadership base in cities and towns, have promoted their visions of economic development and urban expansion. Bankers, merchants, brokers, lawyers, and entrepreneurs, as representatives of the major economic interests of southern communities, have played prominent and influential roles in shaping attitudes about urban growth and prosperity, as well as policies. Their ideas, primarily reflecting the goals and concerns of white elites and promoted through major media and voluntary organizations, have influenced public officials, affected competitive strategies for economic development, and informed social policies. A black commercial elite emerged in some cities, particularly in Memphis, New Orleans, and Atlanta.

After the Civil War and Reconstruction, urban boosters, like Atlanta's Henry Grady, promoted southern towns to northern financiers and investors as bases for expanding railroad lines, building factories, and employing cheap, nonunion labor. Although urban competition was a national phenomenon, this particular form of boosterism was prevalent in the South at the beginning of the 20th century. Southern municipalities competed with each other to recruit devel-opment by offering generous tax exemptions and bonds, often at the expense of public education and social programs. Many of these initiatives succeeded in attracting low-wage jobs for hiring displaced agricultural workers, but they failed to make the region more competitive by improving human capital.

During the Great Depression and World War II, federal dollars supported military bases, hydroelectric power development, and other economic stimu-lants that benefited southern towns and cities. In the postwar period, urban elites and boosters welcomed federal dollars for interstate highways and urban renewal. A succession of programs, such as the Title I Housing Act of 1949, the Community Development Block Grant in 1974, and the Urban Develop-ment Action Grant program in 1977, focused on businesses and jobs more than housing. Elected officials and chambers of commerce have promoted building airports, convention centers, hotels, sports arenas, and high-rise office buildings on urban landscapes. These projects typically have treated older and less affluent neighborhoods as "blighted" and in need of redevelopment, but redevelopment proposals often become contentious. Some have sparked neighborhood activism and fueled resistance.

One post–World War II development initiative, the plan for North Carolina's Research Triangle Park (RTP), has attracted widespread interest in a different type of economic development—the knowledge economy. The RTP was conceived as a means of diversifying the state's traditional industrial base, attracting high-technology industry, and creating employment for workers educated in science and engineering that were leaving the state. Faculty members from three universities—Duke, the University of North Carolina, and North Carolina State—the governor, and private funding launched the project in the 1950s. The RTP, founded in 1959, is now the largest research park in the world. The park has expanded to include 7,000 acres. The demands for housing and services for the 40,000 people who work there and their families have affected urbanization in the center of the state, especially in Raleigh, Durham, and Chapel Hill. The RTP serves as an economic development model for other areas, such as Memphis and Birmingham, where city leaders and public-private partnerships have intensified investment and participation in the knowledge economy. In 2009, the RTP hosted the 26th International Association of Science Parks' World Conference on Science and Technology Parks.

Southern economic development and urbanization also have been affected by the banking industry. In the 1980s, changes in federal banking laws, formation of the Southeastern Regional Banking Compact, and the implementation of new technologies to provide banking services, such as automatic teller machines, created opportunities for interstate banking mergers. These mergers led to the growth of large and profitable banking companies in the South. Because of population increases and business growth that occurred during this time, Charlotte and Atlanta became prominent centers of banking. Charlotte's recently acquired nickname—Wall Street South—reflects its position as the second-largest bank town in the United States, second to New York and ahead of San Francisco, although the city lost prestige and jobs with the global financial crises of 2008 and 2009.

Recruiting foreign investment is another post–World War II development strategy with profound consequences for urbanization. Interstate 85 from Charlotte to Atlanta has been described as the "autobahn," referring to the number of German companies located there. A BMW automobile plant, Hoechst chemicals, and others have spawned the growth of homes and businesses along the interstate and away from downtown areas. Japanese car companies have built plants along interstates in Tennessee, Mississippi, and Alabama. But the newly constructed Toyota plant in Tupelo, Miss., scheduled for opening in 2009, was delayed because of the economic downturn of the global economy.

Despite occasional stalls and setbacks, southern boosters can point to major success stories of accomplished southerners. Ted Turner and CNN in Atlanta and Fred Smith and FedEx in Memphis are the basis of stories of southern entrepreneurialism and global achievement. They also fuel aspirations of those who want their cities to become bigger and better and dream of being "world-class." Atlanta boasts of having the busiest passenger airport in the world and claims to be "the world's next great city." Memphis has been the busiest cargo airport in the world for more than a decade. Boosters describe Memphis as North America's Distribution Center. Orlando, in the center of the Florida theme parks, advertises its city as the happiest place on earth. Norfolk boasts of having the world's largest naval station. Tampa's Busch Gardens is recognized as one of the top 10 amusement parks in the world.

Religion. Modernization, migration, urbanization, and suburbanization supposedly contribute to the declining significance of religion, but this clearly is not the case in the American South. The region traditionally associated with comparatively high levels of religiosity and with the dominance of conservative Protestantism continues to be associated with the growth and expansion of evangelical Protestantism and Pentecostalism. Some religious groups, such as Catholics and Jews, historically had a minority presence in the region but are becoming more visible in rapidly growing communities. Wal-Mart, the corporation that changed small-town life all over America, has been responsible for attracting Muslims, Hindus, and Jews to Bentonville, Ark., as executives from suppliers have relocated from Boston and New York to be near their largest client. Some of these migrants are establishing new congregations and meeting in unlikely places. Bentonville's growing Jewish community obtained a former Hispanic Assemblies of God church building for its synagogue and named it Congregation Etz Chaim, Tree of Life.

Southern communities are not the only ones transformed by migrants seeking economic opportunity and religious continuity in urbanizing settings. During the Great Migration, African Americans who relocated in industrializing cities, including St. Louis, Chicago, and Detroit, often took their religious beliefs with them. Subsequently, the Church of God in Christ (COGIC), with modest beginnings in the rural South, has become the largest Pentecostal church in North America and the fastest-growing religious denomination in the United

States. For decades, COGIC church mothers established churches in diverse urban settings, planting churches and winning converts. These churches maintained networks of education and support within cities outside the South and between newly established urban congregations and the COGIC headquarters in Memphis. These churches also played an important role in the civil rights movement.

In recent years, the growth of suburbs and exurbs has contributed to the phenomenal increase of megachurches. Some of these congregations occupy former sports arenas; others build new campuses or expand older ones. They offer coffee shops, sports activities, and musical concerts for the 2,000 or more people who attend weekly services. Megachurches are not exclusively southern, but it is estimated that half of all megachurches in the United States are located in southern metropolitan areas, and Sunbelt states account for three-quarters of megachurches. They tend to be prevalent in sprawl cities, such as Atlanta, Houston, and Orlando. These expanding metropolitan areas, located near affluent populations, offer cheap land for buildings and parking lots as well as access to major highways.

Resilience. The first decade of the 21st century has brought many challenges to southern cities and metropolitan areas. They are confronted with pressures on resources brought by unprecedented population growth and sprawl, destruction in the aftermath of Hurricane Katrina and other disasters, a downturn in the global economy, fallout from the subprime mortgage crisis and restructuring of the financial industry, an aging and deteriorating transportation infrastructure, and severe state and local budget shortfalls. How will they remain viable for future generations? Whose needs will take precedence? How can cities meet current needs without sacrificing future potential?

If the history of urbanization in the South is any indication, southern cities will be resilient. In many ways, narratives of disaster and recovery define southern cities. Columbia, Charleston, Savannah, Richmond, and Atlanta rebuilt after the Civil War. Memphis recovered from the devastation of yellow fever. Charleston and New Orleans established the first two historic preservation districts in the South during the Great Depression of the 1930s. Cities from Atlanta and Selma to Jackson and Memphis, as well as others, have worked on racial reconciliation since the 1960s-era civil rights movement. Southern cities have embraced technology and innovation. In musical innovation, Memphis and Nashville stand out. Houston and Cape Canaveral embraced NASA. St. Jude Children's Research Hospital has flourished in Memphis. Atlanta has the Centers for Disease Control and Prevention. Research and treatments occurring in urban medical centers located in Memphis, Nashville, Houston, Birmingham, Durham, and other communities call positive attention to a region once associated with the debilitations of hookworm and pellagra among rural citizens, brown lung disease in textile workers, and black lung disease in miners. In the post-Katrina South, innovative and collaborative planning strategies, including charrettes (in which a group of designers drafts a solution to a design problem), have brought together professional planners, engineers, developers, and local residents to create pedestrian-friendly, sustainable communities for recovery.

A sense of place, and a commitment to rebuild, lies beneath ongoing efforts by residents to reclaim and reinvent southern cities. Some critics suggest that speculative investment practices escalate after crises and aggravate the conditions that make places seem more alike and less distinctive. In a similar vein, others argue that growth and diversity move southern cities toward a homogenized culture. But there is plenty of evidence to contest these claims in a region of economic productivity, cultural innovation, and social change. It is up to those who study the South to continue to wonder about what makes southern cities so vibrant and remarkable, to explore meaningful connections between the past, present, and future, and to explain how new forms of cultural identity and expression are related to processes related to urbanization and the global economy.

WANDA RUSHING
University of Memphis

Joshua Ambrosius, "Feeding the Lambs: Youth Engagement and Development Activities of Southern Megachurches," Southern Growth Policies Board (15 May 2008); Michael Barbaro, "In Wal-Mart's Home, Synagogue Signals Growth," *New York Times* (20 June 2006); W. J. Cash, *The Mind of the South* (1941); James C. Cobb, *The Selling of the South: The Southern Crusade for Industrial Development, 1936–1980* (1993); Peter A. Coclanis, in *Globalization and the American South*, ed. James C. Cobb and William Stueck (2005); Edward Cohen, *The Peddler's Grandson: Growing up Jewish in Mississippi* (2002); Pete Daniel, *Agricultural History* (Fall 1994); Mike Davis, *Magical Urbanism: Latinos Reinvent the U.S. City* (2001); Farah Jasmine Griffin, *Who Set You Flowin'?: The African American Migration Narrative* (1995); David R. Goldfield, *Cotton Fields to Skyscrapers: Southern City and Region, 1607–1980* (1982), *Still Fighting the Civil War: The American South and Southern History* (2002); Wendy Griswold and Nathan Wright, *American Journal of Sociology* (May 2004); Steven Hoelscher, in *Landscape and Race in the United States*, ed. Richard H. Schein (2006); Bruce Katz, "Concentrated Poverty in New Orleans and Other American Cities," Brookings Institution (4 August 2006); Tara McPherson, *Reconstructing Dixie: Race, Gender, and Nostalgia in the Imagined South*

(2003); Raymond A. Mohl, *Alabama Review* (October 2002); John Shelton Reed, *One South: An Ethnic Approach to Regional Culture* (1982); Wanda Rushing, *Memphis and the Paradox of Place: Globalization in the American South* (2009); Stewart E. Tolnay, *Annual Review of Sociology* (1 January 2003); Lawrence J. Vale and Thomas J. Campanella, eds., *The Resilient City: How Modern Cities Recover from Disaster* (2005); Rupert B. Vance and Nicholas J. Demerath, eds., *The Urban South* (1954, 1971); Charles Reagan Wilson, *Judgment and Grace in Dixie: Southern Faiths from Faulkner to Elvis* (2007); Jamie Winders, in *New Faces in New Places: The Changing Geography of American Immigration*, ed. Doug Massey (2008).

Banking

Urbanization and economic growth in the South are closely connected to changes in the banking industry. Phenomenal growth that took place in the region's metropolitan areas in the last two decades of the 20th century also occurred in southern banking. Charlotte, N.C., rose to prominence as the second-largest banking center in the United States, after New York. During that time, the banking industry also made significant gains in Atlanta, Ga., and Birmingham, Ala., but in 2008 the nation's financial crisis raised new concerns in southern cities about the banking industry and its impact on local communities.

The ascendance of southern cities in banking followed a series of changes in state and federal banking laws that began after the Civil War. With enactment of the National Banking Act of 1864, investors in several southern cities, particularly Charlotte and Atlanta, opened new banks under federal charters and converted state-chartered banks to federal ones. However, the practice of chartering new state banks resumed later in the 19th century, primarily because state banks established lower capital and reserve requirements and they were less restrictive in lending and investing activities. In any case, new southern banks based in urban centers provided much of the capital needed for expansion of the region's textile industry and stimulated growth of southern cities. Consequently, Atlanta quadrupled its population between 1870 and 1900 at a growth rate higher than any other city in the South. Still, the postbellum era was a difficult economic time for the South and its banks.

Congress created the Federal Reserve Bank in 1913, locating two of the 12 district banks in Atlanta and Richmond and establishing branch offices of those district banks in other southern cities, including Charlotte, Birmingham, Miami, Nashville, and New Orleans. As the national economy grew rapidly in the 1920s, the country's banks entered into a series of mergers and consolidations. In this expansionary era, as the nation grew more urbanized and population density increased, tensions grew between rural-based banks and expanding urban banks and branches. Consequently, several southern state legislatures, dominated by rural constituencies, passed laws restricting branch banking. In 1927, Congress passed the McFadden Act, which subjected branching by nationally chartered banks to state approval. This federal law also inhibited interstate branch banking by preventing out-of-state banks from establishing branches in another state without that state's approval.

The combination of bank mergers in the 1920s and bank failures in the early years of the Great Depression reduced the number of nationally and state-chartered banks in the United States by 50 percent. This era represented the greatest period of consolidation ever experienced by the banking industry until the last two decades of the 20th century. However, the Bank Merger Act of 1960 and its 1966 amendments limited mergers if consolidation limited competition, and the Bank Holding Company Act of 1970 limited activities of previously unregulated one-bank holding companies.

At the same time, states further restricted the expansion of bank branching. With the exception of North Carolina and South Carolina, southern states maintained some of the most restrictive branching laws in the nation, and did so at a time when the South was emerging from World War II and experiencing significant growth and greater prosperity. Federal and state limitations on consolidation and geographic expansion of banks limited the formation of capital for southern businesses, but demand was growing. Consequently, southern businesses were forced to import capital from larger banks in the Northeast and Midwest, further widening the gap between southern banks and those headquartered in other regions.

In response to economic disparities between the South and most other regions of the nation, southern academics, including sociologists, historians, economists, and others, advocated southern regionalism as a means of uplifting the South through economic development and industrialization. In 1971, the governors of nine southern states organized the Southern Growth Policies Board, a nonpartisan public-policy think tank, based in Research Triangle Park of North Carolina. In 1980, the Southern Growth Policies Board convened the Commission for the Future of the South to improve the economic and educational prospects of the region. A commission report recognized trends toward nationwide interstate banking. "Changes in federal laws to allow interstate banking seem likely during the 1980s. The region's banks need to prepare for this eventuality to protect their competitive situation and at the same time assure a supply of money for expansion of trade and industry. As a precursor to interstate banking, the southern states should develop reciprocal banking agreements within the region as permitted under current federal law with an eye toward the eventual development of regional, multibank holding companies." These recommendations laid the foundation for the Southeastern Regional Banking Compact.

A number of economic and technological changes in the banking industry also drove regulatory change. In 1980, the Depository Institutions Deregulation and Monetary Control Act began a phaseout of previously prescribed interest rate ceilings on time and savings deposits. Although this regulatory change benefited customers by allowing financial market forces to price the interest rates to be paid on savings accounts, the change came at a time when interest rates were very high, and the greater cost of money strained bank profitability.

Also, brokerage firms had created money market mutual fund accounts as an effective competitor to bank savings accounts. Subsequently, Congress passed the Garn–St. Germain Depository Institutions Act of 1982 that created a new type of money market bank depository account that allowed banks to be more competitive with brokerage firms. However, the net effect to banks of the deregulation of interest rates was an increase in the cost of deposit funds and pressure on profits.

In the 1970s, technological advances like the automated teller machine (ATM) and information technology systems began to change how customers interacted with their banks and started the process of eliminating geographic boundaries to banking. These advances influenced bankers and bank regulators in the South and elsewhere to consider ending geographical restrictions at county and state levels, as a convenience to customers and as an opportunity for banks to diversify risk and increase profitability through additional market options.

In August 1983, representatives from the leading southeastern banks and the state banking associations convened in Atlanta in a two-day symposium on the subject of interstate banking in the Southeast. Afterward, lawyers representing larger banks in Florida, Georgia, North Carolina, and South Carolina prepared banking legislation creating a regional compact. The model legislation authorized acquisitions by bank holding companies in any "southern" state of a bank or bank holding company in another "southern" state. The defined southern region varied slightly from state to state but usually included the states of Alabama, Arkansas, Florida, Georgia, Kentucky, Louisiana, Maryland, Mississippi, North Carolina, South Carolina, Tennessee, and Virginia, and sometimes West Virginia and the District of Columbia. Under the new law, a qualifying "southern" banking company had to have its principal place of business in a southern region state and had to have total deposits in the southern region in excess of 80 percent of total deposits of holding company–owned banks.

As of June 1985, the *American Banker* listed only two southern banks in the top 25 but noted that 19 southern banks had moved into the top 100. These included three banks from North Carolina, three from Georgia, four from Virginia, five from Florida, two from Tennessee, and one each from Alabama and South Carolina. However, the scope of the large New York and California bank holding companies still eclipsed the holding companies from the South. As of 30 June 1985, Citicorp, the largest in the country, was nearly 10 times the size of the largest bank in the South, NCNB Corporation.

Interregional mergers began in summer 1985. By 1995, when full nationwide interstate banking was permitted, most of the largest southern banks had

A 1980s church-fan advertisement for AmSouth Bank, which was founded as the National Bank of Birmingham, Ala., in 1873. In 2006, Regions Bank acquired AmSouth, forming one of the top 10 bank holding companies in the United States. (Charles Reagan Wilson Collection, Center for the Study of Southern Culture, University of Mississippi)

combined into a few superregional bank holding companies. The Southeastern Regional Banking Compact provided southern banking companies a window of opportunity in which to grow and remain independent under a protective cover for 10 years until full interstate banking was finally permitted in 1995 by the passage of the Riegel-Neal Interstate Banking and Branching Act. In 1998, the merger of Bank of America with NCNB of North Carolina created the first coast-to-coast banking merger in U.S. history.

Two big banking companies headquartered in North Carolina, NCNB, which became Bank of America, and First Union, which merged with Wachovia, were the most successful southern bank holding companies in terms of the size and scope of their banking and other financial operations. SunTrust, based in Georgia, and Regions Financial, based in Birmingham, were ranked in the nation's top 10 banking institutions. In the financial downturn of 2008, however, the banking industry shed thousands of jobs and created financial turmoil. In a new wave of mergers and acquisitions, Bank of America acquired Merrill Lynch for $50 billion, and Wachovia sold itself to Wells Fargo for $15 billion.

THOMAS D. HILLS
Atlanta, Georgia

Dan Fitzpatrick, "How Charlotte Became a Banking Giant, Outpacing Pittsburgh's Banks," *Pittsburgh Post-Gazette* (25 June 2006); David R. Goldfield, *Cotton Fields* and Skyscrapers: Southern City and Region, 1607–1980 (1982); Howard W. Odum and Henry Estill Moore, *American Regionalism: A Cultural-Historical Approach to National Integration* (1938); Margaret M. Polski, *The Invisible Hands of U.S. Commercial Banking Reform: Private Action and Public Guarantees* (2003); Michael E. Porter, *Clusters of Innovation Initiative: Regional Clusters of Innovation* (2001); Bernard Shull and Gerald A. Hanweck, *Bank Mergers in a Deregulated Environment: Promise and Peril* (2001); Pat Watters, ed., *1980 Commission on the Future of the South* (1980).

Black Middle Class

The term "black middle class" is commonly used, but our understanding of who falls into the category changes over time, and with regional variation. The "mulatto elite," consisting of former slaves with white ancestry, formed the foundation for the black middle class just after the Civil War. Although the members of this elite parlayed the skills they had learned as personal servants to white slave owners into stable careers serving white clients once slavery was abolished, their claim to a middle-class status was rooted in ancestry and family name, not in occupational status. By the early 20th century, as rural southern blacks migrated into northern cities, the mulatto elite was replaced by the emergent black middle class—among them doctors, teachers, insurance agents, funeral directors, and entrepreneurs committed to serving the swelling population of northern blacks, whom many whites refused to serve. The basis for their claim to a middle-class status was achievement rather than ancestry. A similar black middle class emerged in segregated southern cities. In both cases, position within the black middle class was based on the status that education provided, not on income. Black professionals earned far less working in segregated black communities than their white counterparts did working in white society. It was not until the 1960s, in the aftermath of the passage of civil rights legislation and in a period of national economic expansion, that a black middle class closely aligned with conventional indicators of class position, such as income and education, began to evolve.

The black middle class has grown so dramatically since the second half of the 20th century that it now makes sense for scholars to devote attention to uncovering variation within the group as opposed to theorizing about the black middle class as a monolithic social category. One important source of variation among members of the black middle class is regional location. Middle-class blacks living in different regions of the United States do not experience their class position in the same way. Atlanta provides an excellent case for examining middle-class blacks in the South. The city figures prominently in the return migration to southern states currently under way, the metropolitan area possesses a vibrant economic base, and the city has managed to create and maintain institutions that blacks have traditionally relied on to attain a middle-class status, even as integration policies in the 1960s made it possible for upwardly mobile blacks to begin to think about accessing mainstream paths to the middle class.

In Atlanta during the first half of the 20th century, upwardly mobile blacks reacted to racial exclusion from trade jobs in rapidly expanding sectors of the economy (for example, plumbing, printing, factory work) by becoming entrepreneurs. Two prominent Atlanta businessmen stand out in this regard: Alonzo Herndon and Hemon Perry. Neither man came from middle-class origins, but both men arrived in Atlanta and quickly took the city by storm. Herndon opened an elegant barbershop outfitted with leather benches and crystal chandeliers. Known as the Crystal Palace, the barbershop had a clientele that was exclusively white and male. As the city tightened restrictions governing black barbers and white clients, Herndon moved on to the insurance industry, establishing the Atlanta Life Insurance Company in 1905. Atlanta Life still exists today, and the mansion Herndon and his wife, Adrienne, and their son occupied on the northwest side of Atlanta has been preserved as a national historic site. Hemon Perry, who dropped out of school in the sixth or seventh grade, founded in 1911 what was at the time the largest black business: Standard Life Insurance Company. Today, entrepreneurs still make up a significant chunk of Atlanta's black middle class.

Acquiring a college education has positioned many blacks to enter the middle class, and Atlanta is home to more historically black colleges and universities (HBCUs) than any other city. Originally, there were five such institutions, all located on the southwest side of Atlanta: Spelman College, Morehouse College, Morris Brown College, Clark University, and Atlanta University. Morris Brown was shuttered recently, and Clark University and Atlanta University have merged to become Clark-Atlanta University. Founded in 1869 by the American Missionary Association (AMA), Atlanta University was a popular choice among middle-class black families, due in part to the institution's decision to establish a private secondary school, the Atlanta University Laboratory School, which served as a feeder for Atlanta University. The influence of the AMA was made visible at Atlanta University through an emphasis on "middle-class morality." Under the belief that blacks' successful admission into the black middle class would have to be cultivated and nurtured, the course "Good Morals and Gentle Manners" (renamed "Elocution and Deportment") was required of all students, along with sexual abstinence, sobriety, and a strong work ethic. Graduates of Atlanta's HBCUs tend to remain in the city (or to return), where they have had an impact on politics, religious life, and social movements, as exemplified by Morehouse graduates Martin Luther King Jr. and Maynard Jackson, the first black mayor of Atlanta.

Religious life has also contributed to the emergence and maintenance of a black middle class in Atlanta. Friendship Baptist Church, Ebenezer, Wheat Street, Bethel AME, and First Congregational are well known as worship sites for the city's growing black middle class. Under the leadership of the AMA, First Congregational Church in particular provided its members with a "cultural blueprint" for living a middle-class lifestyle and serving as spokespersons for the black community. Unlike Baptist churches, missionary churches promoted a quiet, reserved approach to worship. Moreover, members were evaluated based on adherence to the church's doctrine, even when they were not in church, as any egregious public behavior would tarnish not only the individual's reputation but the church's as well. Individuals found to be in violation of the doctrine could be excommunicated. For example, although First Congregational forgave a male church member accused of stealing, he was nonetheless expelled. The church minutes stated: "We feel that our duties to this church require us to be very watchful for its purity and zealous for its good name and inasmuch as the warning given by suspension in two instances has not availed to change his course, therefore resolved that [he] be and he is hereby excommunicated from this church."

The black middle class is often considered to be a single, homogeneous group, but there is considerable variation by region in the emergence and maintenance of the black middle class. In Atlanta, small businesspersons, HBCUs, and religious institutions have been instrumental in shaping the lives of middle-class blacks, not only in the South but in the nation.

KARYN LACY
University of Michigan

Lawrence Graham, *Our Kind of People: Inside America's Black Upper Class* (1999); Joseph Jewell, *Race, Social Reform, and the Making of a Middle Class: The American Missionary Association and Black Atlanta, 1870–1900* (2007); Karyn Lacy, *Blue-Chip Black: Race, Class, and Status in the New Black Middle Class* (2007); August Meier and David Lewis, *Journal of Negro Education* (Spring 1959); Gary Pomerantz, *Where Peachtree Meets Sweet Auburn: A Saga of Race and Family* (1996).

Boosterism

Equal parts city promoter, civic benefactor, southern loyalist, salesman, speculator, and hustler, the urban booster led the efforts to awaken southerners to the possibilities for profit and progress in the development of the region's cities. Active mainly in the late 19th and 20th centuries, the town promoter was typically a male business owner, land agent, banker, professional, or newspaper editor and was typically a member of various fraternal organizations, commercial associations, and civic leagues. Burdened by the South's rural, tradition-bound, and often ambivalent population and by the skepticism of Yankee financiers and industrialists, the urban booster often resorted to the rhetoric of the confidence artist while making his pitch, making him an almost tragicomic figure throughout much of the South's history. Whether boosting the village of Bunkie or the metropolis of Atlanta, he traditionally wrangled investment through a mixture of puffed-up claims of municipal progress and wildly exaggerated promises of returns for investors. Although the booster usually failed to deliver, he nonetheless played a critical role in the urbanization of Dixie.

In the South's colonial period, when slave-based, plantation-centered agriculture dominated the economy and the region's planter aristocracy shared a Jeffersonian ambivalence toward urbanization, the town promoter generally lacked both the means and the support for city building. The potential for town promotion improved somewhat in the antebellum period, especially when boosters sought to portray the development of southern cities as part of the emerging sectional rivalry with the urban and rapidly industrializing North. Their arguments, enunciated most persuasively by New Orleanian J. D. B. De-Bow in *DeBow's Review*, tied urban development to regional patriotism, touting city growth and railroad building as a means of lessening southern dependence on northern manufactured goods. Such rhetoric failed to generate significant support among the members of the slaveholding elite, mainly because they feared urbanization could threaten slavery. As a result, the South had only around 50 of the nation's 400 urban centers by 1860.

The Civil War, while devastating to the South's few cities, created circumstances that led to the zenith of the urban booster's fortunes. In the aftermath of Confederate defeat and the abolition of slavery, town promoters frenetically peddled urbanization to a largely receptive audience, promising residents and outsiders alike a field ripe for unprecedented urban development and industrialization. This vision of a "New South" was championed primarily by southern entrepreneurs, business and civic elites, land speculators, and newspaper editors in the decades between the war and the turn of the 20th century. In the postwar years, boosters argued that, with its plantation economy destroyed, the South would develop a new economy more in line with the industrial capitalism that dominated the urban North. *Atlanta Constitution* editor Henry W. Grady, the de facto spokesman for a New South based on industrial development and urbanization, conveyed the message of industrialization as a panacea for the region's ills and also a stern regional patriotism and a moderate stance on racial issues.

With the South's economy in shambles, urban boosters searching for capital had few options but to turn to their recent adversaries in the North. Town promoters were among the first to play up sectional reconciliation as the surest way to garner northern financing of southern urbanization and industrialization. Addressing an audience of northern business leaders in the 1880s, Henry Grady explained the progress made with a combination of Yankee dollars and southern acumen: "We have sowed towns and cities in the place of theories, and put business above politics. We have challenged your spinners in Massachusetts and your iron-makers in Pennsylvania. We have fallen in love with work." As evidence, Grady and his fellow boosters pointed to the bustling city of Atlanta and to emerging boomtowns like Birmingham.

In the New South years, urban boosters employed a variety of tactics to solicit northern capital. Mainly they peddled southern towns as potential bases of operation for extractive industries, mills, factories, and railroads, glorifying the region and its cities as repositories of untapped wealth ripe for vast returns on modest capital outlays. Boosters supplied ample evidence of the postwar South as a transformed region—a place fully awakened to progress, efficiency, science, modernization, sectional reunion, and racial harmony. Poor whites were generally a crucial component of these campaigns and were hawked as an acquiescent, low-wage, nonunion workforce derived from hardy Anglo-Saxon stock. To appease southern members of their audience, town promoters preached a parallel dedication to the "Lost Cause" and an unshakeable commitment to the defense of southern cultural traditions. The successful booster courted Yankee-financed railroads, factories, and textile mills for his city but also exhibited his credentials as a southern patriot by spearheading efforts to erect a suitable monument to the heroism of fallen Confederate soldiers.

Most municipal governments in this period convinced themselves that unless they secured the next railroad, mill, or plant, their town might fall off the map. As a result, they worked hand-in-glove with boosters, offering potential investors financing from city bonds to aid construction of a new rail line into town or tendering free land, cash bonuses, and generous tax exemptions for any new industry. In the mania to court development, town officials privileged spending on development over allocations for adequate public services or much-needed infrastructure improvements. Chambers of commerce and fraternal organizations—including those devoted solely to boosterism, such as commercial clubs, investment associations, and civic leagues—offered organizational structure and legitimacy to urban promotion schemes. They generally worked with local governments to craft propaganda pamphlets disguised as city guides to hype their hometown as the next great progressive and cosmopolitan metropolis, one that in only a few short years had risen from a bucolic village to become "the Standard Bearer of Southern Progress." Most guides cataloged an array of extraordinary statistics, citing spectacular profits in land, ore, coal, or lumber alongside radically inflated and constantly rising population counts as proof that an easy dollar could be had in "wide-awake" places throughout Dixie. Noting that much of what it contained was as "startling as fiction," a typical Virginia booster pamphlet claimed that there had never been a real estate failure in the boomtown of Roanoke, which was "unparalleled in the history of the world." Some boosters even pushed undeveloped "paper cities," offering plots to the "discerning" investor in a wholly imagined town that existed only as nearby pastureland and yet was destined to become the next Atlanta. In towns that did exist, boosters engaged in a rebranding campaign, christening boomtowns "magic cities" and marketing industrializing urban areas as the next Pittsburg, Lowell, or Chicago of the South.

Few question the fact that booster campaigns in the late 19th-century South resulted in dramatic urban growth, railroad construction, and industrialization. Those developments, however, never came close to matching the growth taking place throughout much of the rest of the nation. Well into the 20th century, southern urbanization and industrialization lagged at least 50 years behind the rest of America. Moreover, when compared to what boosters promised, the New South's urban achievements appear as abject failures. Development also came with a high price—growth at any cost strapped the region with numerous "cities" that were little more than overgrown country towns. Little evidence of the racial harmony advertised by boosters was apparent, with race relations better characterized as tumultuous at best and maintained through draconian segregation laws. Population growth arrived mainly through annexation of the surrounding countryside, and industrialization materialized primarily in extractive industries or processing plants, both of which trapped the region in a colonial economy and left its population in low-wage, low-skill jobs.

In the early 20th century, a new wave of urban boosters sought to remedy the many municipal ills that threatened future investment in most southern towns and cities. Carried out under the banner of progressive reform, promoters turned to city planning, cityscape upgrading, park building, historic preservation, road paving, and improvement of city services as a means to ensure order, stability, and tradition along with continued economic progress and development. For the first time, women joined the campaign in significant numbers. Banding together in ladies' clubs and civic improvement leagues, they were among the first to campaign for better schools, improved health regulations, and civic beautification. Lobbying for municipal bonds to cover the expense of such improvements, urban boosters argued that failure to act would result in civic malaise, stagnation, and decay. In the South's new cities, promoters sought to convince potential investors of the permanence and stability of their particular municipality, downplaying its boomtown origins in favor of hyping it as an organically growing metropolis nurtured by a caring citizenry devoted to steady and rational growth.

During the Great Depression and World War II, urban boosters sought to steer New Deal and Department of Defense dollars into municipal development projects. In the postwar period, promoters turned to architectural boosterism, using federal urban renewal dollars to tear down areas of town populated by poor whites or African Americans in order to construct civic centers, convention facilities, hotels, airports, and skyscrapers. Those moves paralleled a new campaign by boosters to lure tourists into southern towns and cities, especially after interstates made these destinations more easily accessible. City promoters in New Orleans, Charleston, and Savannah moved quickly to make their hometowns tourist friendly, and boosters in less obvious locales advertised their towns as necessary historic stops that any visitor to Dixie would be remiss to ignore. As part of a larger marketing campaign following the civil rights movement, boosters also sought to dilute negative connotations associated with the term "South" by replacing it with "Sunbelt." In the last decades of the 20th century, as the region's cities gained population and industrial investment at the expense of midwestern and northern towns, the South realized many of the promises made by urban boosters in the 1880s and 1890s. Foreign investors—attracted by Dixie's largely nonunionized workforce and obsequious municipal governments—have stepped in to replace northern financiers, bringing a new era of industrialization in the form of car factories and tire and chemical plants. More recently, boosters have successfully added the solicitation of northern retirees to their pitches, advertising southern cities and towns as hospitable, low-tax, and low-crime places in which to spend one's golden years. As one historian has aptly remarked, however, the realization of boosters' dreams is a decidedly mixed blessing that threatens to rob the region of its culture and transform it into a "tinfoil-twinkling simulation of Southern California."

RAND DOTSON
Louisiana State University

Blaine A. Brownell, *The Urban Ethos in the South, 1920–1930* (1975); Blaine A. Brownell and David R. Goldfield, eds., *The City in Southern History: The Growth of Urban Civilization in the South* (1977); Rand Dotson, *Roanoke, Virginia, 1882–1912: Magic City of the New South* (2007); Don H. Doyle, *New Men, New Cities, New South: Atlanta, Nashville, Charleston, Mobile, 1860–1910* (1990); Gaines M. Foster, *Ghosts of the Confederacy: Defeat, the Lost Cause, and the Emergence of the New South* (1985); Paul M. Gaston, *The New South Creed: A Study in Southern Mythmaking* (1976); David R. Goldfield, *Cotton Fields and Skyscrapers: Southern City and Region, 1607–1980* (1982); Lawrence H. Larson, *The Rise of the Urban South* (1985).

Central Florida, Disneyfication of

Since 1970, the population of central Florida has exploded, and, as a result, its ever-expanding built environment has flowed over former agricultural scrublands like lava from a volcano. Beginning with the location of the Disney Company's eastern Disneyland some 24 miles west of the formal city limits of Orlando, this city has stretched itself into a regional metropolis, the center of which cannot easily be discerned. Indeed, Orlando is not really a city anymore, or at least anything recognizable as such. Rather, it is a veritable archipelago of more or less metropolitanized places, or urbanized bits, only loosely connected by a web of interstates, expressways, and highways. In this sense, the metropolis of Orlando *is* central Florida, stretched along the transportation infrastructure in all directions.

Disney began this growth process, shaping the very social and material substance of the region. Central Florida has been remade, if unevenly, in the image of what the Disney Company represents: a footloose, tourist-based, fantasy-driven, imagineered built facade overlaying an overwhelmingly low-end, dead-end, service-sector social economy peopled by many who are barely making ends meet. In fact, a major reason that the built environment has expanded in so many directions so rapidly has been the search for affordable housing by those who fulfill the fantasies of visitors to the ever-more-numerous themed attractions of the region, from Disney World to Universal Studios to Sea World.

Yet there is far more to the story than this summary. The Disneyfication of central Florida should be considered a harbinger of future urbanism in the United States as a whole. Orlando as a more or less centralized city has not only been hollowed out and stretched beyond recognition but its traditional role as the focal point of business and public interaction has been supplanted by the several privatized, Disneyesque "downtowns" of the theme parks. In this, the story of Orlando is not that much different from other cities attempting to attract tourists and professionals, and their money, by sanitizing their former industrial pasts, both social and built. Indeed, this story of the construction of festival marketplaces on old wharves, the rendering of warehouses into high-end boutiques, and the renewal of blighted inner cities through sports stadia, aquaria, and the like is now a common enough occurrence not to need repeating here.

But the story of the development of Orlando as the Disneyfication of central Florida demands telling, if only as prophesy. Unlike other cities attempting to initiate postindustrial revivals, Orlando never had an industrial past. The city jumped from a small, sleepy, agricultural, crossroads town to a postindustrial metropolitan giant without the usual transition through the industrial stage. Because of this, Orlando should be considered the quintessential, more finished, more clearly apparent example of the ultimate end product of the still evolving, more dimly perceived, and unevenly understood postindustrial trends in other U.S. cities.

And that underscores the Disneyesque quality of what is taking place in central Florida. After all, the Disney Company is nothing if not the master of facade and fantasy. The Orlando metropolitan region has undergone a boom in the last three decades as a direct result of its image as a safe, clean, happy city of ever-contented residents. Like the many theme parks that lay the ground for this image, the metropolitan region as a whole increasingly is imagined as Disney imagineers would have it. The editing out of "unsavory" social and built realities via high entry fees, highly regulated social relations, and fantastic built facades hides more reality than it reveals. Just as in the theme-park imagineering process, so it is with Orlando.

Critics see central Florida as the nation's urban future. The main reason Orlando is now considered to include as many as four counties in central Florida (Orange, Osceola, Lake, and Seminole—and, in reality, most of eastern Polk County) is that its service sector–dominated tourist economy does not provide its ever-increasing workforce enough income to live more centrally. The race for housing is to the more rural, less central parts of those counties mentioned. As a result, terms like inner-city poverty and suburban wealth make no sense in postindustrial Orlando. The various urban bits of central Florida either should be considered relatively randomly rich or poor or, in fact, quite the opposite of what would be expected according to traditional models of urbanism. Low-end service workers cluster in the most rural parts of Osceola, Polk, and Lake counties, while professional service workers cluster in the more urbanized areas of Orange, Seminole, and Brevard counties. Among these counties are areas of vast wealth, like Disney's Celebration City in Osceola County, and vast poverty, like the so-called western Black Zone of Orlando and the predominantly black

TABLE 1. *Population Growth, Central Florida, 1970–2000*

	Orlando MSA	City of Orlando	Suburbs
1970	522,575	98,965	423,610
1980	804,925	128,291	676,634
1990	1,224,852	164,693	1,060,159
2000	1,644,561	185,951	1,458,610

Source: U.S. Census Bureau, various years.

town of Eatonville, in the middle of the wealth of Orange and Seminole counties (Table 1).

This randomly placed, social and spatial polarization of Orlando has been successfully hidden beneath the happy facade of Disneyfication. Just as the glitter of postindustrial festival marketplaces and wharves and stadia in other cities generally hides urban problems that have been displaced but not solved, so the many unhappy realities of life in central Florida simply are imagineered away. The region as a whole has been, in this regard, successfully themed.

Perhaps the best example of such large-scale imagineering of the greater metropolitan life is Disney's own town of Celebration, an even more specific harbinger of urban things to come. On territory once a part of Disney property—and therefore somewhat "in" but not "of" Orlando city—an entire town is being constructed from scratch lands, according to the most recent and best "new urban" practices of urban designers and architects in the United States. This new urban place is physically designed to recover something called "community," commonly understood by new urbanists to have been destroyed in the chaotic, strip-malled, automobile-addicted, Las Vegas–obsessed modern city. The belief is that reclustering the built environment will bring about a renewed city social life. The main ideological theme of the place is that the residents of the town will rediscover the joy of neighborly socializing through forced proximity and, most interestingly, by attending workshops organized by the Celebration Foundation on such topics as "how to be a good neighbor."

Celebration represents a grandiose plan to social engineer. The town covers 1,983 hectares in traditionally rural, cowboy Osceola County, surrounded by another 1,902 hectares of protected conservation greenbelt. Despite larger claims, it appears to be little more than a randomly located urban bit of Orlando. Its 20,000 to 30,000 or so residents are, and will be, virtually all upscale, professional suburbanites, physically and socially isolated from just about everything and everyone outside the town. In this sense, it is as much isolated from its surroundings as the much poorer black town of Eatonville. Both are urbanized yet disconnected communities within a metropolitan region of other disconnected communities. That such a creation might help solve the problems of American cities, as Celebration's designers contend that it should, remains to be seen.

In addition to adding to the archipelago of disconnected urban bits that constitutes Orlando, Celebration shows a significant deepening of such social and spatial disconnectedness as a result both of its very magnitude and of its designers' thematic intent. Celebration represents the most profound example of the ongoing Disneyfication of central Florida. This is an entire town that is designed along the lines of a theme park. From its high entry fees (housing costs are some 30 to 40 percent above the average for the metropolitan area), to the physical isolation of its customers/residents, to its fantastic built facades and overall imagineered nature of its social relations, Celebration is the first large-scale attempt to Disneyfy real, lived life. Jobs and stores are there, as is a downtown, along with bedrooms. Like a medieval castle, residents may never have to leave the gates. Celebration embodies an attempt to edit out the bad parts of real, lived life by imagineering in only the good, the neighborly, the happy.

KEVIN ARCHER
University of South Florida

Kevin Archer, *Economic Geography* (1997), in *Growth, Technology, Planning, and Geographic Education in Central Florida: Images and Encounters*, ed. R. Oldakowski, L. Molina, and B. Purdum (1997); Douglas Frantz and Catherine Collins, *Celebration U.S.A.: Living in Disney's Brave New Town* (1999); Andrew Ross, *The Celebration Chronicles: Life, Liberty, and the Pursuit of Property Value in Disney's New Town* (1999).

City Planning

The South possesses a rich tradition of urban planning that extends back to the colonial era. Indeed, some of the most innovative town plans of that period were located in the southern colonies. Williamsburg, the small but influential capital of colonial Virginia, introduced baroque civic design to the New World in a plan devised by Theodorick Bland. James Oglethorpe's Savannah plan of 1733 reflected the English philanthropist's commitment to a middle landscape ideal—blending city and country. The town's spacious lots and gridiron streets included five public squares that are considered America's first urban parks. Along the Mississippi River, colonial plans reflected French influence, with streets oriented to the water, especially in the 1722 design of New Orleans by

Jean Baptiste Le Moyne, focusing on the magnificent place d'armes dominated by St. Louis Cathedral.

As in other parts of the United States, planning gave way to less-imaginative rectilinear grids during the 19th century. Along the railroads, new towns and town extensions expanded in checkerboard fashion, efficient for real estate developers but boring in other respects. Savannah, for instance, abandoned its pattern of civic squares in the mid-19th century in favor of an undifferentiated gridiron of streets. The South's relatively slow rate of urbanization became a blessing in disguise, preserving older parts of cities such as Charleston, Savannah, and New Orleans, with their parks, trees, and public waterfronts.

A new era in civic design opened during the New South years around 1900. Electric street railways, perfected by Frank Sprague in Richmond in 1888, made suburbanization practical in the South and nationwide. Developers seeking to set their projects apart from the city hired a new generation of landscape planners. These designers introduced parks, greenways along streams, and tree-shaded curving street patterns. In Atlanta, for instance, the neighborhoods of Inman Park, by English native Joseph Forsyth Johnson, and Druid Hills, by the Boston-based firm of Frederick Law Olmsted, took shape during the 1890s. At the same time, Olmsted pupil George Kessler began Roland Park in Baltimore, which was expanded in 1901 by Frederick Law Olmsted Jr. Perhaps the most influential suburban planners in the South were Boston-based John Nolen and his protégé Earl Sumner Draper. Their many neighborhoods include Crystal Springs in Roanoke, Va., Irving Park in Greensboro, N.C., Emorywood in High Point, N.C., Sequoyah Hills in Knoxville, Tenn., Farmingdale in Charlottesville, Va., University Park in Gainesville, Fla., and the magnificent thousand-acre Myers Park suburb (1911) in Charlotte, N.C.

At this time, planning remained a nongovernmental affair in the South. Private developers rather than taxpayers footed the bill for suburban planning. The planners themselves often urged communities to go further and create unified citywide plans. Sometimes business associations or women's clubs gingerly took up such efforts, but few went very far. In Roanoke, for instance, Nolen drew up a 1907 city plan for the Women's Civic Betterment Club, but it languished until a city-planning agency was chartered in the late 1920s. Planners experienced somewhat more success creating entire new towns for industrial clients, such as Nolen's Kingsport, Tenn. (1917), for a chemical firm, and Draper's Chicopee, Ga. (1927), for a textile manufacturer.

What began to pull urban governments into planning was the issue of race. The growing mania for segregation after 1900 spurred southern cities to adopt the new tool of zoning. Baltimore wrote the nation's first ordinance creating separate black and white districts in 1910, followed by Richmond in 1911. By 1915, when the U.S. Supreme Court officially approved zoning as a proper use of government's police power, racial zoning laws already existed in a dozen southern cities, including Atlanta, Birmingham, and Winston-Salem. In 1917, however, the Supreme Court ruled in a Louisville, Ky., case, *Buchanan v. Warley*, that zoning on the basis of race was unconstitutional, although this did not stop southern city governments from segregating the races, whether through less overt zoning language or other planning and building-permitting tools.

The next major stimulus to urban planning as a governmental activity came from Washington. To win New Deal projects in the 1930s and postwar stimulus dollars in the 1940s and 1950s, cities found they needed full-time planning staff. The 1941 Lanham Act, for instance, offered $150 million for construction of community facilities for defense workers but required localities to file planning documents in order to get the cash. Similar strings were attached to other federal aid for hospitals, airports, and urban expressways. Nationwide, only 39 cities spent as much as $5,000 annually on planning in 1936; by 1948 that number zoomed to 110.

The two juiciest postwar federal funding initiatives were the interstate highway program begun in 1956 and the demolition programs known as "urban renewal," which offered abundant dollars to clear "blighted" districts. In the South, even more than in other parts of the United States, these were used to displace African Americans. Blacks possessed little political power prior to the 1965 Voting Rights Act. Government bulldozers plowed through historic neighborhoods such as Brooklyn in Charlotte, destroying homes and black-owned businesses. In most southern cities today, large highway interchanges and government buildings have supplanted African American neighborhoods.

The excesses of the urban renewal and interstate highway era brought a deep change in philosophy of the planning profession nationwide. Since the 1970s, planners have made citizen involvement their watchword. Rather than seeing themselves as "engineers" interested in quick implementation of technological solutions, planning professionals often have become "facilitators," helping neighborhood residents organize and take part in government. This has had impact on southern cities far beyond physical growth issues, a transformation chronicled in careful detail for Birmingham, Ala., by historian Charles Connerly.

The South played a leading role in two other reactions to the era of wholesale demolition: historic preservation and New Urbanism. Neighborhood preservation began in the South with creation of America's first two historic districts — in Charleston, S.C. (1931), and New Orleans (1936). During the 1960s and 1970s, citizen groups in city after city across the South and nationwide seized upon this planning mechanism as a tool to halt demolition and spur reinvestment. In Savannah, for example, the area of Oglethorpe's original squares was protected with historic district zoning in 1968. In 1979, local planners combined historic district zoning of Savannah's Victorian District with grassroots organizing to spark revitalization while not displacing low-income residents.

The New Urbanism movement began the same year with the founding of the new town of Seaside, Fla. Visionary planners Andres Duany and Elizabeth Plater-Zyberk set out to rediscover the principles of early 20th-century neighborhood designers, especially John Nolen. Also called "traditional neighborhood development," the movement seeks to create pedestrian-friendly districts that mingle single-family and multifamily dwellings and also include retail centers and parks. By the first decade of the 21st century, the Congress for New Urbanism could point to successful projects by hundreds of firms worldwide, including many in the South, such as Ion outside Charleston, S.C., Kentlands near Gaithersburg, Md., and the Walt Disney Company's Celebration at Orlando.

TOM HANCHETT
Levine Museum of the New South

DAVID GOLDFIELD
University of North Carolina at Charlotte

Charles Connerly, *"The Most Segregated City on Earth": City Planning and Civil Rights in Birmingham, 1920–1980* (2005); John Reps, *The Making of Urban America* (1998); Christopher Silver, *Journal of Planning Education and Research* (Number 1, 1996), *Journal of Planning Literature* (Number 4, 1987); Christopher Silver and John Moeser, *Separate Pasts: Black Communities in the Urban South, 1940–1968* (1995); Christopher Silver and Mary Corbin Sies, eds., *Planning the Twentieth-Century American City* (1996); Bruce Stephenson, *Visions of Eden: Environmentalism, Urban Planning, and City Building in St. Petersburg, Florida, 1900–1995* (1997).

Commercial Civic Elite

Merchants and other members of the economic elite were a major influence in the development of American cities. Shipowners, money lenders, brokers, shopkeepers, small manufacturers, skilled artisans, and the "propertied classes" shaped colonial towns and were even more important in the towns and cities of the expanding new nation, driven by entrepreneurial energy and speculative fevers. In the late 19th and early 20th centuries, a commercial civic elite had clearly emerged in southern cities—composed of white property and business owners and other prominent citizens concerned primarily with the downtown business district and organized into civic clubs, trade associations, and a variety of voluntary organizations. The concerns and aspirations of this group dominated the editorial voices of the major local newspapers and promoted notions of economic growth, urban expansion, and social and spatial order. Collectively, members of the commercial civic elite were the driving force behind city planning, urban boosterism, and other efforts to shape the city and compete successfully with other cities for population, jobs, and economic opportunity.

The composition of the commercial civic elite varied somewhat from city to city and from decade to decade, but it consisted primarily of those whose social and economic interests were concentrated in the local urban area but extended beyond any section, neighborhood, or business—the larger merchants, bankers, brokers, and others who shared business middle-class goals and priorities, including physicians, educators, clergymen, and city officials. The early 20th century was particularly notable for the rise of civic clubs—Rotary, Kiwanis, Civitan, and others—and these associations were especially popular in the urban South, providing excellent venues for social and business contacts and the shaping of common attitudes toward urban development. Membership was intentionally spread across a variety of businesses and professions and satisfied both economic self-interest and the desire for civic service and recognition. And these organizations were both prominent and influential in local affairs. In Atlanta, for example, the Presidents' Club was composed of the chief executives of local civic groups and weighed in on most major issues facing the city. Although women were sometimes appointed to city committees, formed auxiliaries to some civic clubs, and contributed articles to the local press on education, health, and other "domestic" matters, their influence was determined by social restrictions of the time and civic club membership was restricted to white males.

Competition among cities was always a feature of American urbanization and became more vigorous in the industrial age, as manufacturing and new transportation networks became the primary determinants of economic prosperity. Here, too, southern city leaders—acutely aware of regional competitors—were committed to seeking new business, dominating surrounding markets, and securing the best roads and rail connections. Chambers of commerce usually led the way in generating publicity, organizing trade missions to the hinterlands, and persuading new business to locate in the local area. This urban boosterism was energetic and pervasive, and it provided a common goal for the diverse members of the commercial civic elite, who stood to benefit from an urban community that was larger and more prosperous. Interestingly, although urban competition was a national phenomenon, this particular early 20th-century manifestation of boosterism — involving local chambers of commerce, civic clubs, the leading newspapers, and vigorous advertising and promotion — was especially prevalent in the South.

It would be an exaggeration to say that the commercial civic elite promoted a common ideology, but its members did share some general concerns and ideas that tended to be reflected in the major newspapers, business journals, and other circulating media of the time. In the prevailing view, urban expansion and civic progress required improvements in institutions and infrastructure — especially transportation — and reliance on social order, efficiency, the protection of life and property, harmonious social relations, and deference to commercial civic leadership. The notion of the city was "corporate expansive," or stable, unified, and capable of significant growth, both economically and demographically. Members of the commercial civic elite were well aware of cities and urban development elsewhere in the country and region and measured their own communities against rival urban models as an integral part of their civic leadership and boosterism.

Not surprisingly, commercial civic elements were major supporters of early efforts at comprehensive urban planning in the South. New transportation patterns and technology, competing land uses, conflicting interests between downtown merchants and manufacturers all contributed to the desires for efficient physical mobility, social stability, the potential for future growth, and the continued domination of business leadership and its commitment to social control. Professional urban planning provided the ideal opportunity to deal with all of these issues in a "businesslike" manner and was regarded as an integral component of civic enlightenment and urban promotion. It was also a tool for imposing more stringent racial segregation in land-use patterns, moving toward more formal white and black neighborhoods through zoning laws and the "reordering" attendant to growth, thus setting the stage for white movement to the suburbs and also for the formation of more autonomous and organized black communities with their own commercial civic institutions and leadership. Major southern cities often contracted with professional planners like Harland Bartholomew to collect data and prepare maps and recommendations, in a process often supervised by commercial civic elements. In New Orleans, in fact, 13 of the 20 members of the City Planning and Zoning Commission were appointed as representatives of designated "leading commercial and civic organizations." By 1930, official planning commissions existed in 71 towns and cities, and 36 had enacted official zoning ordinances. The momentum for city planning was halted by the Depression of the 1930s but was resurrected in the late 1940s and 1950s.

Every southern city of any size contained African American neighborhoods and widely scattered residential pockets, which became consolidated and more formally separated from white neighborhoods after the 1890s. Especially in cities like Atlanta, New Orleans, and Memphis, a black commercial civic leadership emerged, composed of small businessmen, teachers, clergymen, and publishers of black newspapers and journals, which often touted the virtues of urban growth and civic virtue. Not surprisingly, issues of race were much more likely to arise among black opinion leaders, whether to celebrate local racial amity and progress or to lament instances of bigotry or injustice. As black communities grew larger and became more distinctive in the urban fabric, they also became more self-sufficient, with their own business districts and religious and civic institutions. African American groups and opinions were, however, largely ignored or misrepresented in the leading urban media and in the plans and aspirations of the white commercial civic elite—other than to note the value of racial amity and social stability. Race relations were, after all, at the heart of southern white notions of social control.

Despite the economic strength and civic energy of white commercial civic elements, their power to control urban destiny was hardly unlimited or unchallenged. Depending on the city, other formal and informal groups competed in the arena of urban policy, from political bosses to neighborhood organizations to major manufacturers and railroads. Restrictive land uses were favored by some and resisted by others, downtown merchants sometimes quarreled with outlying businesses, and smaller businesses resisted the dominant influence of the larger local corporations. Even modest disagreements among commercial civic elements could virtually paralyze concerted civic or political action, since the underlying assumption was that this dominant group represented a "right-thinking" consensus. The urban planning process embodied some of this ambiguity and often resulted in highly generalized suggestions for urban improvement that were all too easily undermined by competing interests.

Business middle-class leadership and its influence has persisted in most southern towns and cities to the present day, although it has been altered and buffeted by competing groups, economic upheaval, political unrest, and racial conflict. Members of the commercial civic elite were drawn together by mutual interest in economic success, social stability, and the notion of a unified urban community but found these common interests challenged and undermined by the dynamic evolution of neighborhoods and the growing complexity of southern cities, by the disaffection of working-class whites whose interests were neglected by local business, and by blacks who increasingly challenged the racial status quo. But the ideas, concerns, and goals of the white commercial civic elite were more than an ornamental veneer on the patterns of urban development. Indeed, southern cities were fundamentally shaped—in physical outline, social policies, and economic priorities—by the concepts and actions of the business, professional, and civic elements that represented the major economic resources in the community and who promoted their ideas through the major media and voluntary organizations and by their considerable influence on public officials.

BLAINE A. BROWNELL
Charlottesville, Virginia

Blaine A. Brownell, *Journal of Southern History* (August 1975), *The Urban Ethos in the South, 1920–1930* (1975); Don H. Doyle, *New Cities, New South: Atlanta, Nashville, Charleston, Mobile, 1860–1910* (1990); Thomas W. Hanchett, *Sorting Out the New South City: Race, Class, and Urban Development in Charlotte, 1875–1975* (1998); Patricia Evridge Hill, *Dallas: The Making of a Modern City* (1996); Steven J. Hoffman, *Race, Class, and Power in the Building of Richmond, 1870–1920* (2004); Gregory Mixon, *The Atlanta Riot: Race, Class, and Violence in a New South City* (2005).

Crime and Delinquency

The southern region of the United States has received more attention from scholars than any other with respect to crime—violent crime in particular. Going back 130 years, to Horace V. Redfield's seminal book, *Homicide North and South* (1880), historians, sociologists, and cultural analysts have documented that since its earliest settlement the southern region of the United States has typically far outpaced other regions in its rate of lethal violence. Although not discussed nearly as much, it may also be the case that the southern region has experienced higher rates of other types of crime than other regions as well.

Data on both violent and property crimes from 1995 to 2007 that are reported to the police are readily available from the FBI website. These data are the most widely used source of crime information to estimate regional differences in serious crime. The violent crime data includes measures of murder, rape, robbery, and aggravated assault. The property crime data includes measures of burglary, larceny theft, and motor vehicle theft. Rates per 100,000 people are constructed to correct for population differences across ecological areas. The FBI uses the standard Census Bureau definition of regional areas in the United States to calculate regional rates, and thus the southern region violent and property crime rates are constructed using data for Texas, Oklahoma,

TABLE 2. *Violent and Property Crime Rates for the South and the Nation,*
1995–2007 (per 100,000 people)

	Violent Crime		Property Crime	
	South	Nation	South	Nation
1995	739.0	684.6	5,004.0	4,593.0
1996	707.0	634.1	5,020.0	4,444.8
1997	682.0	610.8	4,865.0	4,311.9
1998	633.0	567.6	4,590.0	4,052.5
1999	600.0	523.0	4,332.0	3,743.6
2000	580.6	506.5	4,162.8	3,618.3
2001	579.9	504.4	4,181.0	3,656.1
2002	571.0	494.6	4,151.0	3,624.1
2003	549.3	475.8	4,115.6	3,591.2
2004	540.6	465.5	4,022.2	3,517.1
2005	542.6	469.2	3,883.1	3,429.8
2006	547.5	473.6	3,780.8	3,334.5
2007	549.2	466.9	3,802.1	3,263.5

Arkansas, Louisiana, Mississippi, Alabama, Georgia, Florida, Tennessee, Kentucky, South Carolina, North Carolina, Virginia, West Virginia, Maryland, the District of Columbia, and Delaware (Table 2).

Focusing first on violent crime trends, consistent with a great deal of prior research, throughout the contemporary period (during most of which crime rates were declining substantially) the southern region as a whole maintained rates of violent crime that are substantially higher than the national average. In supplementary analyses, which compare all four census regions (South, West, Northeast, Midwest), the South is consistently higher than all other regions during this period. This lead in violent crime is long-standing, although likely not as pronounced as it was during earlier time periods. Much of the research on southern violence has debated the efficacy of cultural-versus-structural explanations for this regional differentiation. Proponents of the cultural perspective argue that a cultural tolerance for interpersonal violence in situations involving threats to honor, family, or property was brought to the southern region from the British Isles through the herding traditions of the Scots-Irish. When they migrated to the American South throughout the 18th and 19th centuries, tolerance for violence became entrenched and has survived through a process of intergenerational transmission, although the forces of modernity have certainly acted to dilute its efficacy. Cultural theorists thus explain much of the regional differential in terms of this cultural variation. It is important to note that this regional culture of violence is to be distinguished from other culturally based explanations for violence. Most notably, Anderson's well-known "Code of the Street" thesis describes an oppositional cultural code that promotes the use of violence as a means of status enhancement in ecological contexts where traditional routes to socioeconomic status are more limited.

In stark contrast to this epistemological tradition is the structural argument. Structural theorists such as Colin Loftin and Robert H. Hill assert that the higher rates of violent crime found in the South are simply because the southern region has a more pronounced level of structurally embedded disadvantage, observed in such indicators as poverty, high school dropout rates, unemployment, and so forth.

Aside from the persistent high rate of violence in the South, the data in Table 2 reveal another major pattern that is rarely if ever acknowledged or discussed. Like the violent crime pattern, the property crime rate for the southern region is also higher than the national average for the entire contemporary period. Supplementary analysis confirms that during the entire period the southern region ranked highest in its property crime rate among the four census regions in every year. The evidence of a regional property crime differential for the 18th-, 19th-, or early 20th-century time periods is generally scant, and so there is little basis on which to make comparisons. Thus, determining whether this is a new phenomenon is difficult and beyond the scope of the present analysis. Nevertheless, the patterns depicted in the contemporary data merit attention.

In recent times, the South has exhibited the highest rates of both property and violent crimes, but this trend has not been systematically addressed by social scientists. Two major trends that have characterized the "New South" are a major transformation of the economic system of production and distribution and several waves of in- and out-migration. The consequence of in-migration has been to diminish the size of the gap in socioeconomic conditions between the South and other regions. The consequence of out-migration has been a dilution and perhaps deterioration of the nature and extent of the basics of "classic" southern culture, which may have perpetuated such a long history of interpersonal violence.

Aside from this, even though there have been significant changes in the socioeconomic conditions experienced by the average southerner, the region is still plagued by high rates of poverty, unemployment, and school disengagement, with some communities experiencing rates of these social problems more than three times the national average. Thus, given the widespread evidence for a link between socioeconomic conditions and both property crime and violence, it is plausible that this explains part of the regional differential for both forms of crime. With respect to the cultural influence on violence in particular, a parallel conclusion is probably warranted. That is, although it is certainly the case that cultural dilution has lowered the rates of interpersonal violence in the South over time, the most recent research demonstrates that rates of argument-based murder in particular are still higher in communities in the South where southern-born residents are most spatially concentrated. Since the spatial concentration of the carriers of southern culture seems a reasonable mechanism by which a cultural tolerance for violence would be maintained, the broad conclusion is that both structural and cultural forces are operating to maintain the southern regional lead in rates of serious property and violent crime.

MATTHEW R. LEE
Louisiana State University

Elijah Anderson, *Code of the Street: Decency, Violence, and the Moral Life of the Inner City* (1999); Harrington C. Brearley, *Homicide in the United States* (1932); Raymond D. Gastil, *American Sociological Review* (June 1971); Sheldon Hackney, *American Historical Review* (February 1969); Matthew R. Lee, William B. Bankston, Timothy C. Hayes, and Shaun A. Thomas, *Sociological Quarterly* (Spring 2007); Matthew R. Lee and Edward S. Shihadeh, *Social Forces* (2009); Colin Loftin and Robert H. Hill, *American Sociological Review* (October 1974); Richard E. Nisbett and Dov Cohen, *Culture of Honor: The Psychology of Violence in the South* (1996); Horace V. Redfield, *Homicide, North and South: Being a Comparative View of Crime against the Person in Several Parts of the United States* (1880).

Crunk and Hip-Hop Culture

Southern crunk music, known for group chants, call-and-response, and rapidly punctuated rhythms and bass, is the centerpiece of mainstream southern hip-hop. The music, which gained significant and widespread attention in the late 1990s through the works of various groups, including Memphis's Three Six Mafia and Atlanta's Lil' Jon and the Eastside Boys, thrust the urban South squarely into popular culture. Although most dictionary definitions of the term express uncertainty about its etymology, "crunk" is most likely a southern articulation of "cranked up." Getting "cranked up," or getting "crunk," involves not only the proper rhythms, words, and sounds, but also appropriate dances: buck-jumping, a high-energy jumping, bouncing, and elbow-throwing dance; gangsta walking, a rhythmic, posturing stomp characterized by alternating feet and forward or in-place motion; juking, an improvised combination of moon-walking and break dancing, usually done competitively; and snap-dancing, done to a particular form of southern crunk characterized by a snaplike snare, or sometimes a synthesized sample of snapping fingers, on the third beat of each 4/4 measure, in which performative and improvised body leans, coordinated with leg and arm movements, are interrupted by an emphasized snap on the third beat. As southern crunk has gained popularity, the chanted commands have become more violent and confrontational, and the accompanying dances have become more sexualized. The genre has faced admonishment for its vulgarity and lack of refinement, particularly in relation to hip-hop in other regions and hip-hop historically. Critics charge that the music simply introduces—and encourages—a regionalized form of violence into hip-hop culture; others argue that the physical release provided and inspired by the shouting, confrontation, and high-energy movement of southern crunk is a postindustrial parallel to the function of the Jim Crow–era juke joint, allowing the cathartic expression of aggression, rage, and sorrow endemic to the experiences of marginalized urban youth.

The sounds of southern artists, while influenced by rap sounds emerging from the East and West coasts, were distinct in that they were directly infused with elements of African American culture that had endured from slavery to the post–civil rights era, relatively unchanged, in the black South: field hollers, call-and-response, blues rhythms, and bass lines. While hip-hop artists on the East and West coasts sampled southern rhythm and blues songs for the melodic bases of their songs, southern artists were integrating postindustrial, post–civil rights urban experiences and sounds into these predominantly black and/or rural southern musical and expressive traditions. Crunk music emerged largely from this synthesis of black and/or rural musical and expressive traditions with the regionalized and place-specific experiences of the urban South by black southern youth.

As one of the most expansive global phenomena of the post–civil rights era, hip-hop culture has influenced the everyday language, modes of engagement, and cultural practices of a broad cross section of world citizens. With genealogical roots that can be reasonably traced back to West African communicative and expressive practices, contemporary hip-hop culture has evolved in much the same syncretistic pattern as many African American cultural forms. The popularity of the culture and its consequent commodification, corporatization, branding, and proliferation is continuously at the center of debates about the authenticity of the culture. Similarly, mainstream hip-hop's links to and its use of urban crime, violence, and vice are implicated as causal in a host of social problems facing contemporary youth in America. Yet, both in spite of and because of hip-hop's global popularity and increasing presence in myriad dimensions of everyday life, the culture continues to focus on local and, in particular, on urban neighborhood contexts. Although hip-hop culture was, from its beginnings in the Bronx, self-consciously concerned with place and urban place-based issues, dogged senses of place attachment and ownership multiplied and intersected with authenticity debates to produce the bicoastal lyrical and sometimes physical battles that by the 1990s had come to overshadow if not define urban places outside of Los Angeles, Oakland, the San Francisco Bay Area, New York, and, to a lesser extent, Philadelphia. It was within this moment of heightened tensions between the East and West coasts that a veritable "third coast"—the American South—gained significant attention from listeners outside of the region and major record labels, ultimately challenging the hegemony of the clusters of large urban centers that had come to be symbolized by New York and Los Angeles.

The success of crunk music also parallels a widely held and oft-articulated sentiment by southern hip-hop artists that rap has finally "come home" to the South, not unlike the African American populations that have been migrating—or "remigrating"—to the South since 1970. Further, the mainstreaming of crunk music created the space for southern hip-hop artists to situate the urban South, both narratively and visually, as the setting for a number of situations that were both familiar to urban minorities across the globe yet regionally distinct. Several black southern films, including Craig Brewer's *Hustle and Flow* (2005), Chris Robinson's *ATL* (2006), and Bryan Barber's *Idlewild* (2006), tell a story of black life in the urban South. Collectively, these films, in part because of the success of crunk music, legitimate and authenticate the region's participation in hip-hop culture by highlighting regional distinctiveness and universal cultural and experiential commonalities.

In the battle for representation in mainstream hip-hop, the "third coast's" crunk music compelled national and global recognition of the urban American South. As the sound has reached a critical point of replicability, and perhaps a critical saturation in popular culture, more artists with far less longevity than their predecessors, or the crunk sound, will emerge. Further, southern crunk may continue to be the category into which all southern hip-hop artists are grouped, regardless of their differences. Nonetheless, the music will likely continue to foster discussions of race, urbanism, regional difference, and popular culture.

ZANDRIA F. ROBINSON
University of Mississippi

Andy Bennett and Richard Peterson, *Music Scenes: Local, Translocal, and Virtual* (2004); Murray Forman, *The 'Hood Comes First: Race, Space, and Place in Rap and Hip-Hop* (2004); Murray Forman and Mark Anthony Neal, eds., *That's the Joint: The Hip-Hop Studies Reader* (2004); Nelson George, *Buppies, B-Boys, Baps, and Bohos: Notes on Post-Soul Black Culture* (2001); Wendy Griswold and Nathan Wright, *American Journal of Sociology* (May 2004); Roni Sarig, *Third Coast: OutKast, Timbaland, and How Hip-Hop Became a Southern Thing* (2007).

Deindustrialization

The term "deindustrialization" was first applied to the process conducted by the Allied victors of World War II of removing industrial plants and equipment from Germany. Since then it has come to mean either the absolute or the relative decline of employment in manufacturing and the resource removal accompanying the closing of mines, mills, and factories mainly in North America, Europe, and Asia. In the United States, deindustrialization is usually associated with the 1970s and 1980s when the problems of automobile, steel, and tire production in the Northeast and Midwest dominated the headlines. However, it began much earlier and affects a host of other industries such as electronics, textiles, mining, lumbering, and paper. Moreover, it involves not only job loss, mainly unionized jobs, but also the transformation of social, cultural, political, and environmental relationships that defined communities, from the local to the global.

Although deindustrialization is not a recent phenomenon, a number of factors led to greater academic and public interest in the issue during the 1970s and 1980s. In the United States, GDP growth slowed, unemployment hit double digits at times, and worker productivity dropped. Between 1973 and 1995, real income gains came only for those in the top 20 percent of family income distribution, while on average the bottom 40 percent witnessed real declines. The number of production workers declined in several industries in the 1970s, including primary metals, tires and inner tubes, household appliances, motor vehicles and parts, textiles, apparel, and electrical distribution equipment. Workers who lost jobs had a poor rate of success in getting adequate retraining and in finding jobs of at least equal value, and most experienced downward mobility. Cities in the Frostbelt were particularly hard hit, and African Americans—particularly males—were especially vulnerable in places like Cleveland, Chicago, and Detroit, where the manufacturing sector remained the main source of employment for them.

Some analysts and scholars have disputed the idea that the United States deindustrialized during the 1970s and 1980s, or they argued that the process is

Abandoned furniture store and mural, Jackson, Miss. (Photograph courtesy of David Wharton)

generally beneficial over the long run. From 1973 to 1980, for example, manu-facturing output in the United States increased in real terms 12.3 percent. This was higher than the European economies, second only to Japan's 22 percent. Also, between 1973 and 1979, new net investment in the manufacturing sec-tor increased an average of 6.9 percent per year. The number of production workers in manufacturing increased from 12.2 million to 13.9 million from 1963 to 1980. This group also disputes the claim that foreign trade is responsible for a decline in U.S. manufacturing employment. In the 1970s, for example, the volume of U.S. manufactured goods increased 101.5 percent, while growth in manufactured imports rose 72 percent. Some argue that the declining employ-ment in basic industries like steel and automobiles has come from declining domestic demand in favor of imports.

Within the United States, the South has been seen as the beneficiary of de-industrialization. Typically, the focus has been on firms that closed older mills or factories in the Northeast or Midwest and shifted production to newer facili-ties in the South or West. Since the Great Depression of the 1930s, the South as a region has witnessed a greater share of its nonfarm employees engaged in manufacturing. As states in the Frostbelt like New York, Michigan, and Ohio lost manufacturing jobs, Sunbelt states like Georgia, North Carolina, Texas, and California saw gains. Overall, as of 2006, 5 of the top 10 states in terms of the percentage of jobs in manufacturing were located in the South: Arkansas (third), Mississippi (fourth), Alabama (sixth), Tennessee (ninth), and Kentucky (tenth). In terms of total jobs in manufacturing, as of 2008, North Carolina ranked ninth. In recent years, southern states have landed several large manufacturing plants, including steel in Alabama and automobile facilities in Georgia, Kentucky, Mississippi, South Carolina, Tennessee, and Texas. The automobile plants have largely been foreign companies such as BMW, Honda, and Toyota. Foreign investment has added to concerns about the ability of U.S. manufacturing companies to survive. Explanations for why manufacturing jobs have shifted southward have included cheaper, nonunion labor and a desire for firms to move to where the population and market for products was growing. In some cases, such as in tire manufacturing, firms closed plants in the North as they opened facilities in the South. In other sectors, such as textiles, it was new investment, not runaway shops, that helped drive production out of northern regions like New England.

But the South has experienced deindustrialization. Just as the South competed more successfully against the North for textiles during the second half of the 20th century, now foreign production has decimated textile mills in the South. The apparel industry in the South lost 80 percent of its workforce between 1990 and 2005, while payrolls fell 18 percent in paper mills and 15 percent in furniture. In automobile parts supply, the South and the North have lost jobs to nations such as Mexico and China. Growth in other sectors such as services and information technology offset the losses to give the South net job increases, but the South has not been immune to deindustrialization.

In the United States, the political response to deindustrialization has been focused on legislation designed to address plant closures—assisting workers through retraining or unemployment compensation and providing economic development for communities facing the loss of industry. The United States has generally been committed to free trade and open markets, which have framed the political solutions to the negative effects of deindustrialization. In the 1960s, for example, the federal government created the Area Redevelopment Administration to assist communities fighting high unemployment; its successor is the Economic Development Administration, which continues fighting economic dislocation through infrastructure improvements and financial incentives to businesses. Other federal legislation and agencies provide worker retraining or economic assistance to communities hit with high unemployment. These include the Trade Readjustment and Recovery Act and the Comprehensive Employment and Training Act.

Other attempts have been made outside the federal arena. Several states have enacted various forms of plant closure legislation. Maine became the first to do so in 1971, with legislation that required advance notice of closings. Wisconsin later adopted a similar proposal, as did Connecticut, Massachusetts, Hawaii, the Virgin Islands, and Tennessee. In the 1980s, Connecticut and California crafted legislation to assist workers with retraining, and Connecticut added a requirement that companies with over 100 employees continue paying health insurance premiums when laying off workers.

Recently, there are signs that concern with industrial dislocation is returning. In 2001, following the collapse of a stock speculation bubble and the attacks of 9/11, the U.S. economy once again stumbled. In 2008, in response to a recession, Congress approved $750 billion dollars to rescue failing financial institutions involved in risky mortgage lending. The financial services sector began shedding jobs as firms collapsed or merged. Meanwhile, the downturn affected the automobile industry, and leaders and unions representing workers from General Motors, Ford, and Chrysler all asked Congress for a bailout of their own to avoid bankruptcy. It remains to be seen what the full effects of the latest recession will be for the process of deindustrialization.

GREGORY S. WILSON
University of Akron

Barry Bluestone and Bennett Harrison, *The Deindustrialization of America* (1982); Jefferson Cowie and Joseph Heathcott, eds., *Beyond the Ruins: The Meanings of Deindustrialization* (2003); Steven High, *Industrial Sunset: The Making of North America's Rust Belt, 1969–1984* (2003); Steven High and David W. Lewis, *Corporate Wasteland: The Landscape and Memory of Deindustrialization* (2007); Bruce J. Schulman, *From Cotton Belt to Sunbelt: Federal Policy, Economic Development, and the Transformation of the South, 1938–1980* (1994); Paul D. Staudohar and Holly E. Brown, eds., *Deindustrialization and Plant Closure* (1987); Gregory S. Wilson, *Communities Left Behind: The Area Redevelopment Administration, 1945–1965* (2009).

Education

Scholars have given a variety of explanations for why education in the South differs from education in other regions of the United States. Some have emphasized geography as the causal factor, others economics or ideology or social structure, and still others some combination of these factors. Southern differences frequently are attributed simply to the rural nature of life. The urbanization of southern education took place mainly in the New South period and after (roughly 1875 to the present), and this fact provides one more angle from which the South's educational distinctiveness may be considered.

In broad outline, educational developments in southern cities were similar to those in other American cities. Southern cities experienced a progressive reform movement in education in the early 20th century, just as nonsouthern cities did; city schools in all regions were racked by the Great Depression of the 1930s as well as by the other economic gyrations of the 20th century; and educational institutions have grown more numerous and diverse in this century, both in the South and outside of it. Since the 1954 *Brown v. Board of Education* decision of the U.S. Supreme Court, southern and nonsouthern school systems have been faced with the challenge of desegregation. Urban public universities in Charlotte, Birmingham, Tampa, Atlanta, New Orleans, and other southern cities have recently entered the competition for students and funds with nonurban southern public and private colleges and universities, just as newer public universities in Boston, Cleveland, Detroit, Chicago, and Milwaukee have begun to challenge the primacy of their regions' nonurban public universities and private colleges.

Yet, despite this overall similarity from region to region, variations in the South's urban educational experience have distinguished it from the experiences of other regions. Changes regarded as innovations elsewhere have different meanings in the South. For example, the school system in Atlanta, Ga., in the late 19th and early 20th centuries selectively adopted educational innovations such as the introduction of technical subjects into the curriculum. Atlantans at first resisted the new subjects and then slowly accepted them, but only as new avenues of preparatory study for higher education. The reformist idea of providing true vocational education as an alternative offering was slow to be realized.

This hesitancy to embrace innovation wholeheartedly was characteristic of urban higher education as well. In the late 19th and the early 20th centuries, two of the region's urban institutions of higher education, Emory and Vanderbilt, were caught up in a struggle between utilitarian curricular reformers and traditional opponents of that reform. At Emory, which originally was in the small-town setting of Oxford, Ga., the conservatism of President Warren A. Candler (1888–98) undid vocational reforms achieved by his two immediate predecessors. Two decades later, Emory moved from Oxford to the urban setting of Atlanta, a move that was part of a plan by Candler, who by then was a Methodist bishop, to make Emory one of two universities closely tied to the Methodist Episcopal Church, South, and its traditional beliefs and values. Candler and his church had bitterly quarreled with its former affiliate university, Vanderbilt, which under the leadership of Chancellor James H. Kirkland chose secularism over Southern Methodism in order to receive a grant for its medical school from the Carnegie Foundation for the Advancement of Teaching.

At Vanderbilt, even after its divorce from the church and during several decades in which it was led by New South advocates like Kirkland and his successors, opposition to social and educational change was strong. A notable defense of traditional southern values came from the famous Vanderbilt Agrarians, who published their manifesto, *I'll Take My Stand*, in 1930. Ironically, this defense of the values of the rural countryside came from one of the South's preeminent urban universities. One of the Agrarians, Donald Davidson, taught at Vanderbilt for over four decades, from the 1910s to the 1950s, defending traditionalism in education and social life during that entire period. Davidson's rabid defense of segregation in the 1950s, however, showed the darker side of southern cultural traditionalism.

The urban South's experience with school desegregation since 1954 has run counter to the prophecies of doom made by Davidson and the anti-integration politicians. Desegregation has taken place with relative success in Florida's major cities—Jacksonville, Miami, and Tampa–St. Petersburg—as well as in other southern cities such as Charlotte, N.C., and Richmond, Va. Thus, by the 1970s most of the images of hate and fear that accompanied the desegregation of urban schools came from such northern cities as Boston, Chicago, Buffalo, and Cleveland, rather than from the South. Explanations for this difference vary, but whatever the cause, the South's urban experience clearly contains something that has allowed it to meet the challenge of school desegregation without collapsing into spasms of hate. But the success of desegregation efforts must be interpreted in light of so-called white flight from urban public school systems. For example, in 1985 about 94 percent of Atlanta's public school students were black, and in Memphis approximately 77 percent were black. Although some school systems are successfully turning around such trends, the new patterns of segregation will persist in many locales in the foreseeable future.

These new patterns of segregation have been called resegregation by many, and Supreme Court decisions in the 1990s in urban areas in Oklahoma, a border state, and in Georgia, a Deep South state, meant the lessening if not the end of mandatory efforts to desegregate public schools in much of the South. Following this trend, the Supreme Court allowed the end of busing for desegregation in the Charlotte–Mecklenburg County schools, an enormously important reversal of successful desegregation and a rather clear sanction of resegregation, undertaken this time with the weight of the law on the side of districting that portrayed itself as nonracial at the same time that it led to increased racial imbalance in many schools. Further litigation in the first decade of the 21st century, this time in the school districts of Louisville, Ky., and Seattle, Wash., meant the further weakening of attempts to desegregate urban schools, even those that replaced mandatory measures with voluntary policies.

Comparisons of the southern urban educational experience with that in other regions are almost always made with the Northeast or the Midwest, but southern cities, with the exception of Birmingham and a few others, have little in common with the industrial centers of those areas. As 21st-century commercial, regional, and governmental centers, most of the South's cities have more in common with western cities such as Los Angeles than they do with the older industrial centers. Fruitful results should emerge when southern urban educational development is compared to the situation in western urban centers, as well as to the North and Midwest. Louisville and Seattle, as the settings for two of the most recent landmark cases in school desegregation law, may be one significant indication of this trend.

WAYNE J. URBAN
University of Alabama

Mark K. Bauman, "Warren Akin Candler: Conservative Amidst Change" (Ph.D. diss., Emory University, 1975); Charles Boger and Cary Orfield, eds., *School Resegregation: Must the South Turn Back?* (2005); John Kohler, "Donald Davidson, a Critique from the Losing Side: The Social and Educational Views of a Southern Conservative" (Ph.D. diss., Georgia State University, 1982); Kevin M. Kruse, *White Flight: Atlanta and the Making of Modern Conservatism* (2005); William E. Schmidt, *New York Times* (25 May 1985); Twelve Southerners, *I'll Take My Stand: The South and the Agrarian Tradition* (1930); Wayne J. Urban, in *The Age of Urban Reform: New Perspectives on the Progressive Era*, ed. Michael H. Ebner and Eugene M. Tobin (1977), in *Education and the Rise of the New South*, ed. Ronald K. Goodenow and Arthur O. White (1981).

Environmental Justice

Environmental justice activists claim that poor, minority neighborhoods suffer disproportionate burdens of environmental pollution. The reality of environmental injustice has existed throughout American history. Elite white neighborhoods and residents have had access to modern conveniences, higher standards of sanitation, and city services denied to poor blacks both at home and at work. The earliest legal case involving this concept, however, erupted in 1979 through the activism of the African American women in a Houston neighborhood known as Northwood Manor. During the summer of 1977, Southwestern Waste Management Corporation purchased property in northwest Houston and applied for a landfill permit in the area. Part of the resistance by the neighborhood involved filing a lawsuit, *Bean v. Southwestern Waste Management*, which alleged that the landfill violated the African American community's civil rights. Residents believed that Southwestern Waste Management Corporation had located the landfill in their area because they were black. To substantiate the charge of "environmental racism," the neighborhood hired Robert Bullard, a sociologist at Texas Southern University and husband of the neighborhood's attorney. Bullard and the residents completed substantial research on Houston's history of siting landfills, finding that minority neighborhoods were far more likely to host a landfill, or other waste site, than white neighborhoods. The courts did not agree with Bullard's assessment, finding numerous flaws in his methodology and conclusions. The Northwood Manor case failed to stop the landfill, but it began Bullard's interest in the issue of environmental racism, and he would become a key player in the movement.

Three years after this case, the environmental justice movement began to move from the local level to the national front, with opposition from residents to a proposed hazardous waste site in Warren County, N.C., a predominantly African American area, which already had substantial numbers of waste disposal sites. During one of the protests, in October 1982, police arrested over 500 people, including politicians and activists. The protest brought national media attention to the issue of environmental racism but failed to stop construction of the site.

The environmental justice movement gained momentum through numerous official studies and academic conferences during the 1980s and early 1990s. Two prominent studies that verified activists' claims included the U.S. General Accounting Office's *The Siting of Hazardous Waste Landfills* (1983), prompted by the Warren County incident, and the United Church of Christ Commission on Racial Justice's *Toxic Waste and Race in the United States* (1987). Both studies concluded that minority neighborhoods saw greater amounts of pollution and health hazards than white areas. In 1991, in response to growing concern, activists held the First National People of Color Environmental Leadership Summit in Washington, D.C. Over 500 people from across the country adopted the "Principles of Environmental Justice" at the summit. Among other things, these principles "affirm[ed] the sacredness of Mother Earth, ecological unity and the interdependence of all species, and the right to be free from ecological destruction . . . and demand[ed] that public policy be based on mutual respect and justice for all peoples, free from any form of discrimination or bias." Activists built on the accomplishments of the 1991 conference with a second in October 2002.

Across the nation, grassroots activism continued after Warren County, often independent of the scholastic and official debates raging above them. Women of all races and classes have played a pivotal role in many of these struggles. Because of the health threats to children from pollution, women often see their activism as a part of their role in protecting their children and communities. The Mothers of East Los Angeles, for example, a group of Latino women from a poverty-stricken area, successfully opposed the construction of several toxic waste sites during the 1980s. Women also form a large part of the opposition to the chemical pollution in the so-called Cancer Alley, an area home to poor African American communities between Baton Rouge and New Orleans. In addition to these fights for a healthier home and neighborhood, the grassroots environmental justice movement has also focused on workplace pollution and hazards. Poor, minority workers, relegated to the lowest-level and most menial jobs, come into contact with hazardous waste and other pollution far more frequently than elite white workers.

Several national-level groups exist to assist these communities in their struggles. One of the most prominent of these is the Center for Health, Environment, and Justice (CHEJ), founded in 1981 by Lois Gibbs, famous for her activism in relocating her Love Canal community in the early 1980s. Gibbs's CHEJ helps neighborhoods understand the often highly scientific issues they face, develop responses, and empower local leadership. Other organizations, including Bullard's Ejnet.org, also provide information and assistance to activists.

As studies and activism continued, the very definition of the problem grassroots groups faced expanded and developed over time, becoming more inclusive and global. Initially, as seen in the *Bean* case, "environmental justice" existed as "environmental racism." Credited with coining the term, Benjamin Muhammad (formerly Rev. Benjamin Chavis Jr.) defines environmental racism as racial discrimination in environmental policymaking. It is racial discrimination in the enforcement of regulations and laws. It is racial discrimination in the deliberate targeting of communities of color for toxic waste disposal and the siting of polluting industries. And it is racial discrimination in historically excluding people of color from the mainstream environmental groups, decision-making boards, commissions, and regulatory bodies.

The term "environmental racism" was criticized by other scholars, who debated the role of race in environmental hazards. Many scholars felt that poverty played an equal, or perhaps more significant, role in pollution exposure. Several academic studies indicated that the issue of "environmental racism" was far more complicated than previously thought. Scholar and activist Robert Bullard later adopted a more inclusive definition of environmental racism, specifically to include global and class issues in the discussion. "Environmental racism," he notes, "refers to any policy, practice or directive that differentially affects or disadvantages (whether intended or unintended) individuals, groups, or communities based on race or color. Environmental racism is not just a domestic practice. It is global. Environmental racism extends to the export of hazardous waste, risky technologies, and pesticides and the application of nonsustainable and exploited development models to the Third World just as it has been targeted toward people of color, working class people, and poor people in this country."

The EPA later decided to use the more inclusive term "environmental justice" rather than the limited "environmental racism." "Environmental justice," the agency stated, was "the fair treatment for people of all races, cultures, and incomes, regarding the development of environmental laws, regulations, and policies." Thus, environmental justice began as a very narrowly defined "environmental racism," specifically aimed at African Americans, and later grew to drawn attention to hazards borne by all minorities and poverty-stricken populations.

With the increased level of national attention to the issues of environmental justice, President Bill Clinton issued Executive Order 12898 in February 1994. The order, seen as a substantial achievement by the environmental justice movement, demanded that federal agencies "make achieving environmental justice part of [their] mission by identifying and addressing, as appropriate, disproportionately high and adverse human health or environmental effects of its programs, policies, and activities on minority populations and low-income populations in the United States." Activists see the order as only a first step and continue to work for environmental justice and enforcement of environmental laws, at the local level, by removing polluting industries, landfills, and hazardous waste sites from their communities or by preventing their siting in the first place.

ELIZABETH BLUM
Troy University

Bunyan Bryant and Paul Mohai, *Race and the Incidence of Environmental Hazards: A Time for Discourse* (1992); Robert Bullard, *Unequal Protection: Environmental Justice and Communities of Color* (1994); Melissa Checker, *Polluted Promises: Environmental Racism and the Search for Justice in a Southern Town* (2005); Christopher Foreman, *The Promise and Peril of Environmental Justice* (1998); Andrew Hurley, *Environmental Inequalities: Class, Race, and Industrial Pollution in Gary, Indiana, 1945–1980* (1995).

Expressways and Central Cities

Since World War II, southern cities and metropolitan areas have experienced sustained patterns of population and economic growth. Their centers have been physically reshaped by large clusters of tall buildings, and their outer edges have sprawled expansively over cotton fields, river valleys, and forested rural areas. Like cities in the rest of the nation, their recent shapes and forms have been dictated largely by motor vehicles and the high-speed traffic arteries that link together the various segments of the metropolis. In the interstate highway era, especially, urban expressways have had a major impact on southern cities, slicing through dense urban neighborhoods, providing essential pathways for commuters and truckers, and undergirding the suburbanization of southern space.

Southern cities embraced the automobile by the 1920s. Auto ownership became a symbol of mobility, modernity, and progress. Rising car sales and registrations in Memphis, Nashville, Atlanta, Birmingham, and New Orleans, along with the resulting traffic congestion, prompted demands for road modernization in downtowns and new intercity highways. Only New York and Chicago built elevated, limited-access express highways during this period, but southern cities also struggled to relieve street-level gridlock. Atlanta, the South's emerging metropolis, reflected the changing urban pattern of the automobile age. The city's developing road system, especially paved roads, spurred suburban decentralization and undermined central city retailing. Consequent spatial and economic patterns tended to concentrate Atlanta's black population at the center, increasing racial distance between blacks and whites. To combat downtown congestion, Atlanta's municipal authorities built an extensive system of viaducts over street-level railroad tracks, speeding auto traffic in and out of the city but also signifying the dominance of the new mode of transport over the older street railway system.

The urban expressway idea predated the interstate era. By the 1930s, as traditional urban rail transit declined, new ideas in urban planning emerged to accommodate Americans' automobile preferences. Anticipating the large urban market for cars, auto companies encouraged express highways. New Deal public works programs financed road infrastructure around the country. At the 1939 New York World's Fair, General Motors sponsored the popular Futurama exhibit, featuring a large model of futuristic cities with elevated expressways speeding traffic through great skyscraper cities. By that time the federal Bureau of Public Roads (BPR), encouraged by President Franklin D. Roosevelt, had begun planning an enormous interstate highway system linking all the major cities of the nation.

During and after World War II, cities north and south began developing freeways to facilitate traffic and support central commercial districts. In 1944, for example, Charlotte began construction of an east-west, multilane "superhighway." In 1946, noted city planner Harland Bartholomew prepared a master plan for Richmond that included several expressways penetrating the central city. In the same year, New York public works builder Robert Moses submitted an expressway plan for New Orleans. In 1949, Atlanta began building a north-south expressway through the central business district. In early postwar Houston, divided, four-lane highways radiated north, south, and west out of the downtown area. By midcentury, Jacksonville, Fla., had embarked on an expressway construction project. Most large southern cities responded to postwar patterns of population and economic decentralization with new expressways designed to rescue the central business districts (CBDS).

When President Dwight D. Eisenhower signed the Federal-Aid Highway Act of 1956, the interstate highway program launched the nation onto an ambitious path in auto and truck transportation. The new road program envisioned a 41,000-mile system (later increased to 42,500 miles) of high-speed, limited-access highways linking every city of more than 50,000 people. (The highway planners missed a few city connections — the Birmingham-Memphis interstate link is only now under construction.) A long debate over financing delayed passage of interstate legislation for years, a congressional logjam that was resolved only with the creation of a Highway Trust Fund derived from fuel and trucking taxes. Under the law, the federal government picked up 90 percent of road construction costs, with the states contributing the remaining 10 percent. State highway departments were charged with acquiring the rights-of-way and building the interstates, with oversight from the Bureau of Public Roads and, after 1966, from the U.S. Department of Transportation (DOT).

In the mid-1950s, as the interstate program got under way, few Americans fully appreciated the enormous impact that the new road system would have on the nation. The interstates brought major changes to American cities. A key interstate decision, promoted by the BPR in the late 1930s and approved by President Roosevelt, called for urban expressways that both penetrated the central cities and encircled them with beltways. In the 1940s and 1950s, big city mayors, planners, and business people endorsed the expressway idea. Interstates through the cities, they believed, would facilitate slum clearance and urban renewal, eliminate traffic congestion, revitalize downtown businesses and institutions, and link central cities to expanding suburbs. However, the consequences of expressway building rarely matched optimistic expectations.

Penetrating urban expressways had significant and not always positive effects on southern cities. Highway planners at the state level, working with local civic elites, routinely routed expressways through black residential and business districts, but relocating housing was not mandated until 1968, when

An anti-expressway poster from Washington, D.C. — a powerful image that conveys the connection between civil rights issues and expressway construction through black neighborhoods (Image courtesy of D.C. Public Library, Washington Division, ECTC Collection)

much interstate construction was already initiated or completed. Traffic had piled up on city streets in earlier years, but commuters and truckers quickly clogged the interstates as well. Suburban commuters in Atlanta and Birmingham today spend more time on congested expressways than their counterparts in most other cities. Highway planners had hoped that the urban links of the interstate system would revive declining central city economic activities, but instead the decentralizing trends that began in the 1920s accelerated. Business and commerce gravitated outward toward the beltway interchanges and "new downtowns," such as those that have sprouted along the expressways north of Atlanta. In Miami, new commercial areas around the Miami International Airport offer twice as much office space as Miami's older CBD. In every southern metropolitan area, sprawling shopping centers and malls, surrounded by asphalt acres of parking, have all but made downtown retailing extinct.

Southern expressway systems encouraged ever-more-distant suburban sprawl. The 8.2 million residents in 2007 of the Washington-Baltimore metropolitan area have spread across the District of Columbia and 33 counties in Virginia and Maryland. Atlanta is a relatively compact central city, but its 2007 metropolitan area population of 5.3 million sprawls over some 28 counties in northwest Georgia. Houston's extensive freeway system of some 575 miles has facilitated sprawling development across a 10-county metropolitan area. Even the much smaller Nashville metropolitan area, with a 2007 population of 1.5 million, sprawls across 13 counties in central Tennessee. The urban expressways of the interstate system had turned these and other southern cities inside out by the end of the 20th century.

Expressway construction also altered racial and spatial lines in central cities. Whites moved to the suburbs that were mushrooming along freeway corridors, while the black population of the South's central cities rose in postwar years as a result of blacks' migration from rural areas. As interstate expressways penetrated the cities in the 1960s, blacks found their neighborhoods disproportionately targeted by highway builders. In Miami, for instance, a single massive interchange of Interstate 95 spread across 40 blocks of the inner city and demolished the housing of more than 10,000 African Americans, as well as the entire black business center. State highway planners in Tennessee purposely put a "kink" in the urban link of Interstate 40 as it passed through Nashville, leveling much of the black business district and dividing the community. In New Orleans, white preservationists fought to prevent construction of the Riverfront Expressway separating the French Quarter from the Mississippi River but stood by silently when the Louisiana Highway Department pushed the elevated Interstate 10 expressway through the black Treme community less than a mile away. In Charlotte, Interstate 77 leveled an African American community, including four black schools in the path of the expressway. In St. Petersburg, Fla., black housing and 13 churches were targeted for the roadbed of Interstate 275. In Atlanta, Birmingham, and Richmond, expressways destroyed black housing and served as barriers between black and white neighborhoods. In these cities and others throughout the South, black housing demolitions for highways triggered neighborhood racial changes, as dislocated African Americans sought replacement housing in nearby white areas.

The racial implications of urban expressway construction became apparent during the civil rights era. In Montgomery, Ala., blacks complained that Alabama highway officials routed Interstate 85 through an established black community to punish the civil rights activists who lived there. In 1968, the South Carolina NAACP organized the Columbia black community in protest over the route of the Bull Street Expressway, an Interstate 20 spur that penetrated the central city. The Mississippi NAACP fought black housing demolitions for interstates in Jackson and Vicksburg. Led by professors from Fisk University, the I-40 Steering Committee in Nashville charged state and federal highway agencies with racial discrimination in highway routing, but their suit was dismissed in federal court. Antifreeway activism became part of the civil rights agenda in Washington, D.C., where dramatic posters criticized "White Man's Road thru Black Man's Home!"

The fight to save African American communities from damaging express-ways was part of a larger, nationwide Freeway Revolt that challenged the high-way engineers' vision of an auto-dominated future. Several of the major victo-ries of the Freeway Revolt occurred in the South. In 1969, after a decade-long campaign against the planned Riverfront Expressway in New Orleans, the U.S. DOT cancelled the highway to preserve the historic French Quarter. In Mem-phis, antihighway activists took a lawsuit all the way to the U.S. Supreme Court, successfully defeating the plan to build Interstate 40 through Overton Park, the nation's largest urban wilderness park. A similar battle prevented expressway damage to Brackenridge Park in San Antonio. In Washington, D.C., the Emer-gency Committee on the Transportation Crisis, representing over 30 neigh-borhood organizations, helped to defeat almost a dozen freeways planned for the nation's capital that would have ripped through numerous black and white neighborhoods.

The Freeway Revolt brought a few successes, but most southern cities lost the battle to protect downtown and inner-city neighborhoods. Fifty years later, planners and politicians have come to recognize the damaging impact of the interstate expressways. Following an emerging national pattern, Nashville is now planning to demolish portions of its downtown expressway system, open-ing up space for parks and new development. Planners in Birmingham have floated the idea of burying Interstate 20 in a tunnel as its passes through the downtown area. Atlanta and Washington, D.C., have built modern subway sys-tems, and Miami has a lightly used elevated Metrorail, but recently more cities have built or considered mass transit and light-rail systems as alternatives to more expressways. America in the 21st century uncertainly confronts its energy future, but the concrete jungle of elevated and below-ground expressways that dominate every American city remain, providing a testament to the power of the nation's automobile culture.

RAYMOND A. MOHL
University of Alabama at Birmingham

Richard O. Baumbach Jr. and William E. Borah, *The Second Battle of New Orleans: A History of the Vieux Carre Riverfront-Expressway Controversy* (1981); Ronald H. Bayor, *Journal of Urban History* (November 1988); Blaine A. Brownell, *American Quarterly* (March 1972); Charles E. Connerly, *Journal of Planning Education and Research* (December 2002); Arnold R. Hirsch and Raymond A. Mohl, *Urban Policy in Twentieth-Century America* (1993); Larry Keating, *Atlanta: Race, Class, and Urban Expansion* (2001); Raymond A. Mohl, *Journal of Policy History* (Spring 2008); Howard L. Preston, *Automobile Age Atlanta: The Making of a Southern Metropolis,*

1900–1935 (1979); Christopher Silver, *Twentieth-Century Richmond: Planning, Politics, and Race* (1984).

Farmers Markets

Farmers markets have become part of the urban landscape in southern cities, like cities in other regions of the United States. These markets include older established ones, such as the Nashville Farmers Market, which began in the 1800s, and newly created ones, such as the Memphis Farmers Market, established in 2006. Recent growth in farmers markets can be attributed to the growing desire of metropolitan consumers to buy fresh, organic, and sustainable products from local farmers and the desire of local producers to expand their markets. According to the USDA's *National Directory of Farmers Markets*, the number of markets in the United States grew from 1,755 in 1994 to 4,385 in 2006, more than doubling in just 12 years. The availability of and access to fresh produce in southern cities like Atlanta, New Orleans, Charlotte, and Nashville is the result of local and state initiatives to promote nutrition programs, community participation, and sustainability.

Unlike southern roadside produce stands alongside highways near farmland, where rural vendors wait for local buyers and vacationers to stop, seasonal urban farmers markets are housed in sheltered downtown areas near retail and business locations. The transition from the roadside stands to urban markets is part of the collaborative effort of citizen groups and state agricultural agencies to create a bridge between farmers and consumers for marketing locally grown produce, herbs, perennials, cut flowers, baked goods, homemade jams and jellies, salsa, candles, and crafts. Some urban markets offer box lunches, homemade ice cream, and other delicacies. They schedule lively entertainment by local bands, gospel choirs, storytellers, and musicians to help create a loyal customer base, thereby supporting local cultural opportunities as well as agriculture.

Urban farmers markets have become a part of the global landscape— featuring similar agriculturally based products, events, and foods in urban settings across the world. A farmers market in Cape Town, South Africa, has the same flavor and feel and attracts the same kind of visitors found in Memphis. A longtime shopper at the Morningside Organic Farmers Market in Atlanta, Ga., reflects on why he shops the local farmers market: "It is a pleasure to meet the people who grow the food. It is educational and inspirational to talk with someone who picked your food the day before. Somebody who put the seed in the ground, and nurtured it to fruition." This remark expresses the sentiments

The Farmers Market in Memphis, Tenn., an example of regional foods in urban settings (Photograph courtesy of Ivonne Amill-Rosario and Sarai Chisala)

of the many market shoppers driving the growth in farmers markets seen over the past decade. Along with the wave of interest and demand for local food have come more information, resources, and funding opportunities, especially for farmers.

Think Globally, Act Locally and other alternative food networks are part of the movement to relocalize food. Admittedly, a wider variety of foods at lower cost has been the result of the globalized food system. However, along with this system of cheap, mass-produced food have come underpaid farmers and farmworkers. Jim Goodman suggests that the combination of food-safety scares, declining food quality, and the world food crisis will eventually bring food production back to a local level. Those who patronize local farmers markets want to be sure that growers and workers are paid a fair wage and that the food purchased is grown in an environmentally responsible manner.

Urban farmers markets are places of local commerce, community development, and products indigenous to the region. They have become the vehicle that connects people and improves the quality of life in urban settings that seem to be transforming every day. Profitability and sustainability are also the benefits of farmers markets in the South. New Orleans's Crescent City Farmers Market has a $6.8 million economic impact on the city. These markets have not only proven to be a support system for the financial progress of the region but they have become a way to improve the lives of farmers and consumers. Electronic search engines, directories, and special supplemental nutrition programs, such as Women, Infants, and Children (known as WIC), are part of the state initiatives that have facilitated the expansion of this type of local market and the access to fresh produce for southerners.

IVONNE AMILL-ROSARIO
SARAI EUNICE CHISALA
GLORIA SEWAA HICKS
University of Memphis

Patricia Allen, Margaret FitzSimmons, Michael Goodman, and Keith Warner, *Journal of Rural Studies* (January 2003); Crescent City Farmers Market, www.crescentcity farmersmarket.org; Frank J. Lechner and John Boli, eds., *The Globalization Reader* (2004); Memphis Farmers Market, www.memphisfarmersmarket.org; Nashville Farmers Market, www.nashvillefarmersmarket.org; Tim Payne, United States Department of Agriculture, *U.S. Farmers Markets — 2000: A Study of Emerging Trends* (May 2002); Southern Sustainable Agricultural Working Group, *Southern SAWG Newsletter* (April 2008).

Gangs

Southerners derive perhaps misplaced comfort from the notion that the South historically was not a gang-suffused milieu and that gang activity is a northern or West Coast import. It is commonly recognized that gang activity is found in all urban areas in all southern states. What is not generally recognized, however, and never discussed in the media, is that gangs, though previously constituted rather differently, have had a long and boisterous history in the South. In that regard, the experience of three cities, two of them ports, is illustrative.

Baltimore, the northernmost though decidedly southern city, at least in sentiments throughout the 1800s, was among the most celebrated gang-dominated cities of its time. Gangs with names such as Plug Uglies, Rip Raps, American Rattlers, and Blood Tubs arose, as in New York City, at least in part in reaction to the flood of immigration in eastern seaboard states. Constituted primarily of "native Americans" of Anglo-American stock, these gangs were fiercely anti-Catholic and fought new immigrants for political patronage and pride of place in the rapidly changing port city. As nativist groups, these gangs were often allied with the American or Know-Nothing Party and sometimes styled themselves as political clubs inasmuch as they had rallies and parades, played what might be termed "dirty tricks" on immigrant political organizations, and endorsed candidates. Acts of violence, riots, and intimidation against "radical" German and "popish" Irish immigrants were common. Irish gangs, such as the Bloody Eights, allied to the Democratic Party, came into being as a counterweight. As might be expected, during political seasons and at election times violence occurred when political gangs collided. In 1854 and 1858, dozens were killed and hundreds wounded as the Know-Nothings prevailed over the Democrats and became the dominant party in state politics. The specter of mob action set the stage for mass insurrectionary violence directed at Union troops during the Civil War. In the Pratt Street riot (or massacre) of 19 April 1861, four soldiers of the 6th Massachusetts Regiment and 11 Baltimore citizens were killed. Afterward, the Union Army occupied the city and arrested the mayor and other officials. Throughout the war, soldiers continued their occupation and quelled the gangs and all antiwar political expression and activity through arrests and imposition of harsh military rule.

Prosperous and still-exotic New Orleans was also noted for gangs, although in the mid-1800s their activities were more overtly criminal than political. The commonsense assumption that "antipopish" sentiment would not have had much currency in predominantly Catholic south Louisiana was true, and Anglo-Protestant gangs gained no ground there. However, paradoxically, the Know-Nothing Party did gain power in municipal elections in the decade before the Civil War. In antebellum New Orleans, the political alliance between gangs and politics was noted, although it was political corruption that was much bruited about in the press. The elections of 1856 and 1857, when nativist thugs and gangs attacked Irish voters, were notably corrupt. Nativist thugs attacked the Irish American chief of police in 1854 and killed two police officers.

Both before and after the Civil War, notorious criminal gangs flourished in various neighborhoods of urban New Orleans. The Live Oak Boys, who frequented the Gallatin Street area, were a disorganized group of petty criminals, indiscriminately killing and vandalizing vice establishments of that area and preying on their denizens and customers. Other well-organized groups of burglars, thieves, and pickpockets frequented the area, including the Yellow Henry gang and the Spiders, both operating in the 1880s. The Spiders were used as thugs and poll watchers by local politicians. In this period, political factions operated in ganglike fashion but ultimately were overwhelmed by the very tide so feared by their Baltimorean confreres—immigrants and their organized gang activity. Ironically, the most serious and renowned incident of "nativist" gang violence occurred following the murder of an Irish American police chief, David Hennessey, in 1890. In his last words, Hennessey supposedly named Mafia "dagos" as his assailants, and he had been shot in typical Mafia style. In March of the following year, after a rancorous trial and the acquittal of all suspects, anti-Mafia rioters inflicted lynch law on all Italian suspects in the city jail. Eleven were killed, chilling relationships between Italy and the United States for some months. Nonetheless, Mafia activity was by no means suppressed, and the Mafia became the dominant gang, a source of corruption and patronage, and a potent political reality in New Orleans and environs for many decades.

Confederate Richmond was the scene of gangs of lower-class and middle-class boys, primarily white but sometimes interracial—the Butcher Cats and the Shockoe Hill Cats—though the members seem much more like Tom, Huck, and Jim than gangsters in the making. The Butcher Cats lived in the slaughterhouse neighborhood and were lower class in origin; the Shockoe Hill Cats were scions of the ministers, doctors, and businessmen of Richmond. It was widely known that Jefferson Davis Jr. was associated with the more prosperous Shockoe Hill Cats in this territorially oriented class war. Brutalized by the war and its associated dislocations and deprivations and armed with bricks and rocks, the gangs fought arranged battles that swept through the lower-class valley neighborhood and up the more upper-class hill. The combatants used complex battlefield tactics in order to temporarily gain territory. In 1861, local newspapers began a crusade against these gangs and their turf wars, primarily because bystanders had been harmed. After a young black ward of the Davis family was bloodied by a missile, President Davis interceded with the Shockoe Hill gang, but without success, and the wars continued. Later, by the end of the war, the gangs' weapon use escalated, and shotguns and pistols were sometimes used and serious injuries inflicted. Several decades following the end of the war and the federal destruction of the city, the gang had faded from notice.

Other than the Mafia and homegrown gangs of organized criminals, interest in gangs receded in the South. When criminologists wrote about gangs in the 1930s through 1970s they were writing not about southern cities but about New York and Chicago, although their analyses could have been applied to rapidly growing southern cities. Throughout the 1970s, the youth gang problem was associated with the large cities of the Rustbelt regions of the Northeast and the Midwest. During the 1970s and into the 1980s, the gang problem grew almost unnoticed in the West, primarily in California. Between the 1970s and the mid-1990s, gangs shifted loci and expanded. Only in the early part of the latter decade did consciousness about gangs and gang-related issues came to the fore in metropolises throughout the South. Academics in the region, never having dealt with the problem of gangs, were not attuned to the issue.

In the late 1980s, however, gang activity began to be noted by police, citizens, and media in many southern cities. The movie *Colors* (1988) and other media coverage gave form and inspiration to many would-be gangbangers in cities throughout the nation. It was alleged that gangs were "following the interstates" from Chicago and New York, and especially from Los Angeles and San Diego, bringing African American and Latino gangs, "street" drug culture and sales, and associated violence to previously peaceful southern milieus. Gang graffiti was often discounted or ignored by police, who did not understand it and who had no idea what lay ahead. Ironically, this denial has certain parallels with that of white southerners of earlier generations. During slavery, discontent among slaves was attributed to "abolitionists," and during the civil rights era to "outside agitators," the inference being that "our Negroes" were content with the status quo. In the present case, police agencies saw the burgeoning gang problem as mainly caused by migrants from northern and western urban areas, with the implication that race relations and living conditions were so idyllic in the South in the 1980s that local African Americans would have no interest in gangs and certainly would not form gangs without agitation from outsiders. This sort of thinking caused communities to be slow in responding.

City fathers and mothers in many southern cities, even longer in denial than police executives had been, began to press police chiefs for information and solutions. Experts and consultants were summoned from Los Angeles and Washington, workshops and seminars for concerned citizens were held, and by the mid-1990s, most urban locales in the region were actively attempting to deal with gang issues or were at least aware that they had a problem. Individual cities formed specialized, dedicated gang task forces within police departments and statewide networks of gang investigators, and gang-related databases were established. Reports to state legislatures were forthcoming, portraying the problem and outlining programs and solutions. It became obvious that the problem was widespread and beyond the coping capabilities of any one locale. Moreover, with increasing Latino immigration, gangs from various Latino ethnicities filtered into southern cities and somewhat unexpectedly into rural areas, where large numbers of agricultural workers were traditionally employed. As gang-inspired styles, argot, and worldviews spread into farm communities and small towns, the infiltration of gangs into the fabric of rural life in the South became a fact of life. Some rural counties reported high gang activity, though it is difficult to assess the accuracy of these perceptions. Wide variations were reported in numbers of gangs per county in similar rural neighboring counties. Some law enforcement agencies seemed alarmist, but as late as the middle of the first decade of the 21st century, others were still in denial about the existence of gangs within their jurisdictions. But clearly gangs were perceived as more problematic in urban areas and small towns than in rural areas.

Southern gangs often claimed linkage with notorious West Coast urban groups, such as the Crips and the Bloods. Purported affiliation with Chicago gangs such as the Folk Nation and Latin Kings was reported by law enforcement in South Carolina as well. It is important to recognize that gangs that claim to be branches of other gangs may not, in fact, be affiliated with them at all. Although family members sending "gangbangers" "down home" to keep them out of gangs might, in fact, spread gang culture, it also could turn out to be a positive experience for that young person. Local police in South Carolina and other states report that gang migrants had relocated to 40 percent of their communities, though the geographical distribution was uneven. Urban youth new to the region have, in some instances, begun new Los Angeles– or Chicago-style gangs in their new city of residence, but these gangs seldom have any but the most superficial ties to the original gangs. They are "wannabees" in the truest sense. However, they can become problematic groups in their own right as they emerge as actual local gangs. But the very sight of gang-related styles and colors and the in-migration of urban youth from outside the region is unsettling to many police officers and municipal officials, who may draw incorrect conclusions from the presence of "street styles."

In the last decade, police have created and relied heavily on intra-agency task forces and have moved to create interstate and regional task forces that share information. Unfortunately, this information is not shared with academics, as a matter of security, so its accuracy cannot be assessed or evaluated. On the local level, typical tactical responses include prevention, intervention, and suppression. Prevention and intervention include mentoring, counseling, conflict resolution, and the gathering of information and monitoring. Suppression, generally regarded as a measure of desperation, includes the use of informants, buy/busts, surveillance, undercover officers, sweeps, mass warrant service, nuisance abatement, reverse stings, and saturation techniques. These methods are often done in conjunction with the use of Community-Oriented Policing (COPS) techniques to gather intelligence from community members and disaffected gang members. COPS officers typically present workshops on gangs to interested members of the minority community and to the community at large.

Gang types and composition have changed radically from the Old South to the New South. From gangs of white urban working-class toughs in Baltimore, criminals in New Orleans, and class conflict–oriented children in war-torn Richmond, to predominately African American and Latino "wannabees" and genuinely committed gangsters throughout the South, the change is clear. It remains to be seen if these gangs become more politically sophisticated, as was seen in Baltimore in the 1800s and in other urban areas outside the South today, or if they remain involved in conflict and in gang-oriented endeavors. But the presence of gangs is a problematic reality confronting the present and future of the region.

FRED HAWLEY
KAREN A. MASON
Western Carolina University

Herbert Asbury, *The French Quarter: An Informal History of the New Orleans Underworld* (1936, 1989); Justin Davis, Richard Hayes, James Klopovic, Douglas Yearwood, Yuli Hsu, and Brian Perkins, *A Comprehensive Assessment of Gangs in North Carolina: A Report to the General Assembly* (2008), at www.ncgangcops.org; Robert J. Kaminski, Jeff Rojek, Michael R. Smith, and Charlie Scheer, *South Carolina Gang Survey* (2005); Walter Miller, *The Growth of Youth Gang Problems in the U.S., 1970–98* (2001).

Gentrification

Gentrification refers to a process of neighborhood change, generally characterized by the renovation of the existing housing stock, an increase in home values, and dramatic demographic shifts. This process frequently involves the economic and social displacement of existing residents. Gentrification is most commonly seen in neighborhoods near city centers that offer both proximity to high-wage employment and a supply of older dwellings that are good candidates for renovation, although there is growing evidence of gentrification in some small-town and rural settings throughout the South.

Scholars have disagreed on the causes of neighborhood change. One approach attributes gentrification to the presence of potential gentrifiers. These pioneering individuals are affluent and typically childless and seek to minimize commute time. The first wave of gentrifiers are often stereotyped as either artistic bohemians or gay couples. Once the first-wave pioneers stabilize the neighborhood, a second (and larger) wave of gentrifiers, generally consisting of high-wage professional workers with offices in the nearby urban core, triggers rapidly rising property values. The alternative approach focuses on the economic conditions that underlie the gentrification process. As the value of housing in decaying neighborhoods declines, a profit potential emerges that promises both inexpensive housing and large returns on sweat equity investments for the pioneering individuals, a condition known as a rent gap. As the neighborhood is colonized by the affluent, the rent gap declines but home price appreciation may accelerate because of the changing status of the neighborhood.

Little research on gentrification has been conducted in southern cities. Scholars assume that the lessons from studies conducted in established global cities such as New York, London, and Vancouver can be applied elsewhere. However, observation suggests that gentrification in the South has been less prevalent than in other regions. The uniqueness of southern gentrification can be understood by contrasting southern urbanism with the causal process outlined above. Historically, southern cities had less visible gay and artistic communities (with the exception of Atlanta and New Orleans) and were late to develop large concentrations of a high-wage workforce in their downtowns (with the exception of Charlotte). This cultural and economic situation reduced the supply of urban pioneers across the region. Demand for gentrifiable property was further reduced in southern cities by the plentiful supply of inexpensive suburban housing. This suburban preference was a product of both cultural preference and the prevalence of suburban employment options. These twin forces reduced the significance of the rent gap in southern cities.

The few studies of gentrification in the South have focused on the unique forces driving neighborhood change in the region. Several studies document efforts to address the region's shortage of traditional gentrifiers in New Orleans. Developers and corporate tourism interests marketed the revitalization potential of neighborhoods to nonresidents. Such promotional strategies worked in concert with city efforts to use "urban renewal" strategies to remove public housing adjacent to the targeted neighborhoods. Such public-private partnerships are common in southern gentrification. Another study illustrated the use of city-defined historic districts in encouraging tourism-driven gentrification on the Charleston peninsula. The absence of a significant rent gap in southern cities has been overcome by the creation of publicly funded charter schools in Atlanta's Grant Park neighborhood, creative mortgage financing in New Orleans, and corporate loan subsidies in Charlotte's Fourth Ward.

Although the absence of the traditional triggers of gentrification in southern cities has been overcome with public-sector assistance in New Orleans, Charleston, and Atlanta, the overt corporate participation in gentrification characterizes the process in Charlotte. Heather Smith and William Graves (2005) document the efforts of two of the city's largest employers, Bank of America and Wachovia, to initiate downtown revitalization. The banks quickly recognized that the absence of a walkable, high-amenity urban center hurt executive recruiting (most experienced bank executives were recruited from New York and London). Beginning in the early 1980s, the banks provided subsidized loans to gentrifiers and legal services, grant assistance, and political encouragement to the city in an effort to trigger the gentrification process in Charlotte's derelict Fourth Ward neighborhood. These incentives were viewed as necessary to overcome the narrow rent gap and an absence of typical first-wave gentrifiers in Charlotte. This corporate participation in gentrification is now common in larger cities where the rent gap has shrunk. However, the Charlotte example appears to predate its arrival in northeastern cities by 20 years. There is little evidence of corporate-led gentrification elsewhere in the South since this phenomenon is thought to be of greater benefit to financial firms because they, more than most industries, recruit executive talent from global cities with high levels of urban amenities.

Gentrification in small towns is also prevalent in the South. The scattered mill villages of the Piedmont South have been pulled closer to urban orbits as cities have sprawled outward. As cities expand, the once-isolated villages offer large amounts of housing stock to suburban office workers. This process can lead to gentrification of the satellite downtowns in combination with the development of nearby suburban settlement. Across the South, evidence of this small-town gentrification can be found in former industrial centers such as Belmont outside Charlotte, Bynum adjacent to Chapel Hill, Montevallo outside Birmingham, and Whittier Mill in the Atlanta area. This small-town gentrification is particularly significant given the greater visibility of demographic change and the associated improvements in infrastructure and retail selection (for example, coffee shops). In a study that examined three small towns within easy commuting distance of Charlotte (Huntersville, Cornelius, and Davidson), tax values of residential properties built before 1950 showed an increase in property values from 1991 to 2003. When coupled with commercial revitalization in each of the downtown areas, evidence suggests that small-town gentrification is occurring around growing southern cities.

Amenity-based gentrification in rural areas of the South is a hybrid of the tourism-based gentrification seen in New Orleans and Charleston and the small-town gentrification seen adjacent to large southern cities. Kurt Culbertson et al. noted that there are urbanization impacts of cities that extend well beyond the traditional boundaries. Proximity to urban centers and their respective amenities are making more remote places desirable residential choices. When examining retirees and empty nesters, Culbertson et al. suggested that rural migration and revitalization of the inner city might be parallel processes; aging populations downsizing to condos in the city may use the equity to purchase second homes in more distant areas with natural amenities. Influx of new residents can cause a change in the community dynamic. Southern Appalachia and the Sierra mountains served as case studies. Additionally, this process could be extended to portions of the coastal South.

Gentrification is frequently viewed as a revitalizing change to urban life by the middle and upper classes, but the gentrification process displaces the less affluent. The extent of these displacement impacts has not been studied in the southern context, but the strong sense of place, lengthy residential tenure, and limited mobility of southerners probably increase the negative impacts of gentrification. Although the social costs of displacement can be overlooked when gentrification occurs on a small scale, increasing commuting costs and a growing cultural preference for urban living promise to increase the costs in the near future.

CHARLYNN BURD
University of Tennessee

WILLIAM GRAVES
University of North Carolina at Charlotte

Manuel Castells, *The City and the Grassroots: A Cross-Cultural Theory of Urban Social Movements* (1983); Kurt Culbertson, Diedra Cae, Drake Fowler, Heather Morgan, and Sue Schwellenbach, in *Political Economies of Landscape Change*, ed. J. L. Wescoat Jr. and D. M. Johnston (2008); Kevin Gotham, *Urban Studies* (June 2005); Katherine Hankins, *Urban Geography* (March 2007); Heather Smith and William Graves, *Journal of Urban Affairs* (September 2005); Neil Smith and Peter Williams, eds., *Gentrification of the City* (1986).

Globalization

Urbanization in eastern North America began in the early 16th century with Swedish, Dutch, Spanish, French, and British settlements on the Atlantic and Gulf coasts. European attempts to acquire and exploit vast disputed areas of the inland Southeast produced the South's first cities in the 17th century. The Virginia Company received a charter to do business in what became Jamestown, Va. The British developed Charleston as a defensive buffer against possible incursions from nearby Florida, where the Spanish had established St. Augustine. John Oglethorpe, again with British support, founded Savannah for similar reasons. Florida's politically precarious location south of established British colonies and east of French settlements in Louisiana made potential city building on the east and west shores of the peninsula and on the northern Gulf Coast problematic. The Spanish, French, and British built and rebuilt Pensacola several times, for example. A French chartered company, the Mississippi Company, founded New Orleans in 1718, replacing earlier settlements at Mobile and Biloxi. Although France ceded Louisiana to Spain in 1762, French merchants continued to trade along the Mississippi, founding St. Louis on its western bank in 1764, after the Treaty of Paris gave the British all land east of the river.

The first United States census, taken in 1790, identified 24 urban places of 2,500 or more inhabitants. Five were unarguably southern. Listed in order of size they were Charleston, Richmond, Norfolk, Petersburg, and Alexandria, each a coastal or river port where investments in shipping, plantation agriculture, slave trading, and early industry were concentrated. Ten years later, Savannah appears on a slightly expanded list of 33 urban places, along with Washington, D.C., and Georgetown, a tobacco trading center. Washington's compromise location in what the nation's Founders regarded as the "South" suggests that it too could be included in a list of southern cities, along with Baltimore, which shared many of the economic characteristics of other cities of the Chesapeake. With independence, federal and state governments borrowed from Holland and France and to a lesser extent from Spain to pay the costs of the Revolution and to fund westward territorial expansion. British and Dutch investors alone held a third of the securities in enterprises incorporated in the United States in 1803, the year of the Louisiana Purchase, which took place in the context of continental and transatlantic political intrigue, domestic territorial politics, and early American economic development policy. Intending to strengthen the French presence in the Caribbean, Napoleon regained Louisiana in 1800 in a secret treaty with the King of Spain, but after military defeat in Haiti, he sold the entire territory to the United States for $15 million. The Louisiana Purchase and the defeat of the British in 1815, at the end of the War of 1812, solidified New Orleans's position as one of the most important cities and the fifth largest in the nation.

The antebellum South produced 80 percent of the world's cotton, three-fourths of which went to Europe, mainly to England. Southern planters sold to European buyers via intermediaries located primarily in northern financial and shipping centers, where they financed yearly crops, speculated in cotton futures, financed the purchase of slaves, sold cotton to domestic manufacturers, and arranged shipping to Europe. The antebellum southern economy did not encourage large-scale city building. In 1850, 15 southern cities appeared on the list of the 100 largest urban places, which included New Orleans, Lafayette, La., Augusta, Ga., Memphis, Mobile, Montgomery, Nashville, Portsmouth, Va., Lynchburg, Va., and Wilmington, N.C., all located on rivers, canals, and a few railroads, with the majority functioning as conduits for outbound cotton shipments. After the Civil War, nonsouthern investors, including carpetbaggers, borrowed heavily in Europe, arranging loans to Alabama, Arkansas, Florida, Georgia, Louisiana, North Carolina, South Carolina, Tennessee, and Virginia. Seriously overextended, all were in default by 1874. Opportunities to invest in railroads, real estate, mining, manufacturing, and business services in the South beckoned, but foreign investors viewed southern ventures with suspicion, given earlier defaults by states. To attract foreign capital to the South required extra incentives, especially for capital-intensive projects such as railroad construction. Alabama, for example, endorsed bonds to attract English, Dutch, German, and French investment in the construction of two railroads. One connected with the British-backed Louisville and Nashville Railroad, linking its namesake cities more directly to international trade networks at Mobile and New Orleans by eliminating circuitous river journeys to the Gulf.

A transformation of the cotton economy began at mid-century. As early as 1850 southern entrepreneurs began accepting cotton as currency from local farmers and then traded in the commodity themselves. The Lehman brothers of Montgomery, for example, established New York offices before the Civil War. After the war, with increased cotton acreage in the hands of small tenant farmers, local brokers became even more active, taking advantage of expanding railways, telegraphic communications, improved ports, and the newly invented mechanical cotton compress. Strategically located in inland cotton-growing areas, compresses made rail shipment of heavy bulk quantities of cotton to southern ports possible. Southern brokers arranged for financing, storage, and sale of cotton grown in the interior and its shipment to European markets through their own foreign branch offices. Southern coastal ports (Wilmington,

N.C., Mobile, New Orleans, Galveston, and Houston) became transshipping points for cotton from interior markets (Memphis, Greenville and Columbia, S.C., Montgomery, Little Rock, Shreveport, Vicksburg, and Augusta). A low-level interior network of southern cities grew with these innovations in the cotton trade. Because southern cotton merchants had to engage in futures trading to stay profitable, the region was dependent on sources of national and international credit, which was available only in the nation's financial centers.

Foreign investments in southern industry had a modest impact on urbanization in the decades just before and after 1900 but drew the South more deeply into the global economy. Historically, foreign investments in America, whether in the South or not, were not universally successful and were met with mixed reactions—at times welcomed, often criticized, and frequently subjected to change at the behest of interests on both sides of the Atlantic. For example, when international marketing of manufactured cigarettes intensified around the beginning of the 20th century, the American Tobacco Company and Imperial Tobacco formed British American Tobacco to manufacture cigarettes for markets outside the Untied States and Britain. British American produced cigarettes in Richmond and Petersburg exclusively for markets in China, India, Malaya, and Latin America. Antitrust actions forced American Tobacco to sell its shares in British American Tobacco, whereupon it became a British-owned and -operated global enterprise. When the company's operations in China and India became increasingly unpredictable because of growing anti-British sentiments, it reduced its dependence on those Asian markets by purchasing Winston-Salem's Brown and Williamson Tobacco Company to gain entry into the American market. In the early 1930s, it moved its U.S. head office to Louisville. The United States today exports about 30 percent of its cigarette production, which accounts for about 20 percent of all world exports. Although the corporate structure of the cigarette industry today is complex, cigarette production continues in Greensboro, Winston-Salem, Richmond, and Louisville, but no longer in Durham, once home to American Tobacco.

Another late 19th-century venture saw British steelmakers invest in ironworks in Alabama (Birmingham and Bessemer) and Tennessee (Cleveland and Isabella, near Chattanooga). Additional British investment in railroads, to transport coal from Kentucky (Middlesboro), Virginia, and West Virginia to Norfolk for export, established important foundations for later southern industrialization and urbanization. In Tennessee, the British constructed the largest sulfuric acid production facility in the world. In North Carolina, the French constructed an aluminum plant in Badin, named for the managing director of a major aluminum manufacturer in France. The Badin investment was probably encouraged by the federal government to foster competition with the Alcoa Company, then the only domestic manufacturer of aluminum. Austrians invested in phosphate mining in Florida and Tennessee to counter German cartel prices for that commodity. Following the Civil War, foreign investment in the southern textile industry was limited, despite convenient supplies of cotton, a source of low-cost, compliant labor, and the growth of a national domestic mass market for lower-cost textiles and apparel. Southern entrepreneurs, some descended from families of plantation owners, recognized this neglected market and constructed mills from the 1850s into the 1880s. Nonsoutherners brokered goods to retailers and eventually established larger southern mills to serve increasingly large-scale retailers in the nation's growing metropolitan centers. Finally, in the 1920s, the British firms J. and P. Coats, American Thread (controlled by the British), and Linen Thread constructed mills in Georgia and Tennessee. In the last half of the 19th century, the textile industry in the South created not cities but mill towns in rural areas, transforming rural farm populations to rural nonfarm populations. The furniture industry also took advantage of a dispersed labor force and located plants in small towns convenient to supplies of wood. Later, concentrations of larger furniture and textile plants and cigarette manufacturing produced numerous small towns and medium-sized cities, particularly in the Piedmont areas of South Carolina, North Carolina, and Virginia. In 1850, only 15 of the nation's largest 100 cities were located south of the Ohio River cities of Louisville and Cincinnati, Ohio, east of the Mississippi, and south of Baltimore and Washington, D.C. The number declined to 11 in 1870 and 1900. In 1900, however, four additional cities—Dallas, Houston, Little Rock, and San Antonio, all west of the Mississippi—were on the list, for a total, again, of 15. By 1930, the total had increased by only one, to 16. New Orleans alone ranked in the top quarter, from 1850 to 1930, a rank maintained in part because of its enhanced importance to international shipping upon completion of the Panama Canal. Three Florida cities, Jacksonville, Miami, and Tampa, appear on the top 100 list for the first time in 1930, all in the bottom half. The presence of Florida and Texas cities hinted at a new era of southern urbanization to come, but depression and war delayed its arrival for more than two decades.

Southern cities made up a quarter of the 100 largest urban places in 1950, with four cities in the top quarter: New Orleans, Houston, Dallas, and San Antonio. The use of the urban place definition, however, does not reveal the reality of postwar dispersed metropolitan growth. A presidential commission report in 1972 anticipated the eventual formation of 25 urban regions in the United States, with eleven projected for the South. In 2000, the U.S. census identified some 30 metropolitan areas in east and central Texas; the northern Gulf Coast; central, Atlantic, and Gulf Coast Florida; the Piedmont and southern coastal plain in North and South Carolina; northwest Georgia; northern Alabama; east, middle, and west Tennessee; and northeast Arkansas. Federally sponsored Depression-era improvements in the South's infrastructure, low taxes, relatively low-wage, nonunion labor, and attractive state and local incentive packages drew domestic capital to the region. These advantages, and the open-market provisions of the Bretton Woods agreements, eventually attracted foreign capital. With market openness compromised somewhat in the 1970s, when the United States imposed tariffs on some imports, the pace of foreign investment in the South actually quickened. To avoid tariffs and gain access to American markets, foreign firms located plants in a business-friendly South. Textile companies in Spartanburg and Greenville, S.C., attracted foreign manufacturers of textile machinery and chemicals. Other states emulated South Carolina's success in attracting foreign investment by offering valuable incentives, from tax breaks to publicly supported job training to right-to-work legislation. When the textile and furniture industries, which had once attracted foreign investments, eventually moved production to lower-cost areas of the world, the automobile industry entered the region. Interstates 65 and 75 provided convenient links between Michigan automakers and suppliers throughout the South. When Corporate Average Fuel Economy regulations went into effect in the 1970s and sales of small fuel-efficient cars from abroad surged, Japanese manufacturers, under pressure from domestic manufacturers, limited imports of economy models and began producing larger models. To meet growing demand for imported automobiles of all sizes, German, Japanese, and Korean automakers sought locations for assembly plants in the United States and were warmly received at locations in or somewhat near Nashville, Chattanooga, Jackson, Tupelo, Tuscaloosa, Birmingham, Columbus, Spartanburg, and San Antonio. After acquiring American domestic truck manufacturers, Volvo began producing heavy trucks in Dublin, Va., and located its North American truck headquarters in Greensboro, N.C. The inevitable growth of global container traffic on the East Coast gave renewed importance and employment boosts to upgraded colonial-era ports in Charleston, Savannah, and Norfolk/ Hampton Roads, and to newer ports in southeast Florida, which, along with Houston on the Gulf Coast, rank among the top 25 container ports in the nation. Inland transportation hubs that service NAFTA-related trade now contribute to growth in New Orleans, Memphis, Mobile, Jackson, Miss., and San Antonio. When the Canadian National Railroad acquired the Illinois Central Railroad, a key north-south corridor connected urban centers in Canada, the

American Midwest, and the South to Mexico. Memphis is particularly well positioned on both north-south and east-west international intermodal corridors. Memphis, Atlanta, and Houston are also major international air cargo hubs.

No southern metropolitan area has attained unambiguous world-city status, although Miami does resemble one: it is an international banking center, the location of the secondary headquarters of many global companies, an information-processing center, and a producer services node. It is also the focal point for Latin American trade because of a unique resource: its cadre of experienced Cubans who settled in the city following the Cuban Revolution. They elevated and secured Miami's importance to the Caribbean, besting the older, established port cities of Houston and New Orleans. Globalization's impact also is evident in Houston, Dallas, Richmond, and Atlanta, together home to a disproportionate share of Fortune Global 500 companies headquartered in the South. Many of these global headquarters are in two of three southern "cyberstates," Texas, Florida, and Virginia, where employment in data-processing enterprises is especially high. In the early years of postwar globalization, academics took note of information processing, design of advanced production technology, and other innovations as drivers of economic development. The work of University of North Carolina sociologist Howard Odum inspired the planning and building of Research Triangle Park near Raleigh, Durham, and Chapel Hill, which drew on the research strengths available at three nearby universities. It has since become a model for many other research parks where state and local governments and private developers seek to link existing university talent to innovative entrepreneurship in hope of attracting global investments.

A common assessment of globalization's recent impact on southern urbanization argues that metropolitan regions of the South are powerless and temporary resting places where American, European, and Asian corporate wayfarers pause on their way to more desirable business climates. Another, but not necessarily more optimistic, view argues that in a world in which enterprises, capital, and labor are footloose, interest groups in all places—nations, metropolitan regions, subregions, cities, small towns, and rural areas—actively facilitate and resist globalization and at times unwittingly become victims of it. Among developers, the anticipated or actual arrival of international enterprise generates regional, state, and local pressures to become globally competitive. State, regional, and local authorities favor the use of local resources to finance infrastructure improvements, social services for diverse and growing populations, and the promotion of initiatives designed to portray globalization as an inevitable and desirable reality. Globalization redefines city and metropolitan boundaries, coercively uproots populations from existing work and community ties, and redeploys them in internationally oriented activities situated in transitional and increasingly unfamiliar urban spaces. Recent globalization has created new urban venues in which protagonists of various points of view will continue to debate and transform southern culture.

DAVID F. MITCHELL
University of North Carolina at Greensboro

Dwight B. Billings, *American Journal of Sociology* 88, Supplement: *Marxist Inquiries: Studies of Labor, Class, and States* (1992); James C. Cobb and William Stueck, eds., *Globalization and the American South* (2005); Peter A. Coclanis, *Journal of the Historical Society* (Fall 2005); Douglas A. Irwin, *Journal of International Economics* 60 (2003); J. R. Killick, *Business History Review* (Summer 1981); Daniel S. Margolies, *Henry Watterson and the New South: The Politics of Empire, Free Trade, and Globalization* (2006); James L. Peacock, Harry L. Watson, and Carrie R. Matthews, eds., *The American South in a Global World* (2005); William Sites, *Sociological Theory* (March 2000); Mira Wilkins, *The History of Foreign Investment in the United States to 1914* (1989), *The History of Foreign Investment in the United States, 1914–1945* (2004).

Growth

For more than a century and a half, urban growth in the South has held out the expectation of bringing social patterns and values into line with national norms. As the points of contact between agricultural hinterlands and the international economy, the cities of the 19th-century South were strongly drawn toward comparable centers of the North. During the years leading up to the Civil War, trading towns of the Mississippi River and the Upper South were reluctant to share the venture of southern independence, with its destruction of internal commerce. In the 1880s and 1890s, hopes for a New South were held most strongly by civic leaders in ambitious cities like Atlanta and Birmingham, who hoped to emulate northern industrial cities.

Through the middle decades of the 20th century, social scientists waited for urban growth to undermine the cultural values and social patterns that had set the South apart from the rest of the United States. According to the common analysis, the combined forces of industrialization, urbanization, and expansion of a cosmopolitan middle class would help to close the cultural gap. In the words of sociologist Leonard Reissman, the emergence of large cities should move the South to "a level of modernity comparable to the nation as a whole."

Indeed, the South between 1900 and 1970 urbanized more rapidly than the North, moving toward the same degree of urban development found in other

TABLE 3. *Urbanization in the South and the Non-South, 1900–2000*

	Urbanization of the South (percent of total population)	Urbanization of the Non-South (percent of total population)	Ratio, South/ Non-South
1900	18.0	50.0	.36
1940	36.7	65.7	.56
1950	44.0	65.8	.67
1960	57.7	74.4	.78
1970	64.4	77.2	.83
1980	66.9	77.1	.87
1990	68.6	78.6	.87
2000	72.8	82.4	.88

Source: U.S. Census Bureau, various years.

parts of the country. In technical use, "urbanization" refers to the proportion of the population of a state, region, or nation living within urban areas. Table 3 compares the degree of urbanization in the South with that of the remainder of the United States and shows a surge of urbanization that crested in the 1950s and 1960s. The differential closed at a slower pace in the 1970s and has remained roughly constant since 1980.

This remarkable record of urban growth has meant new economic roles and influence for established centers and the emergence of new urban rivals. The "Census South" (16 states and the District of Columbia) contained only one metropolitan area with 1 million residents in 1940. Sixty years later, the same region counted six metropolitan areas of 2 million and 14 with populations between 1 and 2 million. The South's combined metropolitan population in 2000 was 62,601,000, or 22 percent of all Americans. At mid-century, studies by Otis Duncan and by Rupert Vance identified Atlanta and Dallas as the only southern cities to rank as high as the third level in the national urban system. By 2000, the southern states accounted for five of the country's 12 largest metropolitan areas (Table 4). The same five metro areas ranked in the nation's top 10 in terms of global economic connections.

At the other end of the urban hierarchy, dozens of small southern cities have grown large enough to earn recognition as metropolitan areas (defined as single or adjacent core cities with 50,000 residents along with the counties with which they have close economic ties). The South counted 58 metropolitan

TABLE 4. *Largest Southern Metropolitan Areas, 1940 and 2000 (rank order)*

	1940	2000
1.	Baltimore	Washington, D.C.–Baltimore (4)
2.	Washington, D.C.	Dallas–Fort Worth (9)
3.	New Orleans	Houston-Galveston (10)
4.	Houston	Atlanta (11)
5.	Atlanta	Miami–Fort Lauderdale (12)
6.	Birmingham	Tampa (21)
7.	Louisville	Orlando (28)
8.	Dallas	San Antonio (30)
9.	Memphis	Norfolk–Virginia Beach (31)
10.	Wheeling	Charlotte (34)

Source: U.S. Census Bureau, various years.

Note: National size rank in parenthesis for 2000.

areas in 1950 and 120 in 2000. Additions to the list during the 1970s included Victoria, Tex.; Alexandria, La.; Florence, Ala.; Hickory, N.C.; and Bradenton, Fla. The 1980s saw the addition of Decatur, Ala., and Naples, Fla., and the 1990s added Blacksburg, Va.; Sumter, S.C.; and Jonesboro, Ark.

Many of the new southerners have been attracted by the changing economic base of these growing cities. By the middle 1970s, the point of national transition from the post–World War II boom to an emerging global economy, three-quarters of the major metropolitan centers in the region depended on tertiary activities (trade, finance, transportation) or quaternary activities (government, research). A comparison of the 10 largest urban centers in the South in 1940 and in 2000 shows some of the changes (Table 4). The old river ports and heavy industrial cities of New Orleans, Louisville, Memphis, Birmingham, and Wheeling dropped off the list. The replacements are the financial and trade center of Charlotte, the recreation-retirement cities of Miami, Tampa, and Orlando, and the military centers of San Antonio and Norfolk–Virginia Beach. Another indicator of the emerging postindustrial economy is the list of medium-sized metropolitan areas (500,000 to 1,000,000 in 1990) that grew more than 25 percent in the 1990s. Austin and Raleigh-Durham are research and education centers, West Palm Beach is a resort-retirement center, and McAllen-Edinburg is a gateway for immigration.

The leading economic sectors in the fast-growing cities demand salaried experts and professionals. Military officers, aerospace engineers, tax accountants, medical researchers, university professors, petroleum geologists, and members of corporate publicity departments are members of a footloose middle class. They expect to make their careers in a sequence of cities, and they are more dependent on the judgments of their professional peers than on the attitudes of their neighbors. They constitute not simply the white-collar class anticipated by social theory, but a modern mobile population with limited attachment to regional traditions.

One of their impacts has been to homogenize the residential areas of southern cities. Families transferring from city to city tend to look for comparable communities. Their taste might run to restored center city neighborhoods like Alexandria, Va., or Inman Park in Atlanta. The majority choose suburbs that are difficult to distinguish from each other or from similar communities outside the South. The sprawl of Houston, the supersuburb of Virginia Beach, and northside Atlanta and northside San Antonio offer essentially the same socioeconomic environment in varying physical landscapes.

Many southern cities are also more international than in the past. New Orleans in the 19th century and Tampa in the early 20th century were important immigrant destinations, but southern cities by and large drew their new residents from the rural South. In the 21st century, however, southern cities are magnets for immigration. For the period 2000–2005, greater Miami had a net population gain from foreign migration of 332,000 — more than San Francisco–Oakland–San Jose. Dallas–Fort Worth gained 232,000 people through immigration — three times the gain of Philadelphia. Houston's gain of 210,000 was two and a half times that of Seattle, and Atlanta's gain of 145,000 was greater than that of Boston.

It is arguable whether many of the largest southern cities retain their distinct "southern" character. Baltimore and Washington, dominated by local elites with southern orientations as late as the 1930s, have been absorbed into the northeastern megalopolis, and Washington's Virginia exurbs now nudge into Harry Byrd country. Houston, Dallas, and Atlanta are high-rise cities, with new downtowns that rise like glass icebergs out of a sea of parking lots. Newcomers to Tampa and West Palm Beach know little and care less about the mill towns and cotton crossroads of the historic South. If anything defines the uniqueness of the South, it is patterns and problems of black-white relations. However, Latino Americans are the largest minority in metropolitan Miami, Austin, and San Antonio, not to mention Texas border cities from Brownsville to El Paso.

In the broadest view, urban development is pulling the South into a new regional alignment. Although the Sunbelt has been a loosely defined and debatable concept since the 1970s, rates of population growth by states and metropolitan areas for the second half of the 20th century show two regions of rapid growth in the United States. A Sunbelt Southeast runs along the South Atlantic coast from Baltimore–Washington, D.C., to Key West. A Sunbelt Southwest angles from Texas and Oklahoma across the southern Rocky Mountains to the Pacific Ocean. The southern states that anchor corners of these Sunbelts— Texas, Florida, Maryland, and Delaware, plus the District of Columbia—all had metropolitan percentages above the national figure of 80 percent in 2000. In contrast, fewer than half of the residents of Arkansas, Mississippi, Kentucky, and West Virginia lived in metropolitan areas. Together with Tennessee (68 percent metropolitan) and Alabama (70 percent), they constitute a region of older cities and older manufacturing, somewhat slower growth, and limited employment in government and high-tech industry.

In summary, urban growth in the early 21st century was simultaneously reducing the distinctiveness of the South and drawing it into new regional and global configurations. Houston is a global energy capital as much as a southern city. Miami is part of the advancing Caribbean frontier. Spartanburg, S.C., is an international manufacturing center. Orlando is one of the top attractors for international tourism. These and other cities may be rooted in a regional past, but they also look toward a global future.

CARL ABBOTT
Portland State University

Carl Abbott, *The New Urban America: Growth and Politics in Sunbelt Cities* (1987), *Political Terrain: Washington, D.C., from Tidewater Town to Global Metropolis* (1997); Blaine A. Brownell and David R. Goldfield, eds., *The City in Southern History: The Growth of Urban Civilization in the South* (1977); Ollinger Crenshaw, in *Historiography and Urbanization: Essays in American History in Honor of W. Stull Holt*, ed. Eric Goldman (1941); Don Doyle, *New Men, New Cities, New South: Atlanta, Nashville, Charleston, Mobile, 1860–1920* (1990); Otis D. Duncan et al., *Metropolis and Region* (1960); David R. Goldfield, *Cotton Fields and Skyscrapers: Southern City and Region, 1607–1980* (1982); William Nichols, in *The American South in the 1960s*, ed. Avery Leiserson (1964); Leonard Reissman, *Journal of Social Issues* (January 1966); Rupert B. Vance and Nicholas J. Demerath, eds., *The Urban South* (1954).

Health Conditions

The southern region of the United States has historically been characterized by a poor health status and unfavorable ratings on most indicators of health and illness. This phenomenon can be traced back to pre–Civil War days when much of the region was isolated from the more "advanced" regions of the country.

Not only did the region suffer from conditions that were not conducive to good health (for example, poor nutrition and environmental hazards), but there was a general dearth of health care resources to address the health problems that were so ubiquitous. The lack of resources was reflected in the absence of public sanitation programs and fewer health personnel and facilities relative to the rest of the country.

Early on, the unfavorable health status of the region was generally ascribed to the rural nature of the population. Southern states remain among the most rural and continue to be characterized by poor health status relative to the rest of the nation. Although the South has undergone a dramatic transformation since World War II, most of the historical health disparities remain. The southern states tend to rank higher than average on most indicators of health status. This is true in terms of the incidence of disease (for example, diabetes and sexually transmitted infections), mortality rates (for example, heart disease and stroke), infant and child mortality, and disability, as well as indicators of poor health such as smoking and obesity.

The diversification of the population of the region is reflected in the variations observed among the southern states in terms of health status. Although the states of the Deep South continue to rank poorly on most health indicators, Florida and Virginia tend to exhibit health indicators more in keeping with national trends. More that anything else, perhaps, this reflects the degree of urbanization in Florida and the growing urbanization of Virginia in the Washington, D.C., area.

Although the South's disadvantageous status in terms of health has persisted for decades, there has been a shift in the concentration of health problems over time. The health problems of the past could be attributed to the rural nature of the South, but today, with the region highly urbanized, the dominant health problems have shifted significantly from concentrations among rural populations to concentrations among urban populations. It is true that certain conditions remain higher among nonurban populations (for example, child death rates and motor vehicle death rates), but these are typically more a function of the rural nature of those areas rather than anything distinctly southern.

When the overall health status of the nation's cities is considered, southern cities do not fare well. Sperling's Best Places index ranks the largest U.S. cities in terms of their health status based on five different dimensions. Although perhaps not the most scientific approach to determining comparative health status, it does appear to be a reasonable indicator in terms of the claims made. This index indicates, for example, that only three southern cities (Austin, Raleigh-Durham, and Nashville) are among the nation's 25 healthiest cities. On the other hand, 13 southern cities are among the nation's least healthy cities. New Orleans and San Antonio were identified as the least healthy, and most of the major metropolitan areas in the South, including Atlanta, Dallas, Houston, and Miami, made the least healthy list.

A 2007 study carried out by *Forbes* indicated that southern cities accounted for 5 of the 10 most obese U.S. cities and 10 of the 20 most obese. Among the leading offenders in this regard were Memphis, Birmingham, and San Antonio. The same study conducted by *Forbes* indicated high rates for one of the precursors of ill health—a sedentary lifestyle—for many southern cities. Southern cities accounted for 8 of the top 10 U.S. cities in terms of being sedentary and 12 of the top 20 on this indicator.

These overall figures, however, mask the variety that exists in health status in southern cities. A major distinction exists between the health status of the urban cores of most of these cities and the suburban areas. An argument can be made for the continued poor health of the South's rural areas, and the region's inner cities follow close behind, leaving the South's suburbs as the one beacon of good health. Indeed, some of the region's inner cities rank among the worst in the nation in health status. Memphis, Tenn., is perhaps reflective of the situation within the region. Tennessee historically ranks among the bottom five states in health status. Shelby County, Tenn., typically ranks among the worst of the state's 95 counties in terms of health status. Within Shelby County, the city of Memphis has much worse health indicators than the surrounding communities and unincorporated areas. Within the city of Memphis, the inner city has health-status indicators much worse than the state and the nation, thereby bringing down the overall rating for the county. On certain indicators, such as infant mortality, sexually transmitted infections, and other infectious diseases, Memphis's inner city is comparable to many Third World countries.

The poor health status of the South's inner cities tends to be correlated with concentrations of low-income minority populations. In much of the South, African Americans are concentrated within the inner city, frequently living in inferior housing and isolated from the majority population (and from access to health services). This is typical of cities such as Memphis and Atlanta. (New Orleans certainly epitomized this pattern of population distribution until Hurricane Katrina disrupted traditional residential patterns.) In other cases, there may be high concentrations of Latinos within the inner cities in some southern states, with Dallas and Houston being prime examples. And a polyglot city such as Miami exhibits concentrations of a wide range of ethnic groups within its inner-city area.

The poor health status of the South's urban areas is statistically associated

A demonstration for health-care reform outside a hospital in Memphis, Tenn., 2009 (Photograph courtesy of Wanda Rushing)

with concentrations of minority groups, but epidemiologists insist that the underlying contributor to poor health status is not race and ethnicity but socioeconomic status. Outside of the older metropolitan areas in the Midwest and Northeast, some of the nation's poorest populations are found in southern inner cities. In many cases, these concentrations of poverty have persisted over generations, with some being traced back to World War II–era rural-to-urban migration. Poor health status becomes perpetuated from generation to generation as a result of unhealthy lifestyles, unhealthy environments, and the impact of isolation and discrimination.

Poverty and its implications for health status are often exacerbated within southern cities as a result of a lack of access to health services. Certain southern cities are known for their health-care systems, but these systems frequently do not deliver adequate care to the sickest within these communities. Indeed, some of the worst conditions in the nation exist within the very shadow of major southern medical centers.

RICHARD K. THOMAS
University of Tennessee Health Science Center

Priscilla W. Ramsey and L. Lee Glenn, *Southern Medical Journal* (13 August 2002); Shakaib U. Rehman and Florence N. Hutchison, *Free Library* (16 June 2006); E. J. Roccella and C. Lenfant, *Clinical Cardiology* (December 1989); Rebecca Ruiz, *Forbes* (26 November 2007); Keith Wailoo, *Dying in the City of the Blues: Sickle Cell Anemia and the Politics of Race* (2001).

Historic Preservation

In the South, an understanding and a respect for the past are such a part of the culture that historic preservation represents more than the perpetuation of physical resources. Historic resources serve as a link to the past, and they reinforce an individual sense of identity and orientation as well as a sense of place. Change can pose a threat to historic resources and to the culture and identity of people within a region. Given an abundance of historic sites and the degree to which the region cherished its past, it is not surprising that the South would provide fertile ground for the evolution of historic preservation. The potential threat to Mount Vernon, George Washington's home, gave Ann Pamela Cunningham the inspiration for the first national preservation campaign, creating a model for preservation efforts across the country. Virginia's Williamsburg became the nation's first outdoor museum, providing an example of restoration that focused on both buildings and the spaces between them, re-creating the character of the historic community. Threats to the historic area of Charleston were a catalyst for creation of the first local preservation ordinance in America, based on land-use control. A few communities soon followed Charleston's lead, but it would be the last third of the 20th century before this preservation tool was widely accepted.

In the aftermath of World War II, new development driven by consumer demand for housing, automobiles, and highways was unleashed. Cities ex-

Historic preservation boosts revitalization of downtowns in cities such as Charleston, S.C.
(Photograph courtesy of Charleston Convention & Visitors Bureau, www.charlestoncvb.com)

panded into the countryside while federal urban renewal programs threatened the historic cores of many cities, endangering and/or destroying many historic resources. Citizen concern about the loss of historic resources led Congress to create the National Trust for Historic Preservation, in 1949, to foster citizen awareness of preservation through programs of advocacy and education. Almost 20 years later, in response to continued loss of historic resources, the U.S. Conference of Mayors prepared a report, *With Heritage So Rich*, which documented the destruction resulting from federal programs and made recommendations for change. Congress reviewed the report, and its response was passage of the National Historic Preservation Act in 1966. The act incorporated most of the report recommendations and provided a program, based upon a federal/state partnership, which provided incentives for increased involvement of citizens in preservation activities. In the interim following establishment of the National Trust, citizens began to organize nonprofit organizations to combat deterioration, urban renewal programs, and an absence of municipal preservation policy. In Georgia, the Historic Savannah Foundation was organized in 1955, and its activities established a model for citizen activism that rescued the 2.2 square-mile central area of the city as a result of a survey, the creation of a revolving fund for the purchase and resale of endangered properties, and the use of covenants to protect restored properties. These efforts not only revitalized the most historic area of the city but also created a tourism industry that, today, brings in $1 billion annually. Thirteen years after this effort began, the National Trust showcased the city as the site of its 1968 annual meeting to provide lessons and inspiration to preservationists across the nation.

The National Historic Preservation Act created a comprehensive national preservation policy that established a nationwide network of state historic preservation offices with provision of federal matching funds to support their work. The act provided for determination of the historic significance of properties and listing on a National Register of Historic Places, financial benefits to those properties listed, the review of the impact of federal programs on historic properties, and incentives for federal tax credits (implemented in 1976) for rehabilitation of historic buildings. The impact of the National Historic Preservation Act was immediate. No longer could local governments obtain federal funds for projects destructive to historic resources without review. As intended, the act provided a stimulus to local preservation initiative and spurred surveys at local and state levels that led to National Register listings and the availability of benefits to listed properties and, at the same time, energized citizens to form community-oriented nonprofit preservation organizations that developed a slate of preservation initiatives. The increased activity caused the National Park

Service, the designated National Historic Preservation Act administrator, to issue a call to the nation's academic community for development of degree programs to prepare individuals to provide the professional guidance and expertise needed by state agencies, elected officials, citizens, and organizations. As a result of the tax credit program, authorized in 1976 for the rehabilitation of historic buildings used for income production, $23 billion in private investment was made by October 2001. The significance of the tax credit program was the creation of financial incentives for the reuse of historic buildings and disincentives for razing them for new construction.

In 1978, the favorable decision of the U.S. Supreme Court on the constitutionality of local government regulation of historic properties encouraged states to adopt enabling legislation, where needed, and communities to adopt local preservation ordinances. An expansion of local government activity was encouraged by the 1980 amendment of the National Historic Preservation Act, creating the Certified Local Government program, including a special category of grants, to bring cities into the federal/state partnership. As of 2003, 1,228 certified local governments were participants with $40 million provided in grants. Increased citizen activism encouraged the creation of statewide nonprofit preservation organizations during this time, with Preservation North Carolina and the Georgia Trust for Historic Preservation leading the way in the South.

The National Trust launched its Main Street Program, in 1980, to revitalize central business districts, within five states. As of 2002 this program had served over 1,600 communities, in 40 states, which had made an investment of $17 billion in downtown revival. Collectively, the Main Street, Certified Local Government, and Tax Credit programs made historic preservation an economic reality and a positive factor in terms of jobs created, the sale/rehabilitation of buildings, sales and income tax collections, income from heritage tourism, and the growth of property values in designated local districts. These indices signaled that preservation was, or could be, a major element of a community's economic success.

Efforts to strengthen the preservation movement and to extend it more fully to all citizens in the last decade of the 20th century included the 1992 amendments to the National Historic Preservation Act, an effort to bring Native Americans and African Americans more completely into the preservation partnership through provisions for Tribal Historic Preservation Officers to have the authority of State Historic Preservation Officers on tribal lands and authorization of assistance to minority colleges and universities. In addition, in 1993, the National Trust, through its Preservation Partnerships Program, sought to help emerging and established statewide and local nonprofit preservation organizations improve their effectiveness. By 2002 the National Trust had facilitated the growth of full-time staffed statewide organizations from 17 to 38 and created a statewide and local partnership including 32 statewide organizations in 31 states and 21 local organizations in 15 states. The National Trust's Southern Field Office reports that all 12 of the states in its area have statewide organizations, with 10 having full-time staff and two having part-time staff.

The story of 20th-century historic preservation is one of expansion, especially in terms of philosophy, legislation, legal standing, economic significance, and the inclusion of diverse resources and all ethnic groups within American society. This process revised definitions of what is historic, articulated areas of significance, expanded the range of resources to reflect the broad patterns of history, and broadened understanding of what constitutes cultural heritage and the means with which to protect it. Terms such as vernacular architecture, cultural landscapes, heritage areas, rural preservation, interior easements, transfer-of-development rights, smart growth, private property rights, cultural diversity, property stewardship, tear-downs, maritime preservation, economic benefit, and heritage tourism have all become a part of the lexicon of contemporary historic preservation. As preservation entered the 21st century, accomplishments included the number of resources identified and protected, an increase in the number of trained preservation professionals from a still-growing number of institutions offering preservation degrees, the development of African American and other minority initiatives on both state and regional levels, increased use of financial and legal incentives to facilitate preservation, broadened attention to a variety of resource types, recognition of landscapes as preservation resources, an increased understanding of the economic impact of preservation activities, and growing recognition of preservation opportunities as environmental and quality-of-life issues.

Concerns and challenges related to preservation, now and in the future, include our society's continuing reluctance to recognize the purpose, need, value, and potential of planning for the development and redevelopment of our environment in recognition of the values of historic preservation. Too many areas eligible for local protection have not been designated, or ordinances may be weak or poorly enforced. The constant migration of new residents to the South feeds development that is often insensitive to historic preservation. The character of historic buildings is often destroyed by conversion to condominiums, and neighborhood character, especially in established areas, is threatened by those who want to purchase properties and make inappropriate changes or demolish them for new construction. Today, the greatest threat to historic areas is from private individuals, not from the federal government. Another problem is the conflict of values among those concerned with preservation of the built and natural environments. Despite problems, preservation is a success and much has been accomplished. The continuation of that success will depend on the degree to which society can be educated to recognize and appreciate the philosophy of preservation and provide the funds necessary for its implementation.

JOHN C. WATERS
University of Georgia

Diane L. Barthel, *Historic Preservation: Collective Memory and Historical Identity* (1996); James M. Fitch, *Historic Preservation: Curatorial Management of the Built World* (1990); Robert E. Stipe, *A Richer Heritage: Historic Preservation in the Twenty-first Century* (2003); Norman Tyler, *Historic Preservation: An Introduction to Its History, Principles, and Practice* (1999).

Homelessness

The term "homelessness" refers to the condition of people who lack fixed, regular, and adequate nighttime residence. The Stewart B. McKinney Act (1987) defines a homeless person as "an individual who has a primary nighttime residence that is (a) a supervised publicly or privately operated shelter designed to provide temporary living accommodations (including welfare hotels, congregate shelters, and transitional housing for the mentally ill), (b) an institution that provides a temporary residence for individuals intended to be institutionalized, or (c) a public or private place not designed for, or ordinarily used as, a regular sleeping accommodation for human beings."

Many studies seek to explain the causes of homelessness as well as the increasing numbers of homeless people. Some of them focus on addictive disorders and homelessness; others focus on people becoming disconnected from social networks because of mental illness, legal difficulties, or substance abuse. Others, however, point to structural factors, such as job loss, foreclosures, inadequate low-cost housing, rising poverty, changes in the social welfare system, and economic recession.

Homelessness emerged as a significant social problem in the early 1980s. Since then, most media accounts have depicted people living in the streets of major cities such as New York or Los Angeles and have overlooked the South. These stories, and popular perceptions, usually call attention to men with substance-abuse problems as the face of homelessness. But homelessness is a social problem affecting southern states and cities, as well as women and children. Homelessness in the South may be somewhat different from that in other regions. Because of the warm climate, the South may attract homeless people from cold climate areas. Also, the South has the highest percentage of children who are unhoused.

According to the National Alliance to End Homelessness, the homeless population in the South, approximately 170,000 people (2007), accounts for more than one-quarter of the homeless population of the United States. Among southern states, Florida, Texas, and Georgia have the highest number of homeless people. The District of Columbia and Florida have the highest number of homeless people per 10,000 population in the South. Their rates of homeless per 10,000 population, 90 and 26 respectively, are higher than for the United States as a whole, which is 22 homeless per 10,000 population. The metropolitan areas reporting the largest number of homeless people in the region are Washington, D.C., Atlanta, Miami, Dallas, and Houston. In the aftermath of Hurricane Katrina, the homeless population of New Orleans reached nearly 4 percent, unprecedented for a modern American urban area. The number of homeless people in New Orleans nearly doubled the pre–Hurricane Katrina number.

According to the 2000 U.S. Census, two-thirds of the homeless population in the South are male, which gives the South the highest proportion of homeless males in the country. African Americans are overrepresented in the homeless population in the South and in the nation. In Miami–Dade County, Fla., and Houston–Harris County, Tex., African Americans made up less than a quarter of the population but accounted for more than half of the homeless population in both counties in 2005. Miami–Dade County and Harris County have the largest Latino populations in the South, but Latinos in both counties are underrepresented in the homeless population.

The fastest-growing segment of the homeless population is made up of families, who account for nearly 40 percent of the homeless population in the United States and one-third of the homeless population in the South. Most of these families are single women with children, not husband-wife pairs, and the majority of family members are preschoolers. Homeless women with children are more likely than homeless single men and homeless single women to cite divorce or family problems as the main reason for becoming homeless.

According to the National Alliance to End Homelessness, homeless family members in the South in 2007 was 32.6 percent of the total homeless population. Maryland, Louisiana, and Virginia report the highest proportion of homeless families in the South, and the number of homeless families in Maryland, Louisiana, and Virginia makes up 48, 46, and 43 percent of the total homeless populations, respectively.

Studies suggest that homelessness among women and men differs in many respects, and gender often influences the effectiveness of homelessness service interventions. Women are less likely than men to live openly on the street. Women are more likely to live in shelters or transitional housing, move among temporary living arrangements, or live out of sight in abandoned cars or in squatter housing. Men are three to four times more likely to have spent a night out of shelter than women. Homeless men also experienced a greater variety of social and environmental risks. Homeless women cite domestic violence as one of the four top reasons for becoming homeless.

The number of homeless youth is increasing, with about 2 million youth per year spending some period of time in emergency shelters or on the streets. Homeless youth are concentrated primarily in large urban centers and frequently have histories of domestic violence, parental criminality, substance abuse, and poverty. They also are vulnerable to physical and mental health problems.

Children age 12 and younger make up the fastest-growing subgroup of the homeless population. Children in homeless families have a high risk of physical and mental illness. They also have histories of abuse, are victims of violence, and witness much of the violence experienced by their mothers. The National Center on Family Homelessness reports that southern states have the highest percentage of children who are unhoused. In fact, 75 percent of all homeless children in the United States live in 11 states in the South and Southwest. Texas, Louisiana, Georgia, and Arkansas have the highest overall risk for child homelessness. Southern and southwestern states make up the majority of states that scored high on overall risk. The increase of homelessness in the South, particularly increasing numbers of homeless children, suggests that low levels of educational attainment and high levels of poverty and violence that have characterized so much of southern history seem likely to continue and will affect the region's future.

DEDEN RUKMANA
Savannah State University

Alice S. Baum and Donald W. Burnes, *A Nation in Denial: The Truth about Homelessness* (1993); Joel Blau, *The Visible Poor: Homelessness in the United States* (1992); Martha Burt, Laudan Y. Aron, Edgar Lee, and Jesse Valente, *Helping America's Homeless: Emergency Shelter or Affordable Housing* (2002); Dennis P. Culhane and Randall Kuhn, *Housing Policy Debate* (1996); S. A. Kidd and L. Davidson, *Journal of Community Psychology* (1997); Christopher Jencks, *The Homeless* (1994); National Alliance to End Homelessness, www.endhomelessness.org/section/data/homelessmap; National Center on Family Homelessness, www.homelesschildrenamerica.org/

report_state-reports.php; Deden Rukmana, *Residential Origins of the Homeless* (2008); U.S. Census Bureau, *Emergency and Transitional Shelter Population: 2000* (2001); James D. Wright, Beth A. Rubin, and Joel A. Devine, *Beside the Golden Door: Policy, Politics, and the Homeless* (1998).

Immigration

Recent rapid cultural, economic, and demographic transformations in the former Confederate states have fostered the view that globalization—already construed as "new"—has at long last come to the "Old South." Although international patterns of trade and commerce have driven the political economy of the South for centuries, shifts in the global economy have been accompanied by emerging patterns of migration and settlement in the region. Whereas before 1970 the Southeast was home to the smallest proportion of foreign-born in the United States, by the 1990s these levels surpassed the Midwest and began to approach those of the Northeast, the country's historical center of immigration. The dramatically growing presence of immigrants in the cities, rural areas, and suburbs of the region has complicated traditional understandings of "southernness" but has also raised deep questions at the national level about civic belonging, the social impact of these new immigration trends, and appropriate policy responses to them.

Perhaps most striking has been immigration to the South from Latin American countries. Between 1990 and 2000, North Carolina, Arkansas, Georgia, Tennessee, South Carolina, and Alabama not only experienced triple-digit increases in their Latino populations but also registered the highest rates of growth of any state except Nevada. Latino newcomers' arrival has complicated the oversimplified understanding of race as exclusively "black" and "white" in what some have called "*el Nuevo*," the New South.

Immigration to the South is inextricably tied to changes in the region's integration into the global economy, which have undermined older forms of production—agriculture, steel, textiles, and apparel. "Free-trade" policies such as the 1994 North American Free Trade Agreement have stimulated the mobility of capital and labor. At the same time, new economic investment has poured into the Southeast, as domestic and foreign-owned corporations have sought cheap labor, new markets, and government incentives. The economy of the "newest" South features foreign-owned auto plants, high-tech research and manufacturing, biomedical research, and new food processing for poultry, hogs, and seafood. In addition, rapid population growth and construction booms in Sunbelt cities like Atlanta have stimulated growth in the construction industry and service sectors with a consequent demand for low-wage labor.

A constellation of social forces and policy effects at the state and local levels that have "deflected" migration away from traditional gateway cities and states to nontraditional "receiving sites" represents another factor stimulating new migration and settlement patterns. Stricter border and immigration enforcement, imposed restrictions on immigrants' social entitlements, and the saturation of labor market niches in gateway cities have all played a role in driving the geographic diversification of migration patterns. In addition, the Immigration Reform and Control Act of 1986, which provided amnesty to millions of migrants residing in the United States, resulted in the unexpected consequence of both galvanizing and dispersing migration patterns, as the legalization of immigrants allowed for increased chances for mobility and settlement in areas with greater opportunities and tolerance.

Although new migration and settlement patterns have occurred throughout this region, migration streams vary by state and locality. Unlike North Carolina and Georgia, where agricultural work as well as economic growth and the construction boom in cities have created labor demand, states of the Deep South—Louisiana, Alabama, and Mississippi—have seen smaller increases in their immigrant populations in absolute numbers. Nevertheless, by the early 2000s, growth rates increased dramatically, as in the case of Louisiana following Hurricane Katrina when President George W. Bush temporarily suspended the Davis-Bacon Act, which had guaranteed construction workers the prevailing local wage when paid with federal money.

Shifts in migratory patterns combined with changes in the regional housing market have also exerted a remarkable impact on the suburbs in some southern states, reversing decades-long trends of "white flight." For example, Prince William County has become the most ethnically and racially diverse county in northern Virginia with its minority population more than doubling, accounting for 94 percent of the population increase between 2000 and 2007. Analysts have only begun to identify the political implications of such demographic changes, but some have pointed to it as a contributing factor to Barack Obama's capture of the state's vote in the 2008 election.

Rapid and massive, settled immigration has caught many communities in the South by surprise, as migrants became increasingly visible in shopping centers, schools, clinics, and other public spaces. This is particularly the case in small rural, suburban, or semirural communities that have historically been home to relatively few foreign-born residents. This public visibility also marks a change in the demographic profiles of those who migrate, as "temporary" male immigrant sojourners give way to growing numbers of more "permanent" families settling in the New South.

Given the particular history and specific political, economic, and cultural conditions in the American South, immigration to this region has taken on its own character among "new immigrant destinations." For example, immigrants' recent arrival in localities has meant that they lack indigenous, communal infrastructures and support networks upon which immigrants have relied in other traditional settlement areas as a source of social capital to facilitate economic mobility and ease the transition to new work and living styles. The dispersed organization of public space—particularly in rural and suburban communities—further impedes immigrants' expanding networks and the building of new social relationships, as does the atomized nature of many of the low-wage occupations in which immigrants work, such as those in the hotel and restaurant sector. In rural areas and suburbs in the South, there are few public spaces where immigrants can gather to socialize and exchange information and contacts, a situation made worse by limited and isolated low-income housing in which immigrants often reside.

There is a gendered component to the particular barriers to social participation in new reception sites of the South. Restrictions on obtaining drivers' licenses, compounded by the lack of reliable public transportation and the dispersed organization of public space can result in women experiencing high levels of isolation and added dependency on male family members or partners for income and mobility. Latina women often arrive after their male counterparts and are less likely to know how to drive. Fear of deportation further impinges upon migrant women's physical mobility relative to men, inhibiting their ability to participate in public life, find better jobs, and gain access to resources that might increase their economic mobility—such as day care and English classes.

Changing race relations represents an additional, continually unfolding challenge in the "newest" South. Recent trends in migration have coincided with an escalation of anti-immigrant frictions. Categorizations like "Asian" and "Hispanic" join diverse (sometimes conflictive) ethnic groups into newly constituted "races," raising questions not only about relations within these categories but between those in them and those who make up the "old" black-white divide.

Scholars have argued that localized and intensified nativism acts as a protective response to the shifting social landscape and erosion of economic security brought on by flexible production and accumulation under globalization. It is not surprising that ethnic and racial tensions have infused local public debates about immigrants' rights and entitlements. Across the region (and, indeed, the nation), state and local decision makers have proposed and enacted policies that restrict eligibility requirements for immigrants seeking social benefits and expand authorization to local police to detain immigrants—sometimes in coordination with U.S. Immigration and Customs Enforcement in actions that have resulted in massive deportations. Often supported by national organizations, like the Federation for American Immigration Reform, local groups like Virginia's "Help Save Manassas" have been forceful voices in the debates surrounding these policies, espousing decidedly anti-immigrant platforms. In some cases, in southern states in which immigrant rights organizations have mobilized, organizers have met with virulent, even violent, opposition.

Latino and Asian immigrants' frequent settlement in traditionally African American neighborhoods (particularly in urban contexts) and their employment in sectors that have historically been majority black as well as the language and cultural barriers across these groups present the potential for interracial animosity. Researchers have only begun to document native residents' perceptions of immigration in new immigrant receiving sites. But a recent study of attitudes among African Americans and whites in Durham, N.C., found that both blacks and whites feel concerned about the rapid growth of the Latino population, with African Americans perceiving more of an economic threat from Latino immigration than whites. Notwithstanding, other researchers have pointed out that, particularly in urban contexts, there also exists the potential for intergroup solidarity between blacks and new immigrants.

As these immigration trends bring with them a new chapter in the history of cultural diversity in the South, questions arise not only about the future of social relations in the region but in the country as a whole. Scholars of immigration have documented that once "chain migration" begins, it often continues, as family members send for their loved ones and local labor recruitment strategies make use of immigrants' social networks. On the other hand, researchers have noted a decline in the growth rate of undocumented immigrants to the United States in the last three years.

As of 2009, the world is caught in a global financial crisis, the impact of which is only beginning to be understood, and sectors that have employed immigrant workers in the South—construction and hotel, food, and restaurant services—are particularly vulnerable to the economy's slowdown. Indeed, there is evidence that the economic recession has begun to exert a negative effect on immigrants' earnings and the remittances they send to their communities of origin. Immigrants tend to be among the most vulnerable groups of workers, and they face added barriers to accessing housing and health care. And these trends suggest that the current recession, coupled with the unfolding impact of restrictive policies focused on immigrants' access to social benefits, holds the real potential of exacerbating these vulnerabilities, eroding the small inroads that immigrants have made in establishing more stable footholds in southern communities. Despite the numerous uncertainties that emerge in the current context, every indication suggests that the presence of racially diverse immigrants confronts and challenges structures in this region of the country and will continue to exert a measurable impact on the evolution of race, class, and ethnic systems in the "Newest South."

JENNIFER BICKHAM MENDEZ
College of William and Mary

Carl L. Bankston III, *Southern Cultures* (Winter 2007); Lawrence D. Bobo and Vincent L. Hutchings, *American Sociological Review* (1996); Leo R. Chavez, *Covering Immigration: Popular Images and the Politics of the Nation* (2001); Natalia Deeb-Sossa and Jennifer Bickham Mendez, *Gender and Society* (2008); Anita Drever, in *Latinos in the New South: Transformations of Place*, ed. H. A. Smith and O. J. Furuseth (2006); Ivan Light, *Deflecting Immigration: Networks, Markets, and Regulation in Los Angeles* (2006); Paula D. McClain, Monique L. Lyle, Niambi M. Carter, Victoria M. DeFrancesco Soto, Gerald F. Lackey, Kendra Davenport Cotton, Shayla C. Nunnally, Thomas J. Scotto, Jeffrey D. Grynaviski, and J. Alan Kendrick, *Du Bois Review* (2007); Raymond A. Mohl, *American Ethnic History* (Summer 2003); Eric J. Oliver and Janelle Wong, *American Journal of Political Science* (Number 4, 2003); Barbara Ellen Smith, in *Cultural Diversity in the U.S. South*, ed. Carole E. Hill and Patricia Beaver (1998); Barbara Ellen Smith and Jamie Winders, *Transatlantic Institute of British Geography* (2007); Víctor Zuñiga and Rubén Hernández-León, eds., *New Destinations: Mexican Immigration in the United States* (2006).

Leadership

Though it was predominantly a rural, agricultural economy until recently, the South required urban centers that spawned their own leadership, which was frequently at odds with the leaders of agrarian society. During the colonial and antebellum periods, the most important cities in the region were mostly coastal trade centers. Baltimore, Norfolk, Charleston, Savannah, Mobile, New Orleans, and other smaller cities provided outlets to northern and European markets for the grain, naval stores, tobacco, rice, and cotton exports produced by the plantation economy. During the colonial era, many of the leading merchants and factors who dominated this trade were foreigners, usually Scotch, British, and French. By the 1820s, as the cotton trade expanded and came under the control of New York City, northerners took over the key urban functions of factoring and shipping the lucrative exports of the plantation economy.

Within the local power structure, urban merchants and factors used their influence through commercial associations and city governments to promote urban growth. Civic improvements in water supply, sanitation, police, and fire control were all subservient to the goal of enhancing the community's commercial prosperity. City governmental agencies were also used to regulate slaves and to guard against their revolt. Though they shared many of the aspirations for urban growth and industrial and commercial development with their counterparts in the North, the leaders of the southern middle class enjoyed less autonomy and less political and economic leverage within a society dominated by large slave-owning planters. Urban merchants and industrial entrepreneurs cooperated with planters in launching new railroads and industrial experiments. During the 1850s, these efforts at economic development were linked to plans for sectional independence from the North.

Ultimately, the move toward urban development was contradicted by the commitment to the plantation economy and slavery. Slave owners realized that slave labor could be adapted to industrial work and urban labor markets only at the risk of losing full control over the slaves. Planters feared a large white working class in the cities that might oppose competition from slaves, and they did not wish to encourage the growth of an independent middle class with interests opposed to the slave regime. The strain between the urban middle class and planters became apparent during the secession crisis when urban representatives opposed secession for fear of severing commercial ties with the North. The dominance of the planter class became apparent when urban leaders ultimately capitulated and served the Confederate cause during the war.

During the war, urban supply and manufacturing centers like Atlanta, Richmond, and Nashville experienced rapid growth and emerged as powerful components of the postwar economic order. Many entrepreneurs who gained experience during the war took their place in a growing cadre of urban middle-class leaders in the New South era. Older seaports like Charleston, Mobile, and New Orleans suffered blockades during the war and continued to stagnate in the decades following it. Along the Piedmont, in northern Alabama, and elsewhere in the interior of the South, towns and cities experienced rapid growth as railroad centers or as textile, tobacco, and iron manufacturing centers. Few of the industrial and commercial leaders who were prominent in the rising cities of the New South came from the planter class. In cities like Atlanta and Nashville they were typically from the yeomanry and small-town merchant and professional classes. Most arrived in their cities after the war as young men and rose to positions of wealth in wholesale commerce, railroads, manufacturing, banking, and insurance. Typically, they were Methodist, Presbyterian, or Baptist, and they celebrated their rise to riches as the reward of hard work and personal piety. By the 1880s, representatives of this ascendant middle-class "new man" articulated a regional vision of economic development, sectional reconciliation with the North, and interracial cooperation. Though they often paid homage to the Lost Cause of the Confederacy, those who proclaimed this New South creed recognized a departure from the Old South and offered the leadership of a young, progressive urban middle class as an alternative to the defeated planter class.

On the local level, prominent merchants, manufacturers, and financiers used their influence through commercial associations, like the chambers of commerce, to direct public policy. Formal control of city government offices was typically held by smaller businessmen whose interests were confined to the local economy. City government continued to serve business interests in efforts to promote urban growth through bonds for railroads, lobbying for federal aid to harbor improvements, tax incentives to new industries, and improved city services. The most visible examples of urban enterprise were the industrial expositions held in Atlanta, Louisville, New Orleans, Nashville, and Charleston in the late 19th and early 20th centuries. Here the New South creed of economic development, national reconciliation, and black progress was displayed in lavish exhibits and reams of publicity. Linked to their vision of New South economic prosperity was a liberal social policy with special application to the black population of the postwar South.

Beginning in the 1880s, with religious revivals and temperance campaigns, the reformers of the urban South sponsored a flurry of new private and government-sponsored charitable organizations. Reform moved toward efforts to improve sanitation and public health in the slums, expand and improve public education, and enforce temperance and sexual morality through government regulation. These reforms were linked to goals of economic progress through a healthy, educated, and generally upgraded workforce. These policies of social uplift, which gained wide currency in the Progressive era, coincided with a growing tendency toward segregation in the workforce, neighborhoods, and public facilities of southern cities. Segregation was approved, if not inspired, by business leaders as a means of assuring social stability in the crowded and competitive cities of the New South.

"Business progressivism," as historian George Tindall has labeled this conservative brand of reform, took firm hold in the early 20th century. Structural reforms in the manner of electing city government officials allowed for "at large" elections of councilmen and the introduction of commission and city manager forms of government. These reforms were intended to model government after the modern corporations and to reduce the influence of ward-level bosses and the poor black and white working-class voters who supported them. In several cities, a southern brand of boss politics prevailed, despite the efforts of business progressives to undermine their ward-level strength. Edward Crump in Memphis, Hilary Howse in Nashville, John Grace in Charleston, and Martin Behrman in New Orleans represented the most durable of such urban bosses. The mobilization effort during World War I and the era of business prosperity that followed gave new strength to "business progressivism." Planning and zoning boards were attached to city government to give the commercial civic elite additional control over the course of physical growth and residential segregation in their cities. Experts in business and planning expanded the powers of local government to cope with a variety of complex urban problems involving air pollution, traffic control, social welfare, and expanded urban services for the rapidly growing suburban population.

The Depression and the New Deal programs of the 1930s accelerated this growth of public authority as federal funds for highway, park, and airport construction, social welfare, and public housing poured into local agencies. World War II strengthened the federal partnership with southern cities, many of which were grateful recipients of government expenditures for aircraft, ships, weaponry, uniforms, and military bases. After the war, a generation of returning veterans and businessmen eager to encourage further federal commitment to southern development began to take over the leadership of their cities. The war against Fascism and the Cold War against communism made the system of racial segregation a national embarrassment. Business leaders were hesitant, nonetheless, to dismantle the system on their own initiative. Many black business and professional leaders had thrived within a segregated society and were slow to push for desegregation.

A younger generation of college-educated blacks, many of them still in school, began in the 1950s to work through the NAACP and other local organizations to batter down the walls of segregation. Through the courts, public demonstrations, and civil disobedience they forced the leadership of southern cities to put an end to formal segregation in schools and public facilities and to a lesser degree in the job market. Urban blacks also regained political power lost after Reconstruction and were able to extract concessions from white leaders. In cities like Atlanta, black political power was sufficient to win key positions within city government. Whatever their formal positions within local government, however, the white business elite remain the most significant group within the power structure of major southern cities and are a force of growing importance within a region undergoing rapid urbanization.

In recent times, black politicians have dominated urban governmental leadership, but the white business elite remains a powerful group within the power structure of major southern cities and has been a growing force within the region. Public-private partnerships finance downtown sports arenas, museums, convention centers, marketplaces, hotels, expensive condominiums, and high-rise office buildings. The commercial civic elite includes such traditional figures as merchants, bankers, and entrepreneurs. Becoming even more prominent in that leadership group have been real estate developers, brokers, and financiers, although the recession of 2008–9 has affected the latter. Tom Wolfe's novel *A Man in Full* explores the social and business mores of Atlanta's leadership elite.

DON H. DOYLE
University of South Carolina

Ronald H. Bayor, *Race and the Shaping of Twentieth-Century Atlanta* (1996); Blaine A. Brownell, *The Urban Ethos in the South, 1920–1930* (1975); Blaine A. Brownell and David R. Goldfield, eds., *The City in Southern History: The Growth of Urban Civilization in the South* (1977); Eugene D. Genovese, *The Political Economy of Slavery* (1968); Floyd Hunter, *Community Power Succession: Atlanta's Policy-Makers Revisited* (1980); Wanda Rushing, *Memphis and the Paradox of Place: Globalization in the American South* (2009).

Maternal and Child Health

Maternal and child health status provides a snapshot of an urban community's social and economic vibrancy. Improvements in maternal and child health benefit society not only by increasing survival rates but by improving the overall quality of life for families and communities and, thus, nations. From a population-health perspective, researchers, who link health to economic development, argue that interventions to improve maternal and childhood health are a social investment that can have positive long-term economic effects as birthrates adjust. Healthy children are better prepared to be educated and be productive citizens, and healthier populations require less to be spent on costly medical care. Maternal and child health conventionally address a broad continuum of topics, including health issues related to preconception, pregnancy, delivery, postpartum, birth spacing, and early childhood. Highlighted here are three current critical urban maternal and child health issues: infant mortality, unplanned pregnancy as it links to preconception health, and sexually transmitted infections (STIs). These issues are especially important in the South, the region reporting high rates of infant mortality, teen pregnancy, and STIs. Given the direct relationship between population health and economic development, the potential economic and community development in the South will continue to be constrained, especially for minority and urban poor subpopulations.

The most troubling health issue afflicting southern maternal and child well-being is the phenomenon of infant mortality—defined as an unexplained death in a child ages 0 to 3 years old. Infants born in the South are more likely to be born prematurely, to be low weight, or to die than infants in other parts of the United States. Moreover, according to the Centers for Disease Control (CDC), the incidence of infant mortality within the Mid-South (West Tennessee, Mississippi, East Arkansas) rivals rates experienced in developing nations. The CDC indicates that the U.S. infant mortality rate was 6.86 infant deaths per 1,000 live births in 2005; in Tennessee the rate was 8.77 in the same year. In Memphis, the rates of infant mortality, according to the Memphis and Shelby County Health Department, showed an overall infant death rate of 13.8 per 1,000 live births in 2006, but the rate for African Americans was 19.0 per 1,000. The underlying reasons for this high rate are wide-ranging and interrelated and include factors ranging from lack of early prenatal care to economic instability and race. What is clear, however, is that low birth weight shares a high correlation with infant morbidity. Unfortunately, the means for preventing low birth weight in babies is imprecise, as solutions relate to both medical conditions as well as social/environmental factors, including the reduction of domestic violence and adolescent pregnancy. One solution favored by community health professionals is breast-feeding, as a source of high-quality nutrition. The benefits of breast-feeding are great for both mother and child; studies now suggest a decreased risk of breast cancer in women who breast-feed, and children who have been breast-fed are less likely to be susceptible to autoimmune diseases. But breast-feeding rates vary by region. According to the CDC, southern states report the lowest percentage of breast-feeding at birth, six months, and one year. Expanded public education efforts to disseminate knowledge on the positive effects of breast-feeding for both mother and child are beginning to appear in the form of grass-roots movements. Although social, ethnic, and cultural factors affect individual decisions to breast-feed, hospital practices also affect these decisions. Southern states score lower in practices supportive of breast-feeding when compared to other regions.

The community response to the infant mortality issues crosses sectors and includes a broad array of approaches/programs, such as nurse home visitation, promotion of early prenatal care, parenting education, domestic violence programs, faith-based family counseling, and even ways to safely give up an unwanted infant (for example, bringing the infant to a hospital or fire station, with no questions asked). In Tennessee, the state is supporting health promotion programs such as Centering Pregnancy (a group prenatal support program) as well as a March of Dimes–designed campaign in Shelby County, Tenn., Community Voice, to educate volunteers about infant mortality, especially as it is affecting the African American community, and to elicit the community's support in sharing what they have learned throughout the community. Southern states also work toward establishing formal, community-based organizations responsible for fetal and infant mortality review in urban areas, in order to identify relevant factors and recommend system changes where needed.

According to recent data from the National Campaign to Prevent Teen and Unplanned Pregnancy, American women are experiencing approximately 3 million unplanned pregnancies each year; the concern is the high correlation between the lack of purposeful and proactive attention to preconception health and child morbidity. Preconception care is key to eliminating many preventable conditions, including neural tube defects that can result in chronic ill health for the child. Preconception health is also important to ensuring medical management of chronic conditions to reduce their potential adverse effect on pregnancy outcomes. The CDC indicates that in 2002 approximately 6 percent of adult women aged 18 to 44 years had asthma, 50 percent were overweight or obese, 3 percent had cardiac disease, 3 percent were hypertensive, 9 percent had diabetes, and 1 percent had thyroid disorder. The potential for preconception health care is greatly diminished among adolescent mothers, who typically have the highest rates of unplanned pregnancy. High rates of adolescent pregnancy, especially for teens lacking family financial resources, can be a serious negative factor affecting the long-term quality of life for both adolescent parents and their children; complications for childbearing women under the age of 20 greatly increase compared to women 10 to 15 years older. The National Campaign to Prevent Teen and Unplanned Pregnancy reports that southern states have among the highest rates of teen pregnancy—the South has nine out of 18 of the highest teen birthrates in the nation, and Mississippi (103) and Florida (97) have the highest southern teen birthrates. The community response to the unplanned pregnancy/preconception health issue is necessarily broad and includes health/wellness promotion, education, and awareness activities; promotion of early prenatal care; faith-based health outreach programs; family-life education in schools; and health campaigns targeting physical fitness, good nutrition, and health screenings.

Other types of disease potentially harmful to children result from the transmission of sexually transmitted infections, including HIV/AIDS. According to the CDC, the presence of HIV in pregnant women if treated properly through antiretroviral drugs can result in transmission rates to the fetus as low as 2 percent. The link between concentrated poverty, high incarceration rates of the urban poor, and substance abuse is thought to be a factor in STI rates in urban areas. STIS include the transmission of bacterial infections such as chlamydia and gonorrhea and viral infections such as genital herpes and genital human papillomavirus (HPV). STIS can increase the risk of preterm delivery and, if untreated, can cause cervical and other cancers, infertility, and other complications. In pregnant women, STIS potentially can be transmitted to the baby before, during, or after delivery. According to the CDC, almost 1.1 million chlamydial infections were reported nationally in 2006; women infected with chlamydia are up to five times more likely to become infected with HIV, if exposed. Mississippi (745.1), South Carolina (611.7), and Alabama (546.9) held three out of four of the ranks of the highest national rates of reported cases of chlamydia in 2007. Testing during prenatal care and regular health screenings can help to prevent the harmful effects of STIS. The community response to this issue includes continued monitoring and follow-up of cases by local public health departments, health promotion activities, and health education about safe sex practices.

Maternal and child health in urban settings occurs within a social, political, environmental, and economic context. According to the Environmental Protection Agency, the developmental environment can determine various physiological parameters in the developing individual that can affect adult health status. Further, evidence shows that a female's in utero and early postnatal environments influence her own reproductive success later in life. Moreover, other urban-related social/economic factors place mothers' and children's health at risk, including urban neighborhood characteristics that directly relate to dietary risks and impede healthy physical activity; food insecurity linked to poverty that compromises the nutritional status of pregnant women and developing children; lack of access to health providers; mental health stressors associated with urban-related social disorganization; poor habitat conditions that compromise well-being and healthy development; limited availability of public or other transportation for accessing health and social services; childcare responsibilities that constrain the mother's ability to comply with care appointments; domestic violence, which tends to be greatest toward women in their reproductive years—violence experienced during pregnancy can result in numerous health complications for the child, including low birth weight and even fetal death; and racial and economic disparities that constrain economic and social opportunities.

Immigrants in the United States create an additional set of challenges for those concerned about urban maternal and child health and health disparities. The growing presence of immigrants, especially young women and children in cities, in suburbs, and in rural areas of the South, raises new questions about social inequality and health care. Responding to different languages, cultural expectations, and lifestyles is a challenge for urban health providers and can further strain community resources.

Individual values, beliefs, and perceptions play an important role in maternal and child health. Some feminists argue that reproduction and sexual health has become too medicalized in the United States. Further, culture and ethnicity affect health beliefs about pregnancy, infant care, immunizations, and wellness, thus influencing maternal decisions about health behaviors and modalities of care for herself and her children—allopathic medicine, naturalistic health approaches, or folk medicine. Culture and ethnicity also affect individual levels of trust/distrust of community health-care providers/institutions, thus affecting the willingness to seek health-care services.

Mothers and children have generally been viewed as having a legitimate claim on society's assistance. The degree of political support has wavered over time and has involved debates about whether women who deviate from normative ideas about appropriate motherhood and sexuality deserve assistance. Historically, debates have been especially strong in some southern states, where officials have been willing to punish "promiscuous" behavior by withholding benefits. However, broad support has generally been sustained for maternal and child health and social services as evidenced by numerous federal- and state-funded programs focused on children and pregnant women, such as Medicaid; Women, Infants, and Children (wic); and Healthy Start. Political ideology directly affects the types of programs supported by communities: for example, comprehensive sexuality versus abstinence-only education programs for teens. Increasingly, public health advocates are calling for more participatory community-based approaches that engage the community as full partners in programs and to ensure cultural sensitivity. Undoubtedly, a systems perspective that respects the effects of place is needed to understand the public health issues affecting southern maternal and child health status and to assess the public policy and community responses to these issues.

JOY A. CLAY
BRIDGETTE R. COLLIER
University of Memphis

Dolores Acevedo-Garcia, Theresa L. Osypuk, Nancy McArdle, and David R. Williams, *Health Affairs* (March/April 2008); Centers for Disease Control, "Eliminate

Disparities in Infant Mortality," www.cdc.gov/omhd/amh/factsheets/infant
.htm, *Morbidity and Mortality Weekly Report* (21 April 2006), "New CDC Study
Finds Gaps in Breastfeeding Support in U.S. Hospitals and Birth Centers," www
.hepprograms.org/perinatal/BreastfeedingMMWR.pdf; Ronald David, *Focus* (Sep-
tember/October 2005); EPA, "Reproductive Toxicology Division," www.epa.gov/
NHEERL/rtd/rtd_longterm.html; Ruth Feldstein, *Motherhood in Black and White*
(2000); Nicholas Freudenberg, Sandro Galea, and David Vlahov, eds., *Cities and the
Health of the Public* (2006); Sandro Galea, Nicholas Freudenberg, and David Vlahov,
Social Sciences and Medicine (2005); Linda J. Koenig et al., *American Journal of Public
Health* (June 2006); Memphis and Shelby County Health Department, "Infant Mortality Statistics," www.shelbycountytn.gov; John Mirowsky, *Social Forces* (September 2002); David Mirvis and David Bloom, *Journal of the American Medical Association* (2 July 2008); National Campaign to Prevent Teen and Unplanned Pregnancy,
*Responding to the Increase in the Teen Birth Rate: Analysis from the National Cam-
paign to Prevent Teen and Unplanned Pregnancy* (January 2009), www
.thenationalcampaign.org/resources/birthdata/analysis.aspx.

Medical Centers

In visiting southern urban centers, one often gets the impression that there is a
hospital on every corner. This may be more perception than reality because of
the prominent locations of hospitals in southern cities, but it could be argued
that the state of medicine in the South has historically been more advanced
than that for most other areas of the economy. Although there are major medical centers all over the nation, southern medical centers appear to play a much
more important role in the economies and culture of their respective communities than they do in other regions of the country. Few cities outside the South
are as closely associated with their medical centers as are many southern cities,
a situation often noted by those in the health-care field. For health professionals
in particular, it is hard to think of Atlanta without reference to the Centers
for Disease Control and Prevention or Memphis without mention of St. Jude's
Children's Research Hospital or Houston without considering the MD Anderson Cancer Center. Indeed, Nashville is often referred to as the "Silicon Valley"
of health care because of the number of important health-related businesses it
has spawned.

Although it is true that most of the nation's prestigious medical schools and
urban medical centers are outside the South, it is noteworthy that southern
cities actually have a proportionate share of health facilities, given the lag the
region exhibits with regard to many other industries. The relative importance

of health care in southern urban centers is perhaps explained by the fact that, although there are a lot of things that a community can do without, health care is not one of them. The growth of major urban centers could also be attributed to the historical lack of large cities outside of a few regional centers. Thus, the growth of medical centers in places as diverse as New Orleans, Memphis, and Louisville reflects their position as regional centers with few communities of any significant size in their sphere of influence. Although this situation is no longer the case, as even secondary medical centers in the hinterlands have access to contemporary medical facilities, these southern urban medical centers were established at a time when there were few other options, and most have retained their regional significance.

The importance of the health-care industry to the South in general and to southern cities in particular is reflected in the fact that the proportion of the workforce involved in health care is higher in the South than in the rest of the nation. Indeed, there are certain southern cities where the employment in health care/social services is notably higher than the average. This is particularly the case for middle-sized southern cities that may not have historically had the industrial diversity of an Atlanta or a Dallas. Thus, the South has "health-care towns" where, according to the 2000 census, the industry is inordinately dominant. These include Little Rock (26 percent higher health-care employment), Birmingham (11 percent higher), New Orleans (9 percent higher), Louisville (8 percent higher), and Mobile (6 percent higher). Others slightly higher in health-care employment include Memphis, Nashville, and San Antonio.

The importance of health care to southern cities is evidenced by the region's disproportionate share of the nation's largest hospitals. Although southern states contain approximately 21 percent of the nation's population, medium and large urban centers in the South contain over 40 percent of the nation's hospitals containing 500 or more beds. Furthermore, the ratio of hospital beds to the population in the largest southern urban areas is more than 10 percent higher than it is for the United States as a whole, indicating the greater significance of health care in southern cities. The importance of health care in these urban centers is reinforced in that there not only more hospitals but they are intensively utilized. The hospitalization rate for the major southern urban centers is 25 percent higher than the national average, reflecting the influence of physicians and hospitals on their respective communities.

RICHARD K. THOMAS
University of Tennessee Health Science Center

American Hospital Association, *AHA Guide* (2009); U.S. Census Bureau, *Census of Population* (2000).

Megachurches

"Megachurch" has become the accepted term used to describe the phenomenon of large-scale Protestant Christian churches and religious life. A "megachurch" is defined as a church having 2,000 or more unique attenders, of adults and children, in all its services on an average weekend. In addition to the size of attendance, these large churches have a host of other common organizational and cultural characteristics. This social phenomenon, which has its roots firmly entrenched in the contemporary southern urban and suburban landscape, is a distinctive contemporary response to cultural shifts and changes in societal patterns throughout the rapidly developing areas of the South, the nation as a whole, and even globally.

The southern region has been especially fertile soil for megachurches because of a convergence of its dramatic population growth, driven by the dislocation of town and country populations into the city, and the region's historic, distinctively powerful, religious milieu. Almost half the nation's megachurches (48 percent) are located in the southern United States. As of 2009, Texas had the largest concentration, followed by California, Florida, and Georgia. These churches mainly cluster around suburbs and exurbs of the largest sprawling metropolitan areas of Houston, Atlanta, Los Angeles, and Dallas, but significant concentrations of them can also be found in the smaller yet rapidly growing urban areas such as Jacksonville, Charlotte, Birmingham, and Austin.

Since 1990, the number of megachurches nationwide has risen dramatically, from roughly 350 to over 1,300 in 2009. Half of the nation's megachurches began after 1970, and nearly all megachurches have relocated or rebuilt their facilities in the past 30 years. These churches can be very diverse in style and visionary approach, but overall they are quite similar in structure, as a result of their size and organizational complexity. The average megachurch has over 4,100 weekly congregants and an annual budget that exceeds $6.5 million. These churches are most often located along major thoroughfares and interstate highways, making them both intentionally prominent and easily accessible. Their expansive worship sanctuaries of hundreds of thousands of square feet and seating for over 1,700 are surrounded by acres of parking and multiple auxiliary buildings and sports fields designed to offer more than just spiritual fare.

Originally, the phenomenon was driven by population increases, which resulted from the Baby Boom, but in recent decades it has continued to be fueled by rapid urbanization and suburbanization. The shift to "supersized" religious structures over the past 30 years is partly a factor of economics—as the cost of delivering quality worship increased so did the size of the congregations. It is also a reflection of the increased scale of all social organizational structures in modern life, including malls, corporations, colleges, and medical centers. In part, the growth of megachurches can also be seen as a symbolic response to the secular claims of the demise of religion. In dramatic fashion, megachurches offer tangible evidence that God is still present. Likewise, an implicit theological motivation could be seen as underlying the phenomenon. The tremendous congregational growth represented in these churches is indicative of spiritual success, which has been interpreted by some as a sign of God's blessing. In any case, the pronounced success of these churches and their leaders has translated into prominence and power in the religious and the secular worlds.

Although these largest churches represent less than half of one percent of all American churches, they garner considerable attention and influence in a country where more than half of congregations have less than 100 attenders. Megachurches have vast resources of money and people, as well as a concentration of active voters. The churches are also surprisingly daring and inventive in terms of programs and organizational structures. Additionally, their senior clergy are popular speakers, prolific authors, and national religious figures. This combination has resulted in megachurches being the catalysts for most of the change in religious expression, music, and organizational forms over the past few decades. In short, the megachurch phenomenon is rapidly reshaping congregational life in the Protestant Christian tradition.

Three-quarters of megachurches still retain the senior pastor during whose tenure the dramatic attendance growth took place. These spiritual leaders are predominantly male, average 50 years of age, are well educated, and are seen as highly entrepreneurial spiritual innovators. They are usually the person who is solely responsible for the distinctive vision, clear mission approach, and well-defined sense of purpose at these churches. These authoritative leaders are assisted by, on average, 50 to 100 clergy and staff with an additional 400 persons who volunteer 10 or more hours a week. The vast majority of megachurches hold conservative theological beliefs and describe themselves as evangelical. The largest denominational affiliation of megachurches is Southern Baptist, but roughly a third of them are nondenominational.

Worship at these congregations most often happens in semicircular theater-style auditoriums devoid of pews, stained glass windows, or traditional religious symbols. The fast-paced professional worship service includes expressive contemporary music led by a team of singers accompanied by electric guitars, keyboard, and drums. This spiritual production is enhanced with sophisticated technology, projected onto huge screens, and is digitally recorded for the Internet or television. The high-quality worship culminates with a polished, entertaining, and occasionally challenging sermon that is both culturally relevant and practical as well as inspirational and biblically grounded.

Megachurches provide countless services, ministries, and activities throughout the week. They sponsor hundreds of programs that meet both the spiritual and physical needs of attenders and the larger secular community. These programs also provide a place for attenders to live out their religious commitments in service to others. Nearly every megachurch offers small groups and intimate fellowship opportunities that structure intentional community building and enhance commitment within the large-scale context.

Participants in megachurches, when compared to national profiles of attenders in smaller Protestant churches, are younger and less likely to be married, as well as more educated and wealthier. Overall, megachurch congregations are more likely to show racial diversity than any other church form. Many megachurch congregants previously belonged to other local churches (44 percent) or joined after being transplanted to an area (28 percent), but nearly a quarter (24 percent) were previously unchurched or had not attended for years. Most congregants state that they participate in megachurches because of the church's vision and mission, the pastor's charisma, the contemporary worship style, and the many activities and educational programs available. The commitment level and spiritual activities of megachurch participants on average is at least equal to those in other sizes of churches.

Megachurches offer congregants new ways of being religious in community. These churches allow attenders to participate on their own terms by choosing the commitment level and distinctive ways that best suit their individual desires. The diverse programs and spiritual options allow participants to select and customize their experiences of the church that best fits the needs of each family member. Many megachurch programs offer supportive training for families, couples, and interpersonal development, as well as the job skills and career advancement necessary for a mobile middle-class congregation. At the same time, the leadership at a megachurch continually encourages participants to increase their involvement, deepen their faith, and commit to live out that faith in service to the church and larger community.

Southern megachurches are quite similar to the national phenomenon as a whole, but they do differ in a few discernible and statistically significant ways. Megachurches in the South are, on average, larger in weekly attendance (more than 300 additional persons), have bigger sanctuaries (by nearly 500 seats), and have annual revenues of $1.5 million more than the megachurches of other regions. They are slightly less likely to be multiracial, yet southern megachurches report an average of 13 percent racial diversity in their congregations. These large churches in the South report greater use of small groups, a more supportive community, and a more family-centered atmosphere than do those outside the region. In keeping with the strong conservative theology that is characteristic of the southern region, these megachurches are more prone to stress personal devotional practices, scripture reading, family devotions, tithing, religious education, and a faith that is uncompromising. Southern megachurches are also more likely to use choirs, print church bulletins, and be slightly less contemporary in their worship style than other megachurches are. Finally, these southern churches claim their worship services to be more reverent, more filled with God's presence, and more joyful than do the rest of the nation's megachurches.

The southern suburban megachurches in particular can be seen as providing a replica of church-oriented village life that becomes a new home to dislocated rural and small-town migrants. These megachurches are also a place of regional and religious socialization for the less-churched northern transplants. Additionally, these churches provide a ready-made social network, complete with intimate small groups and lifestyle programs, which allows for quick integration into a new community composed of persons of similar values and social demographics. All these functions are essential in a rapidly growing and increasingly diverse and disconnected suburban reality. It is no surprise then that megachurches have grown like kudzu in the South, since this distinctive spiritual form ideally fits the contemporary regional reality.

SCOTT THUMMA
Hartford (Connecticut) Institute for Religion Research
Hartford Seminary

Mark Chaves, *Review of Religious Research* 47 (2006); Nancy Eiesland, in *Contemporary American Religion: An Ethnographic Reader*, ed. Nancy Eiesland and Penny Edgell Becker (1997); Anne C. Loveland and Otis B. Wheeler, *From Meetinghouse to Megachurch: A Material and Cultural History* (2003); Donald E. Miller, *Reinventing American Protestantism: Christianity in the New Millennium* (1997); Lyle E. Schaller, *The Very Large Church* (2000); Scott Thumma, in *Religion in the Contemporary South: Diversity, Community, and Identity*, ed. Kendal White and Daryl White, in *Religions of Atlanta*, ed. Gary Laderman (1996), *Southern Anthropology Proceedings* 28 (1995); Scott Thumma and Dave Travis, *Beyond Megachurch Myths: What We Can Learn from America's Largest Churches* (2007).

New Orleans and Hurricane Katrina

On the afternoon of 28 August 2005, Hurricane Katrina made landfall, with winds exceeding 180 miles per hour. The next day, on 29 August 2005, New Orleans flooded. The tidal surge from Katrina's winds was more than the city's ill-prepared levees could handle. By late in the day, more than 80 percent of New Orleans was underwater. It would be two weeks before the water retreated, leaving unimaginable destruction in its wake.

Before the floodwaters of Katrina, New Orleans was an urban center at risk. In the previous 30 years, New Orleans had experienced flat or little economic growth. While tourism and health care continued to be the largest employers, much of the city was in crisis before Katrina made landfall. Of the city's housing stock, approximately 32,000 homes were substandard, the public schools were in constant crisis, and the public health-care system was struggling. At the same time, the infrastructure of the community was in decline—streets, bridges, levees, and the coastline all begged repair.

As with any urban setting, the decline created a climate for other types of social problems. Not only were property and violent crimes on the rise, but New Orleans had one of the world's highest rates of incarceration, matched by a staggering rate of generational poverty. As if a foreshadowing of what was to come, the day the levees broke the Census Bureau reported that Orleans Parish had a poverty rate of 23.2 percent, seventh highest among 290 large U.S. counties. African Americans made up 84 percent of the impoverished.

Well before the turn of the 21st century, the economic, social, and racial travails of New Orleans had combined to push the city to the periphery of an America barreling down the fast tract of a globalizing economy. Beginning in 1960, the city began to experience a net loss of population. By 2005, in short, this geographic place and its people were fast becoming expendable in a world of finance-driven capital. Although its port and shipping continue to be of service to our national economy, the rich diversity and cultural uniqueness of New Orleans are far from the minds and policies of our national and international political leadership. The abstract idea of a disposable place and people became concretely visible for all to see as the city filled with water.

Hurricane Katrina was not "the big one," the doomsday storm that would destroy the city once and for all. Indeed, by the time it reached the eastern edge of New Orleans, Katrina's winds barely exceeded 100 miles per hour, making it a weak Category 2 storm. The relative size of the storm, however, and whether it was the "big one" meant precious little to the hundreds of thousands of people who faced incalculable risks from the waters that surround, run through, and simmer just below this city.

In the early hours of Monday, 29 August 2005, the residents remaining in New Orleans breathed an early sigh of relief, thinking that once again New Orleans had dodged "the big one" one more time. Yet this relief was short lived when, one by one, nearly 40 levees breached and two overtopped. As the water in the city rose to meet the level of water in Lake Pontchartrain, the human story unfolded, graphically illustrating how vulnerable and expendable this city and its people were.

The immediate governmental disaster-response effort to the flooding of New Orleans has been roundly considered a failure. The Bush White House had systematically reduced the size and scope of key units such as the Federal Emergency Management Agency and Housing and Urban Development and had privatized many agency responsibilities. The result was a striking failure to respond effectively and humanely to the catastrophe. State and city governments were also paralyzed by Katrina's wrath. Waiting for a coordinated federal response that did not materialize for more than two weeks, the mayor of New Orleans and the state's governor issued a stream of contradictory statements and accused one another of failing to take the lead. The result was egregious government failure at all levels in the face of an overwhelming humanitarian crisis.

The exact number of those who died in New Orleans during and after the flood—from drowning to kidney dialysis patients left untreated to suicides and random killings of suspected looters by vigilante groups—is unknown.

Urban disasters are particularly devastating events, and a key unit of analysis in assessing disaster impacts is the neighborhood. New Orleans is a mosaic of 72 distinct neighborhoods. Each one has its own complex social, cultural, and political history. Approximately 80 percent of New Orleans's neighborhoods bore the frontal assault of the flood. In a limited way, Katrina was a democratic disaster affecting upper-, middle-, and lower-class neighborhoods. Neighborhood recovery from Katrina, however, has been anything but egalitarian.

Included in the roughly 20 percent of neighborhoods that remained dry are the city's two most distinguished tourist attractions: the Vieux Carre, or French Quarter, and the Garden District. Aptly christened the "Isle of Denial" by some unnamed source, these neighborhood clusters are testament to the saving grace of higher ground in this flood-prone city. Each cluster sits several feet above sea level. Illustrated in the recovery trajectory of these neighborhoods is the intimate correlation between life chances and distance above sea level in New Orleans. Roughly put, the better a person's life chances the more likely he or she will live on higher ground.

New Orleans, La., in the aftermath of Hurricane Katrina, showing Interstate 10
at West End Boulevard, looking toward Lake Pontchartrain
(U.S. Coast Guard, Petty Officer 2nd Class Kyle Niemi)

Not so fortunate are the historic neighborhoods of Gentilly and Fillmore located north of the city, toward Lake Pontchartrain. These clusters began as white suburbs but over time became predominantly middle-class, African American neighborhoods. Most of the housing stock was built on slab foundations, a structural arrangement particularly susceptible to flooding. These neighborhoods, along with New Orleans East, have been slow to repopulate. The demographics of repopulation suggest that the African American middle class displaced by the flood is returning to the city at a comparatively slow rate.

By 2009, four years after the flood, the recovery of New Orleans neighborhoods has been anything but uniform. Repopulation and subsequent rebuilding is uneven. Although the postflood population has increased along the high ground near the Mississippi River, low-lying or "wet" neighborhoods like the Lower Ninth Ward and Venetian Isles have recovered less than one-third of pre-Katrina residents. An evening drive through the Lower Ninth Ward more than three years after the storm is an opportunity to witness what some call the "jack-o-lantern effect." This colorful and telling term was coined to describe those streets where the lights of one or two houses cut through the black night of an otherwise abandoned neighborhood. The irregular and patchy rate of repopulation appears to be closely tied to the size and quality of the housing stock in postflood New Orleans. Not surprisingly, it is also linked to job opportunities, as well as to the more immediate problem of repairing the levees and creating relatively safe topographies.

The most serious issue facing residents and flooded neighborhoods is housing. More than 75 percent of the city's housing stock was damaged by floodwaters. Housing recovery slowed after 2008, after explosive growth in home prices, building permits, and new construction during the initial two years after the storm. After surging upward nearly 60 percent over pre-Katrina levels in the year after the storm, the average sale price of a single family home in 2008 dropped to $171,219, or 82 percent of the pre-Katrina level. Reflecting national trends, the New Orleans housing market is stagnant, with a 40 percent increase in active listings in 2008 compared to prestorm levels. The number of days a house stays on the market before it is sold has sharply increased.

Despite a stagnant housing market and rising property taxes, the balance of recovery is tilted toward homeowners over renters—the combination of federally funded flood insurance and the Road Home Program provided more than $10 billion for home repairs. More than 52,000 building permits and 10,000 demolition permits were issued in New Orleans from August 2005 to

August 2007. But the pace of rebuilding and demolition, reflecting a severe national recession, slowed to a snail's pace in 2008. Only 9,000 building permits and 2,500 demolition permits were issued in 2008. The intersection of a city's disaster recovery and national economic and political trends is graphically evident in the uneven and unequal pace of rehousing New Orleans's displaced residents.

Housing recovery was further slowed by the decision of the U.S. Department of Housing and Urban Development to tear down over 5,000 public-housing units. This has prevented many low-income residents from returning to the city and has contributed to a shortage of rental housing within city limits. Rents in New Orleans have increased by an average of 46 percent since the storm. Moreover, there are approximately 71,000 vacant houses in the city, nearly 65,000 of which are likely blighted. Blight is unevenly distributed across neighborhoods, with rates as high as 85 percent in the Lower Ninth Ward, 50 percent in New Orleans East, and more than 33 percent in the neighborhoods of Mid-City and Gentilly.

In addition to housing, neighborhood recovery requires jobs. Economic recovery in the metropolitan New Orleans region has been impressive but irregular. Manufacturing and construction employment have fully recovered their pre-Katrina levels, and employment in professional and business services and in federal and state government is proportionately higher than it was before the storm. On the other hand, local government employment at the end of 2007 was only one-third and information sector employment was only 57 percent of pre-Katrina levels. Job losses in Orleans Parish are spread unevenly across neighborhoods.

Job losses are highest in heavily flood-damaged neighborhoods like New Orleans East, where total employment at the end of 2007 stood at 43 percent of pre-Katrina levels. Employment decline by industry in New Orleans East provides a snapshot of economic change in hard-hit neighborhoods. Several hospitals were closed in the East, and employment in the health sector dropped from 4,004 in the second quarter of 2005 to 698 in the third quarter of 2007. Employment in the food-service and accommodations sector in this section of the city declined from 1,845 to 342, and retail employment dropped from 3,269 to 914 during the same period.

In addition to housing and jobs, and unique to New Orleans, is the relationship of neighborhood recovery to the rebuilding of the levees. Levee breaches caused by Katrina's storm surge flooded most of the city. Also damaged in this disaster was the belief shared by most residents that the city was adequately protected from serious flooding. The engineering failures that contributed to this devastating flood are well documented, as are efforts of the U.S. Army Corps of Engineers (USACE) to repair and improve the levee system that protects New Orleans. According to a recent USACE report, post-Katrina levee repairs and improvements constitute the largest civil works project ever undertaken. The USACE reported in June 2008 that repairs were complete. According to the report, all levees damaged by Katrina are generally stronger and higher now than when Katrina struck. All is far from perfect, though. The report was quick to add that there are still gaps in the system and that only some areas of the city are better protected now than they were before Katrina.

Neighborhood recovery not only includes improved levee protection, economic growth, and better housing, but it also requires a more-personal and less-tangible resource: an adequate measure of emotional and cognitive stability. Humans do not live apart from one another each seeking a private solution to the problems of survival. We live, rather, in groups. City residents are likely to form a semblance of what Herbert Gans called "urban villages." Such total urban disasters like the flooding of New Orleans splinter these villages, leaving broken social ties in their wake. Loved ones are lost, families are broken apart, friends and acquaintances are gone. Shortly after the floodwaters receded, a colorful idiom emerged on the streets of the city to capture the mental exhaustion being experienced by many residents. "Katrina Brain" was, and to a certain extent remains, a pandemic problem in post-Katrina New Orleans. Suicide rates in the city tripled in the first year after the disaster. A significant number of residents report a sense of grief and loss in neighborhoods where half the houses remain unoccupied three years after the storm. Not only are people suffering from an increased sense of vulnerability, but resources to assist them are greatly diminished. Psychiatrists, psychologists, and social workers were reduced as their institutions cut staff, and many professionals chose not to return.

On the other hand, there are those residents who have forged deeper relationships with neighbors as they struggle together through the rebuilding process. Many find comfort in renewed community activism and participation in recovery planning. Others contribute to rebuilding of community centers and churches. Neighborhood organizations went through a period of renewal and growth after Katrina. Neighbors organized to save their communities from being designated a green space or to reopen schools in their neighborhoods.

The flooding of New Orleans altered the social and geographic landscapes of the city. Few neighborhoods were spared. For some residents, the disaster is a cause for optimism. "Perhaps," they say, "we can make things better." For others, the drowning of the city contributes to increased levels of emotional distress and mental illness. One thing is certain, the recovery of New Orleans and its neighborhoods is closely tied to the struggles of neighbors and neighborhoods to craft a new life after Hurricane Katrina.

NEW ORLEANS LATINOS AFTER HURRICANE KATRINA. Hurricane Katrina made New Orleans a new destination for Latino immigrants by creating an intense and highly visible demand for construction workers. As the floodwaters were pumped out of the city, government subcontractors, businesses, and homeowners hired untold numbers of workers to remove the tons of debris from thousands of flooded buildings. In 2005 and 2006 nationwide, nearly a quarter of all construction workers were Latinos, most of whom were foreign-born. Their employment in New Orleans was facilitated by the U.S. Department of Homeland Security's decision to suspend regulations requiring employers to check employee immigration documentation. Those present in the city at that time witnessed the arrival of the rapid-response Latino labor force, but none could count their numbers.

The prolonged recovery of the city has sustained this demand long after the emergency suspensions of labor regulations were lifted in late 2005. In March 2006, a survey of construction workers found that about half the workers were Latino and a quarter stated that they were undocumented. The increase in the Latino population was confirmed from the first population estimates that included racial and ethnic characteristics. In 2005, prior to Katrina, 3.1 percent and 8.1 percent of Orleans and Jefferson parishes were Latino. The first population estimate that included racial and ethnic characteristics took place in fall 2006 and estimated the Latino populations of Orleans and Jefferson to be about 9.6 percent and 9.7 percent, respectively.

These figures likely underestimate the true populations at that time, since the household survey did not include those staying in hotels and nonresidential buildings and in other temporary arrangements. Furthermore, Latino workers residing in households may not have responded to the interview forms or to interviewers. Although the Census Bureau produced lower estimates of the Latino population for 2006, their methods are likely less reliable than the locally generated population estimates. As of 2009, no more recent or more reliable estimates of the Latino population exist, but the larger post-Katrina enrollment of Latino children in public schools and the increased demand for Spanish translators in clinics, hospitals, and courts all substantiate the claims that the Latino immigrant population has grown and includes more recently arrived immigrants.

The post-Katrina Latino immigrants' arrival has been facilitated by the small but well-integrated pre-Katrina Latino population. These pre- and post-Katrina Latino populations are distinct with respect to their national origins and their degree of incorporation into the city. Some of the Latinos in New Orleans were the descendants of the Canary Islanders who had arrived in the 18th century and who gave many contemporary New Orleanians their Spanish surnames, although they were as assimilated as the other New Orleanians of European ancestry. The more recently arrived pre-Katrina Latinos mostly came from Central America, especially Honduras, Nicaragua, and Guatemala, as well as from Cuba. Although there were a sizable number of Mexicans in New Orleans prior to Katrina, they were underrepresented relative to their proportion of the U.S. population. These pre-Katrina Latino immigrants have similar levels of education and occupation as the non-Latino population and are residentially dispersed throughout the metropolitan area. Thus they had little in common with the Latino construction workers other than their language and immigrant status. Nevertheless, some pre-Katrina Latinos were called to action by the needs of the post-Katrina Latino immigrants who were cleaning up and rebuilding the city.

Post-Katrina Latino immigrants needed this advocacy since their working and living conditions were often quite poor in this devastated city. Reports of Latinos consistently described workers living in crowded makeshift dormitories, apartments, or houses. They were disproportionately men, typically in their prime working years, and if they had families they usually had left their spouses and children in their country of origin. This demographic profile may have changed with time as the first hurricane chasers are joined by their families, although population data to demonstrate this change is lacking. However, reported increases in births to Latinas and increased enrollment of Latino children in schools suggest that more families have moved to New Orleans.

The Latino immigrants who came to New Orleans and other areas affected by Hurricanes Katrina and Rita were highly mobile and mostly originated from within the United States. In the early stages of the recovery they were recruited by U.S.-based contractors, but as the word of ample employment and high wages spread through immigrants' social networks they increasingly arrived with the help of fellow immigrants rather than of employers. Many groups of immigrants moved through the city in response to change in the scale and type of labor demand, wages, immigration enforcement, and working and living conditions in the recovering city.

This mobility, along with the fact that many Latino immigrants speak little or no English and are sometimes unauthorized immigrants, makes this group vulnerable to a variety of social ills. Immigrant advocates and Latinos expressed concern over these problems in a public meeting with the Human Relations Commission of the City of New Orleans, a group established by the mayor's office "to combat discrimination and promote inclusion." Nonpayment of wages by employers, language barriers preventing access to health care and legal assistance, crime victimization, and fear that local law enforcement officers will deport unauthorized immigrants if they report on crime were the major issues raised at this meeting. Some New Orleans residents are eager to see the Latino immigrant population become integrated into the community, but others are ambivalent or even opposed.

By 2009, at the fourth anniversary of Katrina, the new Latino immigrants were still seen as a necessary part of the rebuilding process by those in the most devastated areas of New Orleans. However, in less affected areas, opposition to their presence was growing. In Jefferson Parish, where flooding damage was less extensive and recovery had progressed further, the mobile food vendors selling Mexican and Central American food ("taco trucks") were banned by the city council. The city councilman who proposed the ban saw the trucks as a symbol of postdisaster disarray, though others felt the ban was an attempt to make the immigrants feel unwelcome. Immigrants were similarly targeted by a proposed bill in the Louisiana House of Representatives that would make it a crime to house or transport unauthorized immigrants and would authorize local law enforcement officers to verify the citizenship status of those in police custody. One legislator said, "Too many illegal immigrants are flooding southern Louisiana and taking jobs of residents. All [these laws do] is give the locals [law enforcement] some bite so they can take care of some problems in targeted areas." The legislation did not pass, because of unresolved questions of how it would be enforced and of its constitutionality.

Whether the new Latino immigrants become part of New Orleans cultural fabric is yet to be seen. Some of the Latino immigrants who arrived after Katrina will move on; others will settle down and add to the diverse mixture of Latino immigrants who already have roots in New Orleans. How many Latino immigrants ultimately stay is likely to be related to the recovery of New Orleans. An expanding labor market, especially in construction, affordable housing, good public schools, and safe and welcoming communities will encourage Latino immigrants to settle in New Orleans, and the absence of these would encourage them to move on. Throughout the last decades, Latinos have been settling in communities throughout the South and other regions of the

United States, and there is no reason New Orleans would not experience this as well.

VERN BAXTER

PAM JENKINS

University of New Orleans

STEVE KROLL-SMITH

University of North Carolina at Greensboro

ELIZABETH FUSSELL

Washington State University

Jordan Blum, *Advocate* (1 May 2008); Brookings Institution, *Katrina Index Monthly Summary of Findings* (January 2006, February 2006); City of New Orleans Human Relations Commission, "We Believe in One New Orleans: Report and Recommendations of the Human Relations Commission of the City of New Orleans," Executive Summary (6 March 2008); Craig Colten, *The Unnatural Metropolis: Wrestling New Orleans from Nature* (2005); Gilbert C. Din, *The Canary Islanders of Louisiana* (1988); Katharine Donato, Nicole Trujillo-Pagán, Carl L. Bankston III, and Audrey Singer, in *The Sociology of Katrina: Perspectives on a Modern Catastrophe*, ed. David L. Brunsma, David Overfelt, and J. Steven Picou (2007); Earth Institute, Columbia University, *Hurricane Katrina Deceased-Victims List*, www.katrinalist.columbia .edu; Laurel E. Fletcher, Phuong Pham, Eric Stover, and Patrick Vinck, *Rebuilding after Katrina: A Population-Based Study of Labor and Human Rights in New Orleans* (2006); Elizabeth Fussell, in *Civic Engagement in the Wake of Katrina*, ed. Amy Koritz and George Sanchez (2008); Herbert Gans, *The Urban Villagers: Group and Class in the Life of Italian-Americans* (1982); Luis Emilio Henoa, *The Hispanics in Louisiana* (1982); Susan E. Howell, *Hispanic Social Needs Survey: New Orleans Metropolitan Area* (1997); Pierce F. Lewis, *New Orleans: The Making of an Urban Landscape* (2003); Manuel Pastor et al., *In the Wake of the Storm: Environment, Disaster, and Race after Katrina* (2006); Eduardo Porter, "Katrina Begets a Baby Boom by Immigrants," *New York Times* (11 September 2008); Mark Waller, "New Rules Eliminate Taco Trucks," *New Orleans Times-Picayune* (21 June 2007); Richard H. Weisler, James G. Barbee, and Mark Townsend, *Journal of the American Medical Association* 296 (2006).

New Urbanism

New urbanism is an approach to urban residential design that promotes walkable, diverse, dense, mixed-use neighborhoods, along with infill and transit-oriented development in the tradition of the early 20th-century American towns as an antidote to sprawling suburban bedroom communities and automobile dependency. Urban planning proposals for community-oriented "gar-

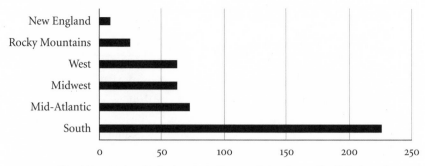

FIGURE 1. *New Urban Projects by Region, 2002* (Source: *Robert Steuteville, Philip Langdon, and Special Contributors,* New Urbanism: Comprehensive Report and Best Practices Guide [2003])

den" settlements by Ebenezer Howard more than one hundred years ago, as well as the City Beautiful movement and other strategies for improving urban life, connect new urbanism to a history of debates about planning. More recent discussions of new urbanism emerged in the 1970s and 1980s, with a push in the 1990s by many professionals—architects, planners, urban geographers, scholars, citizens, governmental officials, and developers—to formalize the design principles. The Charter of New Urbanism, drafted between 1993 and 1996 by the Congress of New Urbanism, describes principles that promote community interaction and cultivate a sense of place through neighborhood design strategies. Residential communities are centered around a community square or park, with shops, offices, playgrounds, open spaces, public transit, and schools within walking distance. The density and diversity of dwellings is important, with five to six homes or apartment buildings per acre, parking and trash in the rear with access via service roads, and street network connectivity featuring narrow streets and vistas.

Geographically, the majority of new urban developments are located in the South. Figure 1 gives the number of new urban projects on a neighborhood scale (at least 15 acres) that were completed, under construction, in planning, or in groundbreaking phases by region in the United States for 2002. The South showed 225 new urban projects. The Mid-Atlantic, Midwest, and West contained 75, 67, and 67 projects, respectively. The Rocky Mountain and New England regions had 29 and 11 new urban projects. Florida ranks first in the South, with 63 new urban projects. North Carolina has the second-largest number of new urban projects, with 34. Texas, Virginia, South Carolina, and Georgia report 27, 21, 21, and 20 new urban projects (Table 5).

Within the South are several prominent new urban projects. Seaside, Fla.,

TABLE 5. *New Urban Projects in the South, by State, 2002*

State	Number	State	Number
Florida	63	New Mexico	7
North Carolina	34	Arizona	4
Texas	27	Kentucky	3
South Carolina	21	Mississippi	3
Virginia	21	Louisiana	2
Georgia	20	Arkansas	1
Tennessee	11	Oklahoma	1
Alabama	7		

Source: Robert Steuteville, Philip Langdon, and Special Contributors, *New Urbanism: Comprehensive Report and Best Practices Guide* (2003).
Note: Includes projects completed, under construction, or in the planning or groundbreaking phase.

is considered the first and most successful new urban town. It is located along the Gulf of Mexico on Florida's panhandle on approximately 80 acres that were inherited by Robert Davis, who partnered with Andres Duany and Elizabeth Plater-Zyberk, two Miami-based planners and the founders of the Congress for New Urbanism, to develop a design concept. They surveyed many traditional neighborhoods throughout the South, such as Grayton Beach and Key West, Fla., Charleston, S.C., and Savannah, Ga. The best feature of each was adopted to form a development that offers beach walkability, an eclectic array of southern architectural styles, porches close enough to sandy walkways to talk to passersby, outdoor activities, diversity of dwelling types (for example, single family homes, apartments, and condos), and shops, including an open-air market. The town's population is estimated at approximately 2,000, with 350 houses and 300 other buildings. Originally, the town was intended to be an affordable residential choice for ordinary people, but it has since become only available to the wealthy due to its popularity.

Planning for Harbor Town in Memphis, Tenn., began in 1988 by developer Henry Turley, who started construction in 1989. Harbor Town consists of 135 acres, located just northwest of downtown Memphis on Mud Island, flanked by the Mississippi River and the Wolf River Creek Harbor. The upscale homes and apartments are built relatively close together, based around the idea of interaction with neighbors and postmodern architecture. The homes in Harbor Town are classically inspired, but each is unique in design while still maintaining fundamental elements such as tall ceilings and doors, raised fountains, vertical windows, and other elements that work harmoniously together. The neighborhood has the feel of a resort town although it is a year-round residential area. Amenities include a small grocery store, a deli, a park along the Mississippi River, tennis courts, a day-care center, a marina, a school, restaurants, a hotel, a fitness center, beauty salons, a dry cleaner, and a health spa—all located within walking distance of Harbor Town.

Celebration, Fla., located southeast of Orlando along Interstate 4, occupies 5,000 of Disney's 30,000 acres in central Florida. Peter Rummell, a Disney executive, convinced Michael Eisner, Disney's chairman at the time, that constructing a neotraditional neighborhood would be the most profitable venture for the area of undeveloped land. Robert Stern and Jacquelin Robertson's 1991 design envisioned a town for 20,000 residents living in four villages that employed a variety of architectural styles. Celebration includes a 2 million square foot open-air shopping mall, the Disney Institute (a place for people to take classes on a variety of subjects), a fitness spa, a performing arts center, and hotels and offices. The town offers nature, walking, and biking trails, as well as a fiber optic computer network and has since become very popular and a well-known example of new urbanism.

New urbanism in the South has also been used in redevelopment projects. The most recent and prominent example is the rebuilding of the Mississippi Gulf Coast since Hurricane Katrina hit in August 2005. Governor Haley Barbour of Mississippi was persuaded by Jim Barksdale, chairman of Governor Barbour's rebuilding commission, to rebuild the Gulf Coast using a new urbanist model. In October 2005, just six weeks after the hurricane, 200 planners, architects, engineers, government officials, and other professionals convened in Naples, Fla., at the Isle of Capri hotel for the Mississippi Renewal Forum headed by the Congress for New Urbanism and new urban planner Andres Duany. After a week of discussions and planning, the forum presented new urban recommendations and plans for the 11 communities of the Mississippi Gulf Coast, including Biloxi, Ocean Springs, and Pass Christian.

Pass Christian, Miss., was one of the first communities affected by Hurricane Katrina to adopt new urbanist planning codes, known as SmartCode, as part of its rebuilding plan. The SmartCode zoning plans were adopted in three-quarters of the city of Pass Christian by November 2008. The last quarter of Pass Christian is considering the SmartCode; if adopted, Pass Christian will be one of the first communities in the United States to adopt a citywide SmartCode.

MELANIE A. RAPINO
University of Memphis

Charter of the New Urbanism, *Congress for the New Urbanism* (2001); Douglas Frantz and Catherine Collins, *Celebration, U.S.A.* (2000); Jim Lewis, "Battle for Biloxi," *New York Times* (21 May 2006); SmartCode in Action, *Harrison County Planner* (November 2008); Mike Snyder, "Mississippi Communities Hope to Avoid Sprawl in Rebuild," *Houston Chronicle* (3 June 2007); Robert Steuteville, *New Urban News* (2004); Robert Steuteville, Philip Langdon, and Special Contributors, *New Urbanism: Comprehensive Report and Best Practices Guide* (2003).

Politics

Throughout southern history, the mercantile classes have formed the core of urban leadership. In colonial times, the business elite dominated the governmental and economic institutions of the South's embryonic cities. For these leaders, the key to urban growth was the economic development of regional hinterlands. In early Baltimore, for instance, city expansion depended upon a thriving grain and flour industry that drew directly from the wheat production of the nearby countryside. Enhancement of the local economy was therefore the primary aim of urban government in the southern colonies.

During the antebellum era, the bond between the business elite and city government persisted. In New Orleans, the South's largest urban center, directors of local corporations often served simultaneously on the city council. In Richmond, 40 percent of the local elite, mainly business and professional men, held governmental offices. Joseph R. Anderson, head of the Tredegar Iron Works, was typical. He became a bank director, an outspoken supporter of various railroad and canal enterprises, and a member of the Richmond city council.

Enlargement of the hinterlands remained important to urban leaders, but many directed greater concern toward developing a regional and national network of cities as well as increasing urban competition. The mercantile elite endorsed railroad subsidies and wharf improvements, which would perhaps attract business away from other communities, but they also recognized the importance to urban growth of better fire and police protection, improved street lighting and drainage, and adequate health statutes. Although municipal services infrequently kept pace with local needs, few questioned their usefulness to urban boosterism. At issue in most urban political contests was the cost of municipal improvements, not their value. Voters commonly removed extravagant administrators from office.

The obligation to regulate urban slaves and free blacks won universal acceptance in the South, but other ethnic tensions periodically took political form. In 1836, differences among the French-speaking Creoles, the incoming Americans, and emigrants from Ireland and Germany prompted the city of New Orleans to divide into three separate municipalities. For 16 years, three distinct governmental entities directed the affairs of the Crescent City while an inconsequential mayor and general council nominally presided. In 1852, inefficiency, disease, and natural disasters contributed to a reunification that solidified the American sections with the annexation of rapidly growing suburbs. Ethnic animosity, however, continued throughout the decade. In the New Orleans municipal elections of 1854, violent opposition to immigration led directly to the victory of the Know-Nothing Party. This organization, with the backing of labor, controlled Crescent City government until the Union conquest in 1862.

Secession sentiment in southern cities was mixed. The commercial leaders in those cities with predominantly northern markets resisted separation. The elite in cities with important trade generally favored disunion. Support for the southern cause, nonetheless, was clearly present in all urban centers.

Urban politics in the Reconstruction South mirrored regional contests that pitted Republicans and their newly franchised black allies against former Confederates and other Conservative Democrats. In New Orleans, the White League, a vigorous and ultimately successful foe of the Republican regime and its metropolitan police, helped to spawn a powerful political machine that dominated local affairs for nearly 75 years. A characteristic urban ring, the Regular Democratic Organization, used election fraud, patronage, political favors, and violence to maintain control. Its leadership of largely first-generation Americans depended upon labor, new immigrants, and (until 1898) subordinate blacks for electoral support. Businessmen who received lucrative municipal franchises provided financial backing.

The Old Regulars' political opponents were more representative of the leadership in other southern communities. Described appropriately as the commercial civic elite by historian Blaine A. Brownell, its members included bankers, real estate entrepreneurs, insurance agents, merchants, and contractors, as well as lawyers, journalists, teachers, doctors, and other middle-class, business-oriented professionals. In the Crescent City, this group constituted a sporadic opposition that achieved its ends mainly through independent governmental boards. In Atlanta, Birmingham, and other cities, the commercial civic elite dominated municipal offices and generally influenced the disposition of city revenue, services, and regulations. Combining the New South creed with urban boosterism, local leaders sought new industry and greater business development within an atmosphere of municipal stability. Urban growth, often accomplished through annexation, was an acknowledged—though frequently contradictory—goal. The new suburbs, a major source of fresh problems, usually received fewer municipal services than did the central business districts and the industrial neighborhoods.

During the early 20th century, the mixing of southern city councils and chambers of commerce intensified. In New Orleans, the evolving Old Regulars under Major Martin Behrmen and in Memphis under the powerful machine of Edward H. Crump clearly inclined toward business interests. Business philosophy and the progressive impulse precipitated structural reform in numerous southern city governments. The city commissioner and the city manager forms of municipal administration, created in Dixie, found favor throughout the region. Governmental change, however, rarely altered political structure in the urban South. The New Orleans machine and the Crump organization continued to dominate the new commission councils in their towns.

During the 1920s, the link between the commercial civic elite and city hall raised urban boosterism to higher levels. The "Atlanta Spirit" became the regional model, although Miami was perhaps the best example of city boom. City leaders used the automobile revolution and the new interest in municipal planning to promote programs for the economic growth of the central business district, the allocation of adequate land for commercial and industrial use, the improvement of local transportation networks, the separation of the races, and the controlled expansion of the periphery. Although these programs infrequently resolved municipal problems, they established patterns for future development.

During the Great Depression, economic demands forced southern leaders to curtail municipal services and to engage in relief efforts. Many regional chief executives joined with their urban counterparts throughout the nation to plead for federal aid to the cities. After the election of Franklin D. Roosevelt, numerous southern mayors espoused New Deal programs. In Memphis, local leaders welcomed cheap electricity from the Tennessee Valley Authority. New Orleans mayor Robert S. Maestri often joked that the Works Progress Administration was a "money tree" for his community.

World War II brought new growth and added challenges to southern cities. After the war, aged political machines in New Orleans and Memphis faltered, and the commercial civic elite began to reassert itself. New-breed mayors such as De Lesseps S. Morrison of New Orleans, Robert King High of Miami, and William B. Hartsfield and Ivan Allen Jr. of Atlanta took charge and advanced programs that were in line with commercial expansion and urban development. All facets of municipal administration, particularly building projects, were geared to the enhancement of the urban image in the South. Within this context of city maturation, the financial problems and political tensions of suburbanization began to appear. To cope with these difficulties, Miami and Nashville adopted metropolitan governments.

The civil rights movement contributed to the outward population shift when white southerners fled to the suburbs to escape integration. In Little Rock, New Orleans, and Birmingham, resistance to desegregation had a debilitating effect upon the local economies. During these crises, governmental and business leadership in the South was sorely lacking until harsh economic reality forced the commercial civic elite to take a moderate stance on desegregation.

During the 1960s, federal legislation on civil rights altered the political structure of the urban South forever and convinced white politicians to reassess their racial views. Candidates who did not address the needs of black voters had little chance for success. An expanding black electorate and white flight to the suburbs increased black political clout in the urban South. By the 1970s, blacks commonly populated city councils throughout the region, and many of the South's largest cities boasted their first black mayors. Although black governmental leaders often worked with and welcomed the support of the commercial civic elite, they devoted greater attention to neighborhood needs. Many white governmental leaders also stressed historic preservation and rehabilitation of core areas as a means to offset the population decrease, and accompanying financial drains, of suburban flight. Increased tourism has been a major goal of such efforts. Memphis, for example, renovated Beale Street into a modern entertainment venue, created music-oriented museums such as the Rock and Soul Museum and the Stax Museum, and built new sports facilities to attract the Memphis Grizzlies national basketball team and the minor-league baseball Redbirds team in an effort to increase the city's appeal as a tourism destination. Willie Harrington, mayor since 1992, and a mostly African American city council oversaw this development, working with white business leaders.

Over the past decades, the commercial civic elite has not surrendered its political power, but it has been forced to vie with other urban interest groups for the allocation of diminishing municipal resources. An increasingly diverse leadership in southern cities has begun to assess the value of economic growth against the importance of metropolitan cooperation, historic renovation, and neighborhood demands. Diversity of political leadership has become a major theme with increasing numbers of women mayors, such as Shirley Franklin in Atlanta and Shelia Dixon in Baltimore. Miami had had Latino (Cuban) mayors since 1997. Finally, the political leadership of no city has faced greater recent challenges than that of Mayor Ray Nagin, whose New Orleans administration has worked for recovery after Hurricane Katrina devastated the city in 2005.

EDWARD F. HAAS
Louisiana State Museum, Tulane University

Carl Abbott, *The New Urban America: Growth and Politics in Sunbelt Cities* (1981); Ronald H. Bayor, *Race and the Shaping of Twentieth-Century Atlanta* (1996); Blaine A. Brownell and David R. Goldfield, eds., *The City in Southern History: The Growth of Urban Civilization in the South* (1977); Edward F. Haas, *De Lesseps S. Morrison and the Image of Reform: New Orleans Politics, 1946–1961* (1974); Carl V. Harris, *Political Power in Birmingham, 1871–1921* (1977); Wanda Rushing, *Memphis and the Paradox of Place: Globalization in the American South* (2009); Christopher Silver, *Journal of Urban History* (November 1983); Eugene J. Watts, *The Social Bases of City Politics: Atlanta, 1865–1903* (1978).

Population Change and Demographics

With over 100 million people, the South is the most populated region of the United States, housing more than a third of the total U.S. population. The South is home to almost 40 million more people than the second-largest region (the Midwest) and almost twice as many people as the Northeast. The South is also one of the fastest-growing regions of the country, growing 17.3 percent in the 1990s. This rate is more than three times the rate of growth for the Northeast over the same time period. Since 1990, Georgia has been the fastest-growing state in the South, with Texas and Florida experiencing the most growth in terms of absolute numbers. In 2007, Texas gained more new residents than any other state in the country.

Between 1990 and 2000, 13 of the 20 fastest-growing metropolitan areas in the United States were located in the South, including Myrtle Beach, S.C., Wilmington, Del., and Austin–San Marcos, Tex. Naples, Fla., grew by more than 65 percent in the 1990s, making it one of the top growers in the nation, second only to Las Vegas. In Georgia, where the population grew by nearly 2 million between 1990 and 2000, almost all of that growth occurred in the Atlanta metropolitan area.

Of course, not all southern cities are booming. On 28 August 2005, Hurricane Katrina hit the Gulf Coast and devastated cities in Mississippi and Louisiana. Less than a month later, on 24 September, Hurricane Rita—the most intense tropical hurricane recorded in the Gulf of Mexico—touched down in Louisiana and southeast Texas. Cities along the Mississippi Gulf Coast, such as Gulfport and Biloxi, were hard hit, and in some cases entirely destroyed, by the 2005 Atlantic hurricane season. In southern Louisiana, New Orleans was devastated. In Orleans Parish, more than 100,000 properties were severely damaged or destroyed as a result of the failing levee system. Displaced residents fled, and many have not returned. Between 1 July 2005 and 1 July 2006, New Orleans lost more than half of its population. Although the population began to rebound slightly in 2007 and 2008, it is too early to speculate on the long-term effects of this ecological disaster. It is worth noting, however, that between 2006 and 2007, St. Bernard Parish on the Mississippi River was the fastest-growing county in the United States, showing that some of the hurricane-affected areas are making a comeback.

Overall, the growth of the South in the last decade is an acceleration of a trend that began in the 1960s. The Civil War, the Great Depression, and the Dust Bowl all contributed to the devastation of the South's economy in the 20th century, with the effects reflected in stagnant or declining populations in many areas. Between 1910 and 1940, about 1.6 million African Americans fled mostly rural places in the South to seek better employment opportunities in industrial cities in the Northeast and Midwest and to escape the racial climate of the Jim Crow era. Called the Great Migration, this period was followed by the Second Great Migration (1940–70), during which an additional 5 million African Americans—primarily from Alabama, Louisiana, and Mississippi—migrated to new destinations in California and points north.

Since 1960, however, the growth of industry and the relocation of businesses to the South have reversed the tide of out-migration from the South. Although the causes of this reversal of economic fortunes remain the subject of debate, most scholars agree that the migration of businesses from the North to the South was facilitated by the completion of the interstate highway system, the spread of home air-conditioning, and the infusion of public capital into large infrastructure development programs by entities such as the Tennessee Valley Authority. At the same time, northern businesses were attracted to the South for its pool of cheap labor and low rates of unionization, both of which resulted from the South's former lack of industrialization. The increasing availability of new jobs has attracted workers from other regions of the country as well as immigrant workers, and this influx of workers has increased both the size and the diversity of the South. The period from 1965 to 2000 has been termed the New Great Migration, to reflect the recent trend of African Americans moving from cities in the North and California to the South. Between 1995 and 2000, Georgia, Texas, and Maryland each attracted more black college graduates than any other state in the United States.

The return of many African Americans to the South occurs at a time when other minorities are also relocating to the South. Excluding Texas (which historically has maintained a large Latino population), the Latino population in the South doubled in the 1990s. During that same time period, the Asian and Pacific Islander population in the South also grew by more than 75 percent. Much, but not all, of the growth of the Asian and Latino population in the South is attributable to immigration, which is particularly notable given that (with the exception of Texas and Florida) immigrants have typically eschewed the South in favor of other destinations. In 1910, when the percentage of U.S. residents who were immigrants was at an all-time high, the immigrant populations in North Carolina, Alabama, Georgia, Mississippi, South Carolina, and Tennessee made up less than 1 percent of the total population in those states. Today, Texas has the second-largest minority population in the United States, and Georgia had the second-fastest-growing minority population between 1990 and 2000.

During the last decade of the 20th century, the United States experienced tremendous growth in its foreign-born population, particularly in areas that had traditionally received relatively little immigration. In 1980, there were 14.1 million foreign-born persons living in the United States; by 2000, the total number of foreign-born persons had more than doubled, to 31.1 million persons. During this same period, the typical dispersal and settlement patterns of foreign-born persons became less predictable. Prior to the 1990s, nearly three-quarters of all foreign-born persons settled in the six traditional receiving states: California, Florida, Illinois, New Jersey, New York, and Texas, usually within the urban centers of Los Angeles, Miami, Chicago, New York, and Houston. Although the total number of foreign-born persons has continued to increase in these places throughout the last decade of the 20th century and into the beginning of the 21st century, a steadily growing percentage has recently begun to settle in nontraditional destinations.

Many of these nontraditional, new-immigrant destinations are in the South. The immigrant population has reached as high as 65,000 in cities like Atlanta, Nashville, and Raleigh, and an even higher number of immigrants reside in the surrounding metropolitan areas. Smaller places such as Dalton, Ga., and Morristown, Tenn., are now nearly one-fifth foreign-born. Whereas prior to 1980 the South contained fewer than 15 percent of the total foreign-born population, by 2000, 27.7 percent of all foreign-born persons resided in the South, a percentage second only to the 37.8 percent that resided in the West. Between 1980 and the end of the 20th century, the number of foreign-born persons in the

South increased by nearly 300 percent, the highest overall percentage increase of the four major regions in the United States for that time period. Today, more than half of all immigrants in the South are Latino, while Asians make up the second-largest foreign-born population.

The South now contains the overwhelming majority of metropolitan areas with the most rapid increase in the number of foreign-born persons. Between 1990 and 2000, states such as North Carolina and Georgia experienced growth rates of 274 percent and 233 percent, respectively, in the foreign-born population, and key metropolitan areas such as Charlotte and Atlanta experienced foreign-born growth rates of 315 and 263 percent, respectively. During the same decade, the foreign-born populations in traditional receiving areas such as New York and Los Angeles increased by a mere 37 and 19 percent, respectively.

This trend continues through the first decade of the 21st century: by 2006, more than 30 percent of all foreign-born persons in the United States resided in the South. The Census Bureau estimates that 11.3 million residents in the South are foreign born. Although the West, at 13.7 million, maintains the largest total population of foreign-born persons, the South continues to outpace all other regions in the percent increase of the foreign-born population. If migration to the South is consistent with current theories of migrant networks, it can be expected that newly established immigrant networks will encourage the continued migration of future immigrants to the South.

Several factors have contributed to this unprecedented growth in the foreign-born population in the South. Among the most cited are the increasingly unfavorable social and economic conditions for foreign-born workers in traditional destinations and the newly favorable market conditions for low-skilled and low-wage workers in the South. Increased anti-immigrant sentiment in traditional receiving areas, as evidenced by the passage of California's Proposition 187, which attempted to keep undocumented immigrant children from public schools, and stronger border enforcement along the nation's southwestern border, combined with greater competition for jobs resulting from the deindustrialization of the Northeast, have pushed immigrants seeking job opportunities and safer living spaces into nontraditional destinations.

Correspondingly, the industrial transformation of the South, from its relatively underdeveloped status for much of the 20th century to the recent lure of northeastern factories, has contributed to the creation of a relative abundance of job opportunities and a comparatively low cost of living, which has thus made the South an attractive destination for many immigrant workers. The lack of sufficient native-born workers (especially in the construction, food processing, and textile industries), high turnover rates, and a perception of immigrants as willing to work undesirable jobs have favored the employment and active recruitment of foreign-born workers.

STEPHANIE A. BOHON
MEGHAN CONLEY
University of Tennessee

Carl L. Bankston III, *Sociological Spectrum* (April 2003); Campbell J. Gibson and Emily Lennon, *Historical Census Statistics on the Foreign-Born Population of the United States: 1850–1990* (1999); Rubén Hernández-Leon and Víctor Zúñiga, *Social Science Quarterly* (Spring 2000); Douglas S. Massey, ed., *New Faces in New Places: The Changing Geography of American Immigration* (2008); Carol Schmid, *Sociological Spectrum* (2003); Audrey Singer, *The Rise of New Immigrant Gateways* (2004); Rebecca Torres, E. J. Popke, and Holly M. Hapke, in *The New South: Latinos and the Transformation of Place*, ed. Heather A. Smith and Owen J. Furuseth (2006).

Poverty, Child

Across the United States, almost one in five children lives in poverty (defined by the federal government as $22,500 for a family of four in 2009). Of the two dozen most advanced industrial nations in the world, the child poverty rate in the United States is second highest, following Mexico. Child poverty in the United States has lasting implications for the health and well-being of individuals as well as of communities. Children in poverty are more likely to suffer from poor health and nutrition, are uprooted from their homes more often, and are more likely to live in unsafe neighborhoods and to struggle in school. As they grow to adulthood, poor children are more likely to drop out of school, to have greater difficulty finding decent jobs, and to become parents in their teens. They run a greater risk of getting involved in crime and are more likely to live in poverty as adults. Another one in five American children lives in low-income families (between 100 and 200 percent of the federal poverty line). These children also face a more difficult trajectory in life: they are more likely to experience food and health insecurity and to have a more difficult time in school and life than their middle-income peers.

Poor and low-income families confront obstacles that add expenses and inconveniences to everyday life. Businesses, grocery stores, and banks are less prevalent in low-income neighborhoods. The lack of businesses increases the likelihood that the working poor, a fifth of whom are employed as cashiers, housekeepers, health aides, cooks, or wait-staff, need to travel farther to work.

Families in poverty are more likely to rely on check-cashing services, which charge much higher interest rates than banks. Additionally, three-quarters of working poor families spend more than one-third of their income paying for their residence, and nearly half of these families have at least one parent who is uninsured.

In the United States, child poverty rates are highest in the South (20 percent), followed by the West and Midwest (16 percent), and the Northeast (15 percent). Analysts point to a handful of reasons for higher child poverty rates in the South, including higher rates of parenting by young, single, and undereducated teens and adults. These proximate causes of poverty are vestiges of the southern legacy of slavery and institutional segregation, of an economy traditionally built on agriculture and hostile to unionism, and of regional efforts to repress dissent by the poor. For many years, the South's one-party system, bolstered by institutional segregation, sustained race- and class-based socioeconomic cleavages that served to politically disenfranchise the poor and led to public policies that ensured the continued prosperity of the privileged few at the expense of the well-being of the many. Historically, the policy implications of this mindset included a disinvestment in public education, deep-seated opposition to welfare relief, and voting rules that discouraged minority voting.

The results of this history show in the condition of southern children and families today. More than half of all African American children in poverty live in the South, where they are twice as likely as their white classmates to be poor. Moreover, there are much higher concentrations of fragile families in the South than in the nation. Southern children are slightly more likely than other U.S. children to have unmarried parents (31 percent versus 28 percent) and parents without a high school diploma (13 percent versus 12 percent).

Southern children can be divided into two distinct cohorts: one rural and the other urban. Nearly 6 in 10 (59 percent) poor children in the South live in the country or in small towns. This group is much more likely to fit our image of southern poverty and is much more racially diverse — made up of both white and black children and leaving children distanced from medical care and highly likely to be malnourished.

Reflecting more general urban migration patterns over the last half century, a growing share of southern children living in poverty are concentrated in large metropolitan areas. Today, 41 percent of all southern children living in poverty reside within the region's 25 largest metropolitan statistical areas (MSAs). Consistent with national trends, urban children in the South are more likely to be black (44 percent) or Latino (28 percent) than white (23 percent). The growth in urban child poverty has been variously attributed to suburbanization and white flight from cities as middle-class populations and employers have moved to the suburbs, leaving poor and minority populations in central cities. Of course, this is not simply a southern phenomenon.

There is also a striking variation in child poverty among southern cities. Among the 25 largest MSAs, Raleigh, N.C., and Richmond, Va., have the lowest percentage of children in poverty in the region, at 13 and 14 percent, respectively. At the other extreme, 30 percent of children in Mobile, Ala., and 27 percent of children in the Memphis, Tenn., MSAs live in poverty. The dramatic variations in child poverty rates likely follow from regionally distinct family-formation and life-course patterns, including marriage, age at parenting, and education levels. Of children born in 2006 in Raleigh, N.C., for example, 77 percent had married parents, 97 percent had mothers out of their teens, and 89 percent were born to mothers with at least a high school diploma. Richmond also has comparatively high rates of marriage (70 percent), adult mothers (93 percent), and mothers who have earned a high school diploma (87 percent). Conversely, in those southern cities where children are most likely to live in poverty—Mobile and Memphis—the percentages of children born to married parents, to mothers older than 19, and to mothers with at least a high school diploma are markedly lower. In Mobile, 42 percent of babies born in 2006 were to married parents. Similarly, 53 percent of this cohort in Memphis was born to parents who were married. Eighty-six percent of children in Mobile and 87 percent of children in Memphis were born to mothers who were 20 years or older. Furthermore, Mobile and Memphis each record low percentages (67 percent and 79 percent, respectively) of babies born to mothers with high school diplomas.

The good news is that, as a region, the South has begun to openly confront child poverty and to recognize that social mobility contributes to economic development. As part of that effort, rates of participation in state-funded pre-kindergarten programs are highest in the South. This is a significant investment in bolstering levels of equality as children enter school. Additionally, interventions that focus on developing educational skills and tools in early childhood are particularly important for poor and low-income children. Evidence-based interventions that strengthen parenting and family formation and provide developmentally enriching early educational experiences to children show the capacity to greatly improve the well-being of preschool-age children.

Rates of child poverty in the American South continue to be a source of great concern. The implications are significant for the health and well-being of children and their communities. The good news is that child poverty is clearly in the lens of a growing number of scientists, social scientists, and policymakers, who are working to build a regional and national agenda for change.

CATHERINE JOYCE

DOUG IMIG

University of Memphis

Earl Black and Merle Black, *Politics and Society in the South* (1987); Valerie E. Lee and David T. Burkam, *Inequality at the Starting Gate: Social Background Differences in Achievement as Children Begin School* (2002); Lee Rainwater and Timothy M. Smeeding, *Poor Kids in a Rich Country: America's Children in Comparative Perspective* (2003); UNICEF Innocenti Research Center, *Innocenti Report Card* (June 2000); Tom Waldron, Brandon Roberts, and Andrew Remear, *Working Hard, Falling Short: America's Working Families and the Pursuit of Economic Security* (2004); Jonathan M. Wiener, *American Historical Review* (October 1979); Gavin Wright, *Journal of Economic Perspectives* (Summer 1987).

Poverty, Concentration of

During his 1964 State of the Union address, President Lyndon B. Johnson directed the country's attention to the millions of Americans who had not benefited from a decades-long economic expansion. Johnson's call for a War on Poverty initiated a flurry of proposals aimed at addressing inequality and poverty and culminated in the adoption of a number of social welfare policies that included Medicare and Head Start. But even as the national poverty rate for individuals and households declined in response to federal and state legislation, serious questions remained about the demographic distribution of poverty and the social problems associated with concentrated poverty in metropolitan areas. In the decades following Johnson's speech, social science research confirmed that rates of concentrated poverty had indeed risen in the country's largest cities, particularly among poor African Americans and Latinos living in them.

Poverty concentration is established in a census tract when the percentage of people living at or below the official poverty line reaches 40 percent. Douglas Massey notes that prior to the industrial revolution, which prompted the migration of large numbers of rural dwellers and immigrants to American cities, poverty was not viewed as a significant social problem because "deprivation existed at low geographic densities." Although some rural areas also have high concentrations of poverty—particularly in the South and the Great Plains regions—the highest number of census tracts in which poverty is concentrated are located in the country's largest cities. The occurrence and consequences of poverty concentration grew in the 1970s as the jobs that drew people to central city neighborhoods were increasingly relocated to the outer rings of metropolitan areas and as individuals and families with sufficient resources followed. Left behind in central cities were people without the economic resources to relocate to the suburbs and those whose geographic mobility was restricted by institutionalized and other forms of racial discrimination in both the labor and the housing markets.

Indeed, poverty concentration in the United States is not solely a consequence of economic shifts and downturns, but also of laws and policies that have historically introduced and accentuated patterns of racial segregation. In the South, Jim Crow laws institutionalized racial discrimination in hiring, education, and housing and by 1970 had resulted in a reversal of late 19th-century conditions when residential contact between southern blacks and whites was common. Thus, as economic restructuring and labor market changes through the 1970s contributed to rising inequality in the United States, historical patterns of housing discrimination and urban residential segregation accentuated the racial dimension of poverty concentration.

Between 1970 and 1990, the proportion of *all* African Americans in the country's 100 largest cities that lived in extreme-poverty census tracts increased from 15.7 percent to 24.2 percent, compared to a change of 1.4 percent to 3.2 percent for all non-Latino whites. Over this same period, the proportion of all *poor* African Americans that lived in concentrated poverty in the inner city rose from 28.1 percent to 41.6 percent. Immigration patterns, particularly among low-skill Mexican laborers, contributed to a shift in the racial composition of the inner-city neighborhoods where poverty was most concentrated, but it was still poor blacks who remained most likely to live in impoverished neighborhoods.

By the year 2000, the number of people living in extreme-poverty census tracts declined by 25 percent. The South, which saw a rise in the number of high-poverty tracts in the 1980s, experienced a 34.7 percent decline in that number between 1990 and 2000, as well as a drop in the percentage of poor urban dwellers living in them. However, according to the U.S. Census, several large cities in the South had remarkably high rates of poverty concentration in 2000. New Orleans, Louisville, Miami, and Atlanta were rated among the top 10 large U.S. cities for concentrated poverty. In these southern cities, the proportion of poor city dwellers that lived in extreme-poverty neighborhoods averaged 36.5 percent, a rate that was far above the national average of 10.3 percent. That is to say, more than 1 in 3 poor people in these cities were living in neighborhoods where at least 40 percent of residents were also poor. Following the national trend, poor blacks had the highest rate of concentrated poverty. In the four cities mentioned, the average rate was 51.1 percent among poor blacks, compared to 36.5 percent for all poor people. Miami featured the most dramatic discrepancy between the poverty concentration rate for poor blacks and that for all poor city dwellers. In 2000, the concentrated poverty rate for all poor residents of Miami was 36.4 percent, compared to an African American rate of 67.6 percent.

A significant consequence of concentrated poverty is a class of American citizens with extremely limited access to the institutions that foster individual and community well-being. Individuals living in high-poverty neighborhoods have a higher risk of cause-specific and overall adult mortality, infant mortality, and tuberculosis than do residents of less economically segregated neighborhoods. Researchers cite poor housing quality, few or inferior health services, and poor nutrition due to the high cost of grocery items in low-income neighborhoods as among the contributing factors. Also, in these neighborhoods, unemployment, drug abuse, crime, dropping out of high school, out-of-wedlock birth, and renting dwellings that exceed 30 percent of income occur at rates much higher than national averages. For example, in 2000, residents of such neighborhoods were 2.3 times more likely to lack a high school degree and 2.6 times more likely to be unemployed than the average metropolitan resident. Figures for the South were similar to the national average: individuals age 25 or older living in high-poverty areas in 2000 were twice as likely as the average urban citizen to be without a high school degree, and employment-age women in those same neighborhoods were much less likely to have a job.

The impact of concentrated poverty on cities and all urban residents is profound. On the one hand, the social problems and urban blight associated with concentrated poverty have contributed to suburbanization and the further concentration of the poor in central cities. On the other, as the population and economic status of suburbs increase relative to cities, the fiscal capacities of city governments also decline, and inner-city neighborhoods become less attractive to private investors and employers. Because of these trends, cities are less capable of fulfilling their historic function of integrating low-income persons into the national economy.

The geography and demographic characteristics of concentrated poverty have shifted over the past several decades. For one, the number of high-poverty tracts located in suburbs has risen. Further, as the share of high-poverty tracts with African American majorities has declined, the share that is predominantly Latino rose to 20 percent in 2000. Although the highest rates of poor Latinos living in extreme-poverty urban neighborhoods are found in the West and the

Northeast, in 2000 several southern cities had higher-than-average proportions of poor Latinos living in concentrated poverty. Across the 50 largest cities in the country, 13.8 percent of poor Latinos were living in neighborhoods where 40 percent or more of residents were also poor. This rate was much higher in Oklahoma City (22.9 percent) and El Paso (21.5 percent) and moderately higher in New Orleans (18 percent), Miami (18 percent), and Phoenix (17.2 percent).

Whether geographic or demographic, changes in concentrated poverty arise from a variety of factors, including economic restructuring, suburbanization, and urban housing market dynamics. But because a high number of census tracts move in and out of concentrated poverty each decade, causal factors are often difficult to isolate. Thus, even as the South has witnessed a decline in inner-city concentrated poverty, questions about the causes of this downward trend and its permanence remain.

DAWN WIEST
CHERISE E. BARTHALOW
University of Memphis

Federal Reserve System and the Brookings Institution, "The Enduring Challenge of Concentrated Poverty in America: Case Studies from Communities across the U.S." (2008); Angela Hattery and Earl Smith, *Journal of Poverty* 11 (1) (2007); G. Thomas Kingsley and Kathryn L. S. Petit, Urban Institute, "Concentrated Poverty: A Change of Course" (2003); Douglas S. Massey, *Demography* (November 1996); Douglas Massey and Nancy Denton, *American Apartheid: Segregation and the Making of the Underclass* (1998); Douglas S. Massey and Mitchell L. Eggers, *American Journal of Sociology* (March 1990); Hanna Rosin, *Atlantic Monthly* (July/August 2008); Gregory Squires, ed., *Urban Sprawl: Causes, Consequences, and Policy Responses* (2002); Todd Swamstrom, Rob Ryan, and Katherine M. Stigers, *Housing Policy Debate* 19 (2) (2008); Loïc Wacquant, *Urban Outcasts: A Comparative Sociology of Advanced Marginality* (2008); David R. Williams and Chiquita Collins, *Public Health Reports* 116 (2001).

Redevelopment

Urban redevelopment, with the related concepts of urban renewal and urban revitalization, denotes the process of transforming an area within the larger urban context. The argument could be made for the renewal of an entire urban space, but that will not be the focus here. Redevelopment tends to focus upon spaces designated as "inner city" prior to redevelopment and "downtown" or "urban core" afterward. Whether that progress will entail providing updated infrastructure to an older neighborhood, providing structurally safe affordable housing in place of unsafe structures, or treating it as an undeveloped/under-developed area that must be developed economically, all can be contentious when discussing urban redevelopment.

The redevelopment of the urban space is not a new concept; it has historical antecedents within the modern city, most notably the restructuring of Paris by Georges-Eugène Haussmann in the 19th century. In the U.S. city, however, urban redevelopment is very much a by-product of Keynesian economic principles employed during the Depression and further catalyzed by low-interest home loans provided to GIs returning from the battlefields of World War II. Urban redevelopment was seen as necessary to create an urban space that would meet the rapidly changing residential and economic needs already being perceived ahead of the postindustrial shifts of the 1970s.

The federal government began its direct involvement in urban redevelopment with the Title I Housing Act of 1949. One of the goals of Title I projects was to create inviting downtown spaces, not just for residents but also for businesses and as entertainment venues. Critiques of the program often focused upon the role of government in general and the federal government specifically in funding and directing social programs. Planners were also criticized for their role in urban renewal, with the argument that they had simply destroyed still-viable, if economically challenged urban spaces and places, rather than focusing upon the sociopolitical context of such urban "problems" and their causes. This was especially true in southern cities such as Atlanta, Memphis, and Tampa, where expressway development bisected and effectively destroyed existing, mostly low-income, African American residential and business communities as part of their urban redevelopment programs and the construction of new, more spatially concentrated and marginally segregated public housing projects.

By 1974, the Title I program was officially replaced by the Community Development Block Grant program, which was then followed in 1977 by the Urban Development Action Grant program. Under these programs, the federal government was no longer the primary impetus behind urban redevelopment but was replaced by state and local government and private interests. Under the grant program, little emphasis was placed on housing on the part of increasingly cash-strapped state and local governments as now-limited funds were made available for private development with a focus largely on job creation and increasing the local tax base.

Overall, the U.S. economy, beginning in the 1970s, began restructuring from manufacturing toward postindustrialism, with an emphasis on services more conducive to spatial stretch than concentration in traditional downtown central business districts. This emerging nodal (rather than hierarchical) spatial economy, focused on communication, information, and transportation, created other competitive spaces within the urban region, with the downtown as merely one competitive area within the agglomeration of the urban space. This played itself out spatially with urban sprawl and the decentralization of economic and political power within the metropolitan area.

This new, postindustrial tendency toward economic and residential sprawl was, in turn, occurring within the context of a just-then desegregating South. As noted, much of the designation of blight from the 1950s to the 1970s disproportionately affected communities of color. In response to now-increasing demands for desegregation and minority empowerment, suburbanization and the economic decline of many parts of the downtown area were simply exacerbated by increasing white residential and business "flight." In this context, local governments turned to actively supporting private enterprises in order to fund redevelopment projects no longer underwritten by the federal government. More and more focus came to be put on attracting tourists with disposable income and on attracting external revenue streams via short-term entertainment and convention activity. In Memphis, for example, this included the redevelopment of Beale Street, where the city bought three blocks of properties and, through a management corporation, turned the area into an entertainment district without accompanying residential space. The now well-recorded, public-private-financed transformation of Baltimore's Inner Harbor from a working industrial port to a tourist and yuppie-dominated festival marketplace also began at this time.

This period also saw a significant influx of population into the urban spaces of the South, now referred to regionally as part of the "Sunbelt." Retirees and younger workers who no longer had viable economic positions in the fading "Rustbelt" of the industrialized North led to population explosions in cities such as Orlando, Tampa, Miami, Atlanta, Charlotte, and New Orleans. Many southern cities had never fully industrialized, and even those that had were rapidly being retooled to meet the demands of a service-based economy. The primary driver for many of these cities would be tourism, particularly cities such as Memphis, New Orleans, and Orlando and now even Baltimore and Atlanta. Not only would this attract capital to the metropolitan region, but niches within the region were actively created to draw economic revenue back into spaces that were viewed as residentially defunct. Traditional economic anchors, like locally owned department stores, newspapers, and banks, no longer drove the economic conditions of the urban space, particularly in downtown areas—the rare exception perhaps being the enormous tourist sink created by

Walt Disney World. New, nationally and even internationally based real estate developers, brokers, financiers, and tourist and entertainment services firms became the primary economic actors in their stead, with government and academic institutions playing sometimes significant supporting roles.

Thus, by the end of the 1970s, private, largely nonlocal developers had become major players in urban redevelopment in most southern cities. Public-private partnerships and mostly privately financed business improvement districts (BIDS) became the name of the urban redevelopment game. In terms of housing, such redevelopment focused increasingly on meeting the market and entertainment needs of those considered most economically viable: younger, more affluent professionals—a new "gentry" for the new, largely privatized city. This signified a major shift toward an emphasis upon entrepreneurial forms of urban redevelopment policy, emphasizing private conceptualization and execution rather than the previous quarter-century focus on a governmental managerial approach.

New policies involved providing tax breaks and other economic incentives (including, at times, complete or partial payment of development costs with public funds) for the attraction of corporate and entertainment enterprises to the downtown area. One of the most visible examples was the bidding war that began in the 1980s for the attraction of preexisting sports franchises with the promise of the public providing new stadia. Other competitions ensued over spatially footloose corporate headquarters and the attraction of developers for downtown entertainment and shopping complexes. Cities such as Tampa, Atlanta, and Charlotte became natural choices for these developments, as areas with burgeoning tourist industries and good business and natural climates conducive to attracting new development. These projects were seen as necessary for the overall betterment of the urban space, even if they occurred at the expense of social programs (since most enterprises involved public funds as part of the deals). Certainly, Atlanta's construction of major sports and infrastructure facilities to the tune of some $400 million (public-private money) eventually to attract the Olympic Games in 1996 is a prime example.

In terms of residential redevelopment, focus has recently shifted to the reduction of the spatial concentration of poverty that was created under Title I. Under the new federal policy Hope VI, enacted in 1992, those determined to be living in neighborhoods with a high density of poverty, such as public housing projects, were dispersed throughout the urban space. In the process, many communities lost important social support networks, and such dispersal also created a transportation crisis, as public transportation could no longer adequately serve the populations it had historically served. This was particularly the case, for example, with the redevelopment of the St. Thomas community in New Orleans and Centennial Place (Techwood–Clark Howell Homes) in Atlanta.

At the turn of the 21st century, public agencies have thoroughly adopted urban redevelopment strategies hitherto the purview of private developers. City governments, reflecting Hope VI policy, have fully adopted the ethos of the new urbanism, the movement within the planning and urban design field that seeks to limit sprawl by rendering the urban built environment more dense and diverse, imitating traditional small-town America. The result has been active and enthusiastic facilitation of gentrification and the resulting scattering of low-income minorities to the winds of fate. Urban governments view this approach as the primary means by which they can manage the future directions of their urban spaces. Many cities are indeed seeing rapid residential growth in their urban cores, such as Memphis, Charlotte, and Jacksonville, mostly with housing catering to higher-income professionals and mostly displacing lower-income communities in their wake. Continued economic development to replace spaces previously used for residences of inner-city populations is also in practice. Following Hurricane Katrina, for example, there are continuing struggles in New Orleans over who will redefine the core urban space—whether to support the return of residents displaced by the storm or to allow developers to focus instead on high-end office space, high-priced condominiums, and additional development for entertainment and tourism. The outcome of these struggles could change the social and spatial characteristics of that city entirely.

In the end, the newly necessary entrepreneurial policies of the privatized, postindustrial city of the South are creating urban environments that are becoming more and more alike on the basis of increasing competition to attract footloose postindustrial people and firms. Each city must have its public-private–financed downtown aquaria, stadia, museums, waterfront walks, convention centers, festival marketplaces, and high-end condominiums for those well-enough endowed to be close to all this high-priced consumptive activity. From Baltimore's Inner Harbor, to Atlanta's Olympic extravaganza remainders, to Tampa's industrial port makeover, to the still-uncertain but quite-likely reconstruction of a more spectacular, high-end, gentrified New Orleans, it is every city for itself in a highly competitive competition—with no public safety net—for the same footloose customers and with, apparently, no alternative in sight in the near to far urban future.

KEVIN ARCHER
University of South Florida

David R. Goldfield, *Region, Race, and Cities: Interpreting the Urban South* (1997); Lawrence H. Larsen, *The Urban South: A History* (1990); David C. Perry and Alfred J. Watkins, eds., *The Rise of the Sunbelt Cities* (1977); Larry Sawers and William K. Tabb, eds., *Sunbelt/Snowbelt: Urban and Regional Restructuring* (1984); Neil Smith, *The New Urban Frontier: Gentrification and the Revanchist City* (1996); Jon C. Teaford, *The Rough Road to Renaissance: Urban Revitalization in America, 1940–1985* (1990).

Segregation, Desegregation, Resegregation

Segregation is the practice of physically separating categories of individuals on the basis of socially determined ethnic, gender, racial, or religious attributes. Segregation can be voluntary or involuntary, sanctioned by law (de jure) and by custom (de facto). Desegregation is the process of undoing the different legal, social, economic, and political practices supporting segregation; resegregation refers to reverting to segregation practices, though sometimes in different ways. In the South, the segregation of blacks was woven into the entire scope and scale of the community. Desegregation attempted to end segregation by challenging it through particular institutions deemed egregious — schools, lunch counters, public transportation. Through the flight of better-educated and wealthier people — white and black — from communities in recent decades, the remaining poor (and usually black) residents were subject to a resegregation perhaps more pernicious than the previous forms of segregation.

Social practices arising around segregation are usually justified by an ideology of one group's superiority over another. In the South, the justification for segregation was the belief in white supremacy, that whites were inherently better — morally, physically, and intellectually — than blacks (the principles of white supremacy continue to permeate the American consciousness today, particularly in white opposition to immigration). Voluntary segregation was more likely in the North, and involuntary physical separation of blacks from whites was the predominant structure of segregation in the South.

Slaves had no choice but to live in close proximity to their masters in rural areas. The few free blacks in the South had a tenuous status and lived in designated sections of towns, barred from most public accommodations. Yet, during this period, free blacks created their own separate communities by forming their own religious, fraternal, and benevolence institutions. These segregated institutions helped to sustain a distinct black identity in the face of white hostility and widespread discrimination.

During the antebellum period and continuing just after the Civil War, the status of blacks was defined by black codes or laws enacted by all states in the Deep South. These statutes defined the near-absolute power slave owners had over their slaves, including their sexual relationships and offspring. Though these codes prohibited slaves from marrying anyone, particularly whites, they also contributed to an ideology of white racial purity, which was given form through appeal to white women. The belief in an inviolate white womanhood or rape myth provided a ready excuse for lynching blacks who were too "uppity," serving to maintain strict racial boundaries separating whites and blacks.

After the Civil War, the Thirteenth Amendment (1865) abolished slavery; blacks were granted citizenship with equal rights, and black males were then granted voting rights (Fourteenth Amendment, 1868). The Fifteenth Amendment (1870) prohibited racial discrimination in voting. These and other federal laws initially protected blacks' civil liberties and civil rights during Reconstruction. But after the withdrawal of federal troops in 1877, the less frequent interventions in the South by Congress and the tightening of local control by white elites allowed the recovery of exclusionary social practices toward blacks.

Between 1890 and 1965, southern states sponsored a system of racial segregation, colloquially termed "Jim Crow." Jim Crow laws covered the segregation of public schools, public places and public transportation, and restrooms and restaurants for whites and blacks. Segregated institutions were established to circumscribe racial mixing in every conceivable facet of social life, covering churches, libraries, schools, theaters, and restaurants. This then followed the pattern of segregation, desegregation, and resegregation: segregation by black codes, desegregation by the federal government during Reconstruction, and resegregation by Jim Crow laws.

Toward the end of the 19th century, industrialization and urbanization fueled growth and demand for more housing and public transportation. In response to the demands, and under pressure from whites uncomfortable with the changes occurring, southern states responded by sanctioning further segregation of the races in political parties, housing, unions, and other private businesses—even to the extent of shopping or working only in certain stores and working only at certain trades. For example, "restricted covenants" barred the sale of homes to blacks (or Jews or Asians), thus ensuring that neighborhoods remained racially segregated. These policies had particular impact in urban areas.

As the 19th century came to a close, several state and local laws were enacted sanctioning discriminatory practices and extending segregation to where someone sat in a railroad car. One challenge to Louisiana's segregated railroad cars eventually made its way to the Supreme Court, *Plessy v. Ferguson* (1896). This case deemed segregation constitutional in public accommodations as long as both races received equal treatment in public. In response, after 1896, all public facilities, including public schools, were therefore subject to segregation, putting an end to informal, sporadic patterns of integration for other non-white racial and ethnic groups. (The introduction of public conveniences such as drinking fountains, restrooms, and phone booths resulted in additional Jim Crow laws.)

In *Rice v. Gong Lum* (1927), the Mississippi Supreme Court maintained that white children must be segregated from all other races, including Asians. Originally brought in to displace black laborers after the Civil War, the Chinese immigrants thought they were well liked by the local townspeople until they tried to send their children to a white school. Racial segregation in the South did not allow for any ambiguity in terms of defining who was white.

Over the next 50 years, between 1896 and 1956, black leaders responded to the systematic exclusion of blacks in the South in two ways: by accommodation or by protest. One prominent black leader, Booker T. Washington, argued on the side of accommodation in a speech he delivered in 1895. In the "Atlanta Compromise" speech, he argued that blacks and whites should be like the separate fingers of the same hand. This image reinforced the basic premise of segregation but also allowed for a notion of racial equality within separate institutions. The rising new middle class of black professionals (ministers, teachers, business owners) began to have a vested interest in segregated businesses and were inclined to be conservative by subscribing to the accommodation viewpoint, largely because of economic self-interest.

Those blacks who did want to protest against segregation did so, in sporadic challenges—against a railroad company, grocery store, or restaurant—usually in response to a personal instance of exclusion. Unlike the mass mobilizations of the 1950s and 1960s, these types of protest sought to create small, individual openings within the existing system of race relations. Early civil rights protests objected to racial segregation as perpetuating racial prejudice and vindicating the treatment of blacks and other nonwhites as inferior. These initial, almost tentative dissents did not stem the incremental growth in segregation but did help to question the morality of such a system in a supposedly democratic society.

By the early 20th century, creating "separate but equal" facilities became increasingly costly for southern states and cities, particularly as the increasingly urbanized South tried to keep up with the demand for more public schools and other services. Funding for black schools fell further and further behind that for white schools, and many southern states were no longer able to sustain even a pretense of separate but equal. Recognizing these economic realities in maintaining separate school systems along with a range of other public facilities, black attorneys formulated challenges to segregation demanding that states actually provide and maintain equal separate institutions as indicated by *Plessy*.

There had been some advances on that front: the Supreme Court was beginning to overturn Jim Crow laws on constitutional grounds, starting with a ruling overturning a Kentucky law requiring residential segregation (*Buchanan v. Warley*, 1917), and more generally in *Shelley v. Kraemer* (1948) in which it held that "restrictive covenants" were unconstitutional. The Supreme Court also no longer permitted segregation in interstate transportation (*Irene Morgan v. Virginia*, 1946).

A series of cases aimed at equalizing higher education and black teachers' salaries was initiated in the 1930s by the NAACP and later by the NAACP Legal Defense and Educational Fund (LDF). In *Missouri ex rel Gaines v. Canada* (1936), the black plaintiff was denied access to the University of Missouri Law School even though the state of Missouri did not provide a separate but equal accommodation. Small victories against segregation were claimed whenever state or lower federal courts ruled in favor of black plaintiffs who sought equalization of resources.

After World War II, there was a shift in strategy from equalization of facilities to directly challenging the constitutionality of segregation. The 1954 *Brown v. Board of Education* case argued that even when black and white institutions were allotted equal resources, as they were in Topeka, Kan., separate but equal institutions forever imprinted a "badge of inferiority" on black children. The court held that *all* separate facilities were *inherently* unequal in the area of public schools, effectively overturning *Plessy v. Ferguson* and outlawing Jim Crow in other areas of society as well. This landmark case included complaints filed in two southern states, South Carolina (*Briggs v. Elliott*) and Virginia (*Davis v. County School Board of Prince Edward County*), along with Delaware (*Gebhart v. Belton*) and Washington, D.C. (*Spottswode Bolling v. C. Melvin Sharpe*).

In the South, the *Brown* decision was met with massive resistance at both the state and the local level. Many southern white congressional members signed the "Southern Manifesto," providing justification for a doctrine of states' rights, declaring the federal court illegitimate and its decisions null. *Brown* caused southerners to re-revisit the role of the national government in regulating local issues. Century-old arguments, reminiscent of the debates over slavery, were revived to defend the primacy of states' rights over federal jurisdiction. Words like "interposition" and "nullification"—the same language used to defend slavery—were heard again in defense of segregation. *Brown* also revived fears of miscegenation as a threat to white supremacy. These fears were realized when *Loving v. Virginia* (1967) ended all race-based legal restrictions on marriage.

In conjunction with the massive resistance to *Brown*, public protests against segregation intensified in the South. Partially in response to this increased activism and to circumvent further school desegregation, the White Citizens' Council (wcc) was formed in Mississippi and quickly expanded to other southern states. Some communities simply closed their public schools, while others reopened their public schools as private "council schools" for white children only, sponsored by the wcc. In Prince Edward County, Va., all public schools were closed for a decade after the *Brown* decision in an attempt to avoid desegregation. These tactics to prevent desegregation were largely successful—by 1964, 10 years after *Brown*, only 2.3 percent of southern black children attended desegregated schools.

The southern mass mobilizations of the civil rights movement in the 1950s and 1960s were successful in raising awareness of racial segregation as undemocratic at home and abroad. This appeal to American core values of fairness and equality increased the likelihood of federal intervention when desegregation was blocked. Additional pressure from the federal government was placed on southern political leaders as images of southern police brutality in Birmingham, Ala., in 1963, for example, were beamed around the world and used to fuel anti-American propaganda by the Soviet Union and other undemocratic regimes. In a largely symbolic protest against desegregation, Alabama governor George Wallace became famous for his "Stand at the Schoolhouse Door" attempting to bar the enrollment of black students Vivian Malone and James Hood at the University of Alabama in June 1963.

Resistance to desegregation led to numerous state and federal lawsuits. In 1968, the *Greene v. County School Board* case of Virginia reaffirmed school desegregation as a means to build a color-blind society: no longer would dual school systems be tolerated. In order to achieve racial parity, desegregation would now be accomplished through a variety of means, including extensive busing of students. A few years later, in North Carolina, the Supreme Court upheld busing as a means to desegregate in the South (*Swann v. Charlotte-Mecklenburg Board of Education*, 1971).

Though *Greene* and *Swann* sought to circumvent attempts to avoid school desegregation, they could not address the economic, political, and social factors working against the implementation of integrated schools. In the South, long-established residential housing patterns of racially isolated neighborhoods contributed to the continuance of dual school systems for many years after *Brown*.

Using busing to integrate schools contributed to the virtual abandonment of public education by white and black elites in many southern communities. Desegregation had thereby stripped public schools of the upper economic strata of society, creating institutions that were resegregated, on the basis of economic resources rather than race.

In *Parents Involved in Community Schools v. Seattle School District No. 1 et al.* (2007), the Supreme Court ordered that race could no longer be a factor in assigning students to schools. In a 5–4 decision striking down public school choice plans in Seattle, Washington, D.C., and Louisville, Ky., Chief Justice John Roberts argued that in keeping with the goal of a color-blind society, using race to assign students to schools is unconstitutional. But, as Justice Breyer remarked in his dissent, this redefinition of a color-blind society gives all races equal weight and ignores any past injustices created by racial segregation. The *Parents* opinion obliquely references resegregation in the South by distinguishing between de jure segregation as being created by school systems and de facto segregation as a result of individual choice in terms of buying homes in more affluent, segregated areas.

Resegregation is evident in residential housing patterns and school board policies, and today southern neighborhoods are as much segregated by social class as they are by race. In the absence of racially explicit laws, de jure discrimination is ever present, underpinning the legality of resegregation in the present context.

JEAN VAN DELINDER
Oklahoma State University

Michael J. Klarman, *From Jim Crow to Civil Rights: The Supreme Court and the Struggle for Racial Equality* (2004); Jean Van Delinder, *Struggles before Brown: Early Civil Rights Protests and Their Significance Today* (2008); C. Vann Woodward, *The Strange Career of Jim Crow* (1974).

Segregation, Residential

Following after the enslavement of Africans and then the Jim Crow laws of the Deep South, residential segregation is now a defining feature of racial inequality in the American story. In metropolitan areas throughout the United States, large segments of the African American population are residentially separated from whites; this concentration, often including the segmentation of middle-class blacks, means that American society remains separate and unequal.

Residential segregation is the process by which groups are sorted by race — but also by social class, ethnicity, immigration status, and age, among other social phenomena—across the neighborhoods of metropolitan areas. Neighborhoods are often measured by social scientists using census tracts or block groups, and segregation is measured using a number of indicators, most often the Index of Dissimilarity (D). These measures indicate that in the midwestern and northeastern parts of the United States, racial residential segregation has been high since the Great Migration. For example, Chicago's segregation score (D) went from about 67 in 1910 to 95 in 1940. Scores over 60 are considered high, and scores are interpreted as the percentage of blacks or whites (or any other groups being analyzed) that would have to move to a new neighborhood in a metropolitan area for the area to become integrated. Southern areas—in particular the larger metropolises of the South like Atlanta—also have a long history of high levels of segregation. In 1940, Atlanta had a segregation score of 87, and by 1960 it was 94.

Over the past few decades, black-white segregation has decreased. R. Farley and H. H. Frey report declines in black-white segregation from the 1980s through the 1990s. "In 1980, fourteen metropolitan areas had indexes exceeding 85, whereas ten years later only four metropolitan areas had indexes that high." According to this study, the mean segregation of blacks from nonblacks in 1980 was 69; in 1990, the mean dropped to about 64. More recently, J. R. Logan, B. J. Stults, and R. Farley analyzed data from the 2000 Census. They examined changes in black-white segregation for 255 metropolises, in which D scores ranged from 85 to 20. Logan et al. reported that the mean segregation of blacks from whites decreased from 69 in 1990 to 65 in 2000. According to the Lewis Mumford Center, in the 1990s the levels of black-white segregation declined slowly, while Asian-white segregation remained relatively unchanged and Latino-white segregation increased slightly. Patterns and trends of segregation and hypersegregation highlight the degree of social separation among racial and ethnic groups in the United States.

Segregation scores in the South also decreased over the last 30 years. For instance, in 1980 Atlanta's segregation score was 75, which had decreased from a previous score of 82 in 1970. Even though the decreasing trend continued into 2000, segregation in the Atlanta metropolitan area remained high at about 66. Similarly, in New Orleans from 1970 to 2000, the score fell from 73 to 69. Another example is Memphis, where segregation decreased from 76 in 1970 to 69 in 2000. But these scores also show that in many large, southern metropolitan areas segregation remains high. Thus, like the large metropolises in the Northeast and the Midwest, black-white residential segregation is high in the metropolitan South.

Residential segregation has consequences for those who remain isolated and impoverished in the central cities of the United States. For example, although concentrated poverty decreased during the 1990s, there are many central city neighborhoods that continue to deal with massive social problems, including crime, single-mother families, and poverty. Residential stratification means that the characteristics of the neighborhoods in which many minority groups, especially poor African Americans, reside are not similar to white neighborhoods. Poor living conditions and lack of opportunity prevent minority groups in hypersegregated metropolitan areas from acquiring the resources needed to leave the ghetto.

The social isolation of racial and ethnic minorities, especially the segregation of African Americans from whites, has not been a haphazard process. Racial violence was used to ensure compliance with the spatial isolation of African Americans in metropolitan areas in both the North and the South. Deed restrictions were transformed into restrictive covenants, created in neighborhood associations, which functioned to prevent substantial black access to white residential areas for much of the 20th century. Racially discriminatory practices by lenders and the real estate industry have made it difficult for African Americans to leave the ghetto. And, historically, white banks did not provide loans to African Americans in neighborhoods that were mostly black, a process known as redlining.

In 1968, overt racial discrimination in the housing market was barred. This legislation slowly began to allow middle- and upper-class African Americans a chance to leave the central city. The number of African Americans that relocated to suburban areas began to grow nationwide. African American suburbanization has been considerable. Frey reported in 2001 that about 39 percent of African Americans resided in American suburbs. In 2001, in the South, at the high end, about a quarter of blacks living in the Atlanta and Charleston metropolitan areas lived in the suburbs, while about 8 percent and 6 percent of blacks in Little Rock and Nashville, respectively, lived in the suburbs. Unfortunately, there is increasing speculation that the inner-ring suburbs are deteriorating in American — southern and nonsouthern — metropolises; the movement of poor residents, black and otherwise, from the city may be part of this process, along with the increasing gentrification of city neighborhoods.

The neighborhoods in which people live impact a number of outcomes and opportunities, including one's exposure to poverty and crime, effective schools, and networks and job availability. The unequal nature of these resources and opportunities, embedded in one's neighborhood and larger urban environment, underscores the significance of studying residential segregation. Segregation impedes the life chances of individuals and families, making equal access to services and infrastructure difficult to attain.

The racial isolation of minority groups is the result of a long history of racial discrimination. The experiences of African Americans throughout the 20th century, in the North and the South, are particularly problematic. Residential segregation means that the color line remains in existence, over 100 years after W. E. B. Du Bois recognized it. The persistence of racial residential segregation is a defining feature of urban America. Even with its slow decline, residential segregation continues to impact African Americans as they struggle to live the American Dream.

MELISSA M. HAYES
Georgia State University

ROBERT M. ADELMAN
University at Buffalo

W. E. B. Du Bois, *The Souls of Black Folk: Essays and Sketches* (1903, 1990); Reynolds Farley and William H. Frey, *American Sociological Review* (Number 1, 1994); William H. Frey, *Melting Pot Suburbs: A Census 2000 Study of Suburban Diversity* (2001); Paul A. Jargowsky, *Stunning Progress, Hidden Problems: The Dramatic Decline of Concentrated Poverty in the 1990s* (2003); John R. Logan, Brian J. Stults, and Reynolds Farley, *Demography* 41 (2004).

Sports Stadia and Arenas

Cities, and the process of urbanization, are so intimately connected to the development of professional sports and the venues where games are played that any treatment of professional sports must recognize their symbiotic relationship. The early industrial city did more than amass a sufficient number of spectators to make sports a profitable enterprise; it provided a supply of athletes with which to build teams and the financiers necessary to support them. It was the twin processes of industrialization and urbanization that gave rise to the professional games of today. Urban growth helped shape professional sport, and sport, in turn, helped shape the city.

From a social and cultural perspective, each element of this city-sport duality has had a mutually transformative relationship, which affected urban life while establishing rules and norms conducive to the assimilation of immigrants and rural migrants to the new urban, industrial scene. Workers' agrarian patterns were replaced by strict rules that conditioned work. At the same time, this new order brought with it moments of leisure time and modest incomes to enjoy it.

Sports, and rooting for the home team, provided a focal point around which a diverse population could coalesce and engage in a shared, common experience. A team could help establish a sense of belonging and, indeed, a sense of place. For the captains of industry, sport was thought to teach important behaviors consistent with the industrial workplace. Professional sports, and the place-based allegiances they engendered, helped socialize the urban workforce.

In the South, this dual relationship was slow to materialize. Owing to its agrarian heritage, its legacy of unsavory institutions, and its relative isolation in the years prior to the Civil War, the pace of urbanization in the South lagged behind that experienced in the Northeast and Upper Midwest. Consequently, by 1900, baseball's National League and its rival American League had a combined total of 14 teams, all of which were located in northern and midwestern cities. For southerners, the first half of the 20th century witnessed many industrial leagues, which typically played in open fields of small towns—some textile mill employees were even hired more for their athletic ability than for their contribution to mill output. With relatively few urban areas of sufficient size to support professional sport, southerners' relationship to the major sports of the day—baseball, basketball, and football—was more likely to be cultivated at the collegiate level.

Big league sport did not arrive in the Deep South until 1966, when Atlanta received the relocating Braves from Milwaukee and the Falcons because of National Football League (NFL) expansion; the same year the Miami Dolphins joined the rival American Football League (AFL). These events, however, were reflections of much larger processes that accelerated after World War II, that is, the rise of the Sunbelt and rapid metropolitan suburbanization. These inter- and intraregional shifts brought with them league expansion and franchise relocation in all the major league sports, sparking a wave of stadium and arena construction as leagues realigned to reflect more accurately the nation's population distribution. In the process, new venues—which form the primary connections among teams, leagues, and cities—fundamentally transformed the relationship between professional sports and the places that host them.

Stadia and arenas have evolved in all majors sports. In the late 19th century and the first half of the 20th century, team owners, not wanting government involvement in their business, generally built and owned the playing facilities of their teams. By 1950, shifting populations and deferred maintenance left many facilities either obsolete or in desperate need of repair. The postwar period ushered in the first wave of new construction, in the 1960s, as teams, following their fans to the suburbs and the West and the South, needed new venues in which to play. However, this period also brought new relationships between teams and cities. Expanding metropolitan areas, viewing major league sport as a ticket to becoming "big league" cities, began subsidizing stadium and arena construction. Indeed, the watershed moment came in 1957 when the Brooklyn Dodgers were lured away to Los Angeles with the promise of a public subsidy in the form of land for their new stadium. By the late 1960s, it became commonplace for stadia, frequently located in the suburbs, to be built and owned by the public (usually a local government entity). For their part, teams would enter long-term leases, paying rental fees to cover the payments on municipal bonds issued to build the facilities. From the late 1960s through the mid-1970s, cities such as Atlanta, Dallas, Houston, Miami, and New Orleans were added to the list of big league cities.

The next wave of stadium construction, beginning in the late 1980s, had a somewhat different flavor. After decades of population loss, fiscal crisis beset many central cities. At the same time, sports teams began claiming that, to remain competitive, additional revenues were needed. Without the additional revenues, relocation would be their only option. Desperate for economic development and not wanting to lose the home team, central cities, with the backing of local growth coalitions, began building stadia and arenas in downtown locations, hoping to revitalize central business districts and enhance the asset value of place-based business interests. The result was a series of public-private partnerships that touted the economic benefits of hosting professional sport. Just as important, however, were the contractual agreements between the team and its governmental partner(s) wherein team owners claimed the lion's share of revenue streams (for example, tickets, parking, concessions, and vending), arguing that cities would make sufficient revenues from the additional taxes from increased economic activity generated by the team's new facility. The first such public-private partnership between a team owner and a city came with the construction of Joe Robbie Stadium, home to the NFL Miami Dolphins. This new precedent was quickly replicated in Atlanta, Baltimore, Charlotte, Nashville, New Orleans, Orlando, Raleigh, San Antonio, Tampa, and a host of other cities, North and South, in all the major league sports.

With the typical playing facility costing $500 million and more, why should cities be so eager to capitulate to the demands of professional sports? Are professional sports and their playing facilities economic drivers of metropolitan economies? Do new stadia and arenas stimulate economic development and central city revitalization, as has been commonly touted? After years of research, most analysts conclude that the answer is no. Although professional sports most certainly raise metropolitan visibility, they rarely account for more than 1 percent of metropolitan earnings. As claims of economic development

LP Field in Nashville, Tenn., home of the Tennessee Titans, with the Nashville skyline at dusk in the background (Photograph by Gary Layda, courtesy of Nashville Convention & Visitors Bureau)

benefits have come under increasing scrutiny, teams today tend to focus on the intangible benefits (civic pride, cultural value of sports) of being home to a professional sports franchise, cementing the place of sports into the community's cultural identity.

Whether communities are large or small, in the North or in the South, investment in sports facilities provides textbook examples of the dynamics surrounding public debate, private gain, and the actors who set the urban growth agenda. Urban scholars have long recognized the role of certain interests in influencing a city's growth. The motivation is simply increased profits to the businesses in the community. Variously referred to as the "growth regime," the "growth machine," or the "growth coalition," most cities have a relatively small cadre of individuals representing local business interests who are influential in public policymaking and economic development planning. Such interests usually represent real estate development, banking/finance, the media, utilities, and politicians. The motivation of the first two groups is clear: to increase land value. (In fact, many owners of the early baseball teams were real estate developers who built their team as an amenity to help sell a subdivision by having the team play in the nearby parks.) Media and utility interests are also players in the progrowth coalition since a growing community will need more of the services they provide.

Today, the growth coalitions are not as brazen as they once were. Many of the progrowth interests have been professionalized in chambers of commerce or development partnerships. The media often editorialize on the benefits of certain developments that align with these growth interests, and politicians work to minimize conflict and provide the infrastructure required to facilitate growth, since creating jobs is often important for reelection in local politics.

The reality is that professional sports and their playing facilities have a relatively small economic impact on cities and metropolitan areas. Urban economies are simply too large and sports teams too small to have a significant effect. Rather, sports play a different and important role for both the progrowth coalition and the American psyche. In many ways, their importance today is the same as it was in the late 1800s: they have a unique ability to bring people together. For the community, a home team still plays a central role in defining community identity, character, and pride. For progrowth interests, sport is a glue that holds the coalition together as they attempt to expand existing businesses and bring new business to the area. Having professional sports and state-of-the-art playing facilities in the mix of cultural amenities is critical to the growth game, but not because sport is a big business. It is not. Its importance is as a point around which the coalition can rally in its efforts to attract more meaningful development while influencing regional land prices and enhancing aggregate wealth.

HARRY CAMPBELL
DAVID SWINDELL
University of North Carolina at Charlotte

Michael Danielson, *Home Team: Professional Sports and the American Metropolis* (1997); Charles Euchner, *Playing the Field: Why Sports Teams Move and Cities Fight to Keep Them* (1993); Roger Noll and Andrew Zimbalist, *Sports, Jobs, and Taxes: The Economic Impact of Sports Teams and Stadiums* (1997); Stephen Riess, *City Games: The Evolution of American Urban Society and the Rise of Sports* (1989).

Suburbanization

"Suburbanization" refers to the movement of people and businesses to residential and commercial zones around a city center, often in a pattern resembling concentric circles. Although outlying urban communities have existed in the South since the early 20th century, suburbanization did not begin to affect southern patterns of life until after World War II, when nearly every major metropolitan area—as well as a significant number of the region's smaller cities and towns—witnessed the rise of inner- and outer-ring suburbs.

The postwar South's new economic infrastructure encouraged suburban development. During and immediately after World War II, the population of the region's urban centers—Richmond, Charlotte, Miami, Atlanta, Nashville, Birmingham, Houston, and Dallas—ballooned as millions of southerners moved to the city for either temporary or permanent employment in nearby industries and businesses. Driven by what historian C. Vann Woodward termed "the Bulldozer Revolution"—repeated waves of land clearance and housing construction—southern cities turned into metropolises with distinct city centers surrounded by a burgeoning collection of suburban residential communities. Federal policy encouraged low-interest mortgages and educational subsidies, thus making homeownership feasible for increasing numbers of upwardly mobile southerners. Atlanta served as the archetype of metropolitan development from the 1940s to the 1970s. To accommodate wartime and postwar population growth in the Atlanta area, the city annexed 82 square miles in 1952, adding nearly 100,000 new residents to city rosters. The federal highway program, begun in the mid-1950s, updated and expanded the city's already existing freeway system, leading to expansive growth around Atlanta's city limits. The extension of city services and utilities to surrounding communities encouraged further decentralization. As a result, during the 1960s, the counties encircling Atlanta added nearly 360,000 new residents.

The rise of the suburban South was also directly connected to the civil rights movement of the 1950s and 1960s. Efforts to desegregate downtown businesses and city schools sparked "white flight," or the migration of white residents and businesses to suburban communities. As in other American cities, the results of white flight were profound for the racial and economic geography of southern suburbia, resulting in suburban communities that often contained only a handful of nonwhite families. For instance, public schools and residential zones in Little Rock, Ark., were almost as segregated by race in the 1980s as they had been in the late 1950s, with suburban schools populated by a large majority of white students. In Atlanta, white flight was particularly acute. By 1970, the suburban counties around Atlanta ranged from 95 to 99 percent white, spurring sociologists Douglas Massey and Nancy Denton to observe that metropolitan Atlantans were "like the residents of old, divided Berlin," living and working "in self-contained zones, not exactly antagonistic, but cut off and indifferent to one another." White flight left a disproportionate number of poorer, nonwhite residents in city centers while simultaneously redistributing the economic core of southern cities to suburban districts, resulting in declining tax bases for public education, infrastructure maintenance, and law enforcement. Thus, by the 1970s, the centers of southern cities mirrored the centers of nonsouthern cities like Los Angeles, Philadelphia, and Detroit, experiencing "urban crises" that were characterized by demonstrably higher rates of unemployment, pollution, and crime.

The economic and racial rearrangements that created suburbia also informed the politics of southern suburbanites. Despite the active role played by the federal government in laying the groundwork for suburban growth, southern suburbia turned into a bastion of antistatist sentiments in the postwar period. Such sentiments emerged for distinct historical reasons. In the midst of federal civil rights legislation and desegregation of public spaces and schools, many white suburbanites exalted the ostensibly "color-blind" language of "freedom of choice" and "freedom of association" as political alternatives to adherence to federal court orders and policy. In addition, federal policies aimed at assuaging the urban crisis struck southern suburbanites as wasteful uses of public monies, resulting in a series of grassroots, suburban-centered tax revolts that sought to limit taxation for the purposes of urban planning and educational programs. Religious sentiments also informed the politics of southern suburbanites, with many suburban churches lauding a conservative set of "family values" as an antidote to the social and sexual revolutions of the 1960s and 1970s. Taken together, such political sensibilities transformed southern suburbanites into a powerful voting bloc, particularly for conservative politicians and strategists working for the Republican Party. To be sure, not all suburbanites affiliated with the tenets of conservatism. But enough joined the ranks of the "New Right" to tip the political balance of late 20th-century America, pitching it decidedly to the right.

Variations on such trends, however, also existed. Miami contained a Cuban community, interspersed throughout inner-city and suburban communities. Houston and San Antonio featured a wide variety of Latino communities, many middle class and living in suburbia. African Americans moved to the suburbs in the postwar South in steady numbers as well, albeit on their own terms and for their own reasons. According to one estimate, southern builders constructed 220,000 housing units for African Americans during the 1950s. New housing constituted 57 percent of the housing that black communities expanded into from 1950 to 1960. Of course, as historian Andrew Wiese has noted, "these enterprises did not solve the desperate housing shortage among African Americans in the urban South, but they represented unprecedented efforts to provide more and better housing [for southern blacks]." Most of these new communities were planned by white developers as container communities. In other words, blacks seeking affordable housing were relegated to housing in "all-Negro" subdivisions. Restrictive mortgage practices likewise kept blacks from moving into white communities, but this did not stop African Americans from demanding open housing. Grassroots protest and legal assaults on restrictive lending and housing practices led to the end of such race-based restrictions. Fuller integration of blacks into white-only communities, however, remained only an intermittent facet of suburban life well into the last years of the 20th century.

In recent years, southern suburbia has undergone dramatic social and economic change. Although still populated by generally middle- to upper-class white residents, suburban zones across the South have also diversified. African Americans, Asian Americans, and Latino Americans have moved to suburbia in growing numbers, as have nonnative southerners moving to the metropolitan South from the North, West, and abroad. For the most part, the economic status of suburban communities remains homogeneous, as housing and property prices continued forms of class-based segregation between suburban and urban sectors and between inner-ring suburbs and pricier outer-ring "exurbs." Still, the rise of a more diversified suburbia has made it difficult to generalize about southern suburbanites, or characterize them as automatic supporters of any political party or ideology. As a case in point, during the 2004 election, 63 percent of voters in suburban and exurban counties in the South voted for Republican Party candidate George W. Bush. In subsequent years, however, suburban voters showed the potential for political redirection. For instance, in 2005 and 2006 voters in northern Virginia suburban counties broke with Bush's party, defeating Republican incumbents in the state's gubernatorial and senatorial contests. Whether demographic shifts or more revolutionary changes in political commitments explains such flips in the southern suburban vote remains open to interpretation. Nevertheless, such patterns in voting confirm their status as swing voters and powerful contributors to the future politics of region and nation.

As southern suburbia continues to sprawl, it also continues to change. According to 2008 estimates, 8 of the 10 fastest-growing metropolitan areas in the United States are located in the South. Additionally, more than half of the 50 fastest-growing metropolises in the nation are in southern states. Nearly every southern metropolis has experienced various forms of "gentrification" (or the refurbishment and repopulation of inner-city residences by upper-middle-class buyers) as well as a wide variety of other suburban phenomena—gated communities, megachurches, "big box" retailers, secondary downtowns, and second-ring perimeter highways. Political debates still circulate around matters of private rights and public good, although such debates now include matters related to environmental debilitation and cultural homogenization. Still, in the midst of such diversity and dynamism, southern suburbia illustrates an indisputable connection to the historical forces that made it and, in many ways, continue to shape it.

DARREN GREM
University of Georgia

William J. Cooper Jr. and Thomas E. Terrill, *The American South: A History*, vol. 2 (2002); David R. Goldfield, *Race, Region, and Cities: Interpreting the South* (1997); Kevin M. Kruse, *White Flight: Atlanta and the Making of Modern Conservatism* (2005); Matthew D. Lassiter, *The Silent Majority: Suburban Politics in the Sunbelt South* (2006); Raymond A. Mohl, ed., *Searching for the Sunbelt: Historical Perspectives on a Region* (1993); Andrew Wiese, *Places of Their Own: African American Suburbanization in the Twentieth Century* (2004).

Sunbelt Cities

Kevin Phillips is most often credited with first using the term "Sunbelt"—in 1969 in his book *The Emerging Republican Majority*. Although he was generally referring to the southern and western regions in the United States, Phillips did not specifically define the boundaries of the Sunbelt. Many scholars accept the geographical boundaries specified by Kirkpatrick Sale in his 1975 book *Power Shift: The Rise of the Southern Rim and Its Challenge to the Eastern Establishment* as the area below the 37th parallel stretching from North Carolina to southern California. Sale used the term "southern rim" rather than "Sunbelt." Disagreement on the boundary still exists, with some including, for example, Virginia and all of California.

Scholars also disagree about the history of the politics of Sunbelt cities. One perspective suggests that during the decades around the turn of the 20th century the commercial civic elite governed. According to this view, professional and business elites, including wealthy landowners at times, generally controlled politics in Sunbelt cities. This contrasted with the machine politics of Snowbelt cities, where professional politicians and political parties exchanged favors with business interests and with immigrants to gain and retain power. According to this perspective, several factors contributed to regional differences. For example, most of the population accepted a conservative ideology promulgated by the elite that emphasized that those at the top of the city's economic and social hierarchy should take a dominant role in governing. Also, Sunbelt cities were more likely than Snowbelt cities to adopt reformist political institutions such as nonpartisan and citywide elections that also played a role in maintaining business hegemony. Governance by a commercial civic elite continued to a significant extent into the 1960s and 1970s and then became more combative and often more inclusive, due to the political mobilization of minorities, civil rights legislation, and splits among business interests.

An alternative interpretation of Sunbelt politics suggests that domination by the commercial civic elite was not uniformly the case a century ago. In fact, governing coalitions were often more diverse and politics often more contested than is suggested by the first perspective. Ideological differences, divergent business interests, and competing political organizations contributed to these conflicts. Some Sunbelt cities, such as Memphis, New Orleans, and Albuquerque, developed machine politics similar to those in Snowbelt cities. In Dallas, between 1880 and 1920, organized labor, women's organizations, socialists, and other groups challenged local business leaders and forced compromises from the commercial civic elite. Nor, according to this alternative perspective, have the political systems of all Sunbelt cities unequivocally moved toward a more inclusive democratic politics, even though minorities have generally gained more representation.

Thus, although disagreement exists on the precise boundaries of the Sunbelt and the nature of politics in Sunbelt cities, the general demographic and economic trends during the last several decades have led to growth in most Sunbelt metropolitan areas and relative stagnation or declines in most Snowbelt areas. For example, 23 of the 25 counties that registered the largest population gains during the 1990s were in the Sunbelt. During the same decade, only 3 of the 25 counties that lost the most population were in the Sunbelt. Another indicator of relative growth in the Sunbelt was that between 1970 and 1996 metropolitan areas (areas encompassing both cities and suburbs) in the West and South averaged an annual population gain of over 2 percent, while those in the Midwest grew at an average rate of only .3 percent and Northeast metropolitan areas averaged no growth. Further, the six metropolitan areas that registered the greatest gain in population from April 2000 thorough June 2006 were all located in the Sunbelt.

Central cities in the Sunbelt were also more likely to gain population than in the Snowbelt, partially because they were more likely to expand their boundaries to annex outlying unincorporated suburban residents, something that Snowbelt cities were less likely to accomplish because they were adjacent to incorporated suburbs that could not legally be annexed. The 2000 Census recorded that Sunbelt cities with more than 100,000 residents in 1990 grew at a greater rate than Snowbelt cities in this category. In fact, northeastern cities, on average, declined by 1 percent, while cities in the Midwest grew on average by 3.4 percent during the decade. The picture was much different in the Sunbelt.

Southern cities gained 12 percent, and those in the West grew by an average of 19.5 percent.

Employment has also grown disproportionately in the Sunbelt. Between 1960 and 2000, the Northeast and the Midwest reduced their share of the nation's employment, and the South and the West gained. In 2000, for example, 21 percent of employment was in the Northeast, compared to 29 percent in 1960. The South's share increased during this period from 27 percent to 34 percent. The Midwest also reduced its share of employment, and the West gained. Although the census category includes some areas in the West that are not generally included in the Sunbelt, the general employment trends would be similar if they were excluded.

Several explanations have been offered for Sunbelt growth. Demographic factors have played a role. Immigrants from Mexico, the Caribbean, and elsewhere have contributed to the growth of many Sunbelt cities. In addition, many retirees have sought out retirement locations in Florida, Arizona, and elsewhere in the Sunbelt, attracted by the more moderate winter weather and the availability of air-conditioning to cool them in the summer. Many who are still in the labor force have also found the Sunbelt desirable as a lifestyle choice. The growth of tourism has also fueled growth in some Sunbelt locations, with Orlando and Las Vegas being prime examples.

Government policy played a role in the growth of the Sunbelt. For example, many military installations were placed in Sunbelt communities. And defense contracts went disproportionately to companies in the Sunbelt, in part due to the political clout of Sunbelt members of Congress. The tax code encouraged investment in new facilities, which led some Snowbelt businesses to invest in new facilities in the South and the West. Federal tax benefits to oil and gas industries have helped fuel Sunbelt growth as well. And some companies moved to Sunbelt states in the decades following World War II because they were "right-to-work" states where it was more difficult to unionize.

Certainly not all areas in the Sunbelt have grown during the past several decades. For example, Macon, Ga., lost almost 9 percent of its population during the 1980s and lost a similar percentage during the 1990s. Jackson, Miss., Richmond, New Orleans, and Savannah are other Sunbelt cities with populations of over 100,000 that lost population during both decades. Increasing population does not inevitably lead to general prosperity. El Paso and Tampa both gained population during the 1990s, but in 2003 El Paso's poverty rate was the sixth highest in the nation and Tampa's poverty rate was the 14th highest. Further, Sunbelt cities and metropolitan areas that have gained population often face problems associated with growth. These include environmental degradation, long commuting times, and inadequate financial support to education and other public services.

The economic downturn that became evident by 2007 has, at least in the short run, modified the dynamics of the Snowbelt-to-Sunbelt migration and, more generally, of Sunbelt growth. Between July 2007 and July 2008, more people left Florida than moved there from elsewhere in the county. In the prosperous year ending in July 2007, of the 24 cities in the South with over 250,000 residents, only three lost population. Of those that gained, however, 17 grew at a lower rate than during the previous year. In the Midwest, five of its 15 cities of that size lost population during the year, but of the 10 that gained, only one registered a lower growth rate than during the preceding year. During the same period, growth also slowed in a majority of the Sunbelt counties that had grown most rapidly during the decade.

The decline in the housing market affected many communities in the Sunbelt. Although most major U.S. housing markets fell, several Sunbelt cities suffered dramatic declines in housing prices. In October 2008, an index of 20 major metropolitan areas recorded that compared to a year earlier the average price drop was 18 percent. Of the eight areas of the 20 with higher than average declines in prices, seven were in the Sunbelt.

Many Sunbelt communities also lost jobs and registered higher rates of unemployment as a result of the falling housing market and the economic downturn in general. Some were also hurt by the collapse in financial markets. Charlotte, N.C., was expected to suffer major job losses in 2009 when Wells Fargo completed its acquisition of Wachovia Corporation, which was based in Charlotte. Although Charlotte-based Bank of America grew in assets with the acquisition of Countryside Financial Corporation and Merrill Lynch, it also planned to cut several thousand jobs.

Certainly the real estate and financial collapses have severely hurt many Snowbelt communities as well as those in the Sunbelt, and it is likely that the general trend of Sunbelt growth relative to the Snowbelt will continue. However, distinctions between Snowbelt and Sunbelt communities that some have presented over the past decades have often been overdrawn. The Sunbelt was never as uniformly buoyant as some had suggested, nor was the Snowbelt as uniformly depressed as some analysts implied. Scholars will be well served in the future to limit their use of these categories, because differences among cities within both the Sunbelt and the Snowbelt might be as important as differences between Sunbelt and Snowbelt cities.

ROBERT KERSTEIN
University of Tampa

Carl Abbott, *The New Urban America: Growth and Politics in Sunbelt Cities* (1987); Richard M. Bernard and Bradley R. Rice, eds., *Sunbelt Cities: Politics and Growth since World War II* (1983); Randall M. Miller and George E. Pozzetta, eds., *Shades of the Sunbelt* (1989); Raymond A. Mohl, ed., *Searching for the Sunbelt: Historical Perspectives on a Region* (1990); Larry Sawers and William K. Tabb, eds., *Sunbelt/Snowbelt: Urban Development and Regional Restructuring* (1984).

Transportation, Mass Transit

Cities in the South have undergone tremendous changes as a result of urban transportation, but it was not until the 20th century and the advent of the automobile age that southerners experienced some of the same environmental disruptions that had occurred in places like Boston and Philadelphia decades earlier.

Montgomery, Ala., and Richmond, Va., were the first cities nationally to be able to boast of the operation of an electric street railway. But the unlikely appearance of this new means of horizontal mobility in the South did not effect dramatic changes as would occur in the North. Although Atlanta, Birmingham, Memphis, Nashville, Tampa, Jacksonville, New Orleans, and Louisville all had streetcar transit, their operations were small and failed to generate any significant degree of decentralized housing, consumer services, or commercial activities. The increased mobility that streetcars offered southerners certainly resulted in suburban annexations: Atlanta had its Inman Park and Druid Hills; Houston its Houston Heights and Deer Park; Tampa its Tampa Heights; and Memphis its Annesdale Park. But by the end of the 19th century, the urban South was hardly comparable to northern industrial cities where streetcar patronage had helped create the sprawling, fragmented metropolises usually associated with late 19th-century American urban life.

Failure of street railway systems to bring about decentralization in southern cities was evident in their size and shape. At the turn of the century, only one city in the South—New Orleans—could claim a population of over 100,000, and for every southerner living in a city in the South with a population of more than 25,000, approximately 15 others remained in smaller cities, in towns, or on the farm. Under the influence of street railway transportation, many of these provincial capitals retained circular shapes until well into the 20th century. Atlanta, for example, had basically a circular shape enclosing an 11-square-mile area in 1900, but more significantly the Georgia capital closely resembled the size of Boston during the mid-19th century. Thus, southern cities entered the 20th century almost uninfluenced by the dominant means of urban transportation of that era. In fact, at that time these relatively small American cities better fit the mold of a preindustrial walking city than that of a late 19th-century industrial metropolis.

Not until the first three decades of the 20th century did many cities in the South begin to outgrow their provinciality. Most of this growth occurred during the 1920s when the very symbol of that decade—the automobile—overtook the street railway as the most popular means of urban transportation. In Memphis between 1920 and 1930, automobile ownership increased by 192 percent; in Atlanta there were 215 percent more registered motor vehicles in 1930 than in 1920; and in Birmingham the figure climbed to as much as 337 percent.

Most of the changes automobile use brought to cities in the South were no different from those in other parts of the country. Businesses unable to survive in congested downtown locations sought refuge in the suburbs; traffic congestion tarnished the image of city fathers who promoted their cities as havens of business opportunity; and citizens of Atlanta, Birmingham, Charlotte, Nashville, and elsewhere found the amenities of suburban life more attractive than ever before.

Increased racial segregation was perhaps the one change private use of automobiles wrought in the urban South—and more dramatically than in other places in the country. Writing about Los Angeles, the model automobile metropolis, one urban authority has claimed that the use of motor vehicles created a new land-use structure in which a measure of racial and class justice could be achieved. This was not the case in the urban South. Because whites were generally more affluent than blacks and could better afford private automobiles as well as home mortgages, suburbanization outside southern cities was limited almost exclusively to whites. In fact, the automobile became the means by which whites achieved their desires for separate living. In terms of time and distance, whites and blacks residing in and around southern cities in 1930 were more segregated than ever before.

Ironically, although urban transportation aided the separate-but-equal doctrine in the urban South, it was through that same medium that blacks began to challenge white supremacy. Rosa Parks's refusal to take a seat at the back of a Montgomery, Ala., bus in 1955 and the subsequent successful boycott of the Montgomery City Line buses by blacks not only brought Martin Luther King Jr. to the attention of Americans as a civil rights activist but also gave the civil rights movement credibility and momentum.

The Montgomery bus boycott ended segregation on Montgomery buses in 1956 and eventually led to integration on public transit conveyers in cities across the South. Decades earlier, however, the private use of automobiles in southern cities had established a pattern of racial segregation in suburban housing and educational facilities that integrated public transportation could not undo. Sometime in the 1960s, the majority of urban white southerners shifted from central city areas to outlying suburbs. In 1974, the Southern Growth Policy Board's Commission on the Future of the South concluded that heavy reliance on the automobile had caused the urban regions of the South to be "less dense and more diffuse than the centralized cities that developed in other parts of the country in an earlier industrial age." Indeed it had—but perhaps the impact of the automobile on southern cities was even more significant to urban life there than commission members surmised.

In recent years, the continued reliance upon the automobile has contributed to the expansion of urban sprawl in southern cities. Atlanta's expressways are the most noticeable among regional cities for the increasing invasion of rural lands as suburbs spread. As well, reliance upon the automobile for urban transportation has been linked to environmental problems like pollution and growing health problems such as obesity.

Some southern cities are making use of rapid transit and light-rail to provide new transportation options. Atlanta's MARTA is the country's ninth-longest rapid transit system. It began in 1971 as a bus system, and MARTA now operates bus lines that connect to 48 miles of rapid transit track serving 38 stations, mostly in Fulton and Dekalb counties. Recent years have seen large increases in passengers. Charlotte's LYNX rapid transit service, which began in November 2007, covers 9.6 miles of track, serving rail transit after the streetcars were discontinued in 1938, and Austin is initiating a 32-mile, light-rail regional railway system in 2010 to serve 10 stations surrounding the capital city of Texas.

HOWARD L. PRESTON
Spartanburg, South Carolina

Rick Beard, in *Olmsted South: Old South Critic/New South Planner*, ed. Dana F. White and Victor A. Kramer (1979); Blaine A. Brownell, *Alabama Review* (April 1972), *American Quarterly* (March 1972); Blaine A. Brownell and David R. Goldfield, eds., *The City in Southern History: The Growth of Urban Civilization in the South* (1977); Thomas Hanchett, *Sorting Out the New South City: Race, Class, and Urban Development in Charlotte, 1870s–1970s* (1998); Howard L. Preston, *Automobile Age Atlanta: The Making of a Southern Metropolis, 1900–1935* (1979); Southern Growth Policy Board, *The Future of the South* (1974).

Underclass

The term "urban underclass" refers to a chronically poor segment of the urban population, distinguished from other poor people, first, by typically living in areas where many or most other residents are also poor and, second, by chronic unemployment or underemployment, which gradually produces a situation in which work is no longer a central organizing feature of people's lives. Concentrated poverty makes social and economic institutions more difficult to sustain, contributes to poorer municipal services by weakening the tax base, and makes everyday tasks like buying groceries and other necessities and getting health care more difficult. It also concentrates problems associated with poverty, such as illness, crime, and family disruptions, in impacted neighborhoods, reducing the quality of life for all in the neighborhood regardless of income. For these reasons, it is worse to be poor in a poor neighborhood than it is to be poor in a neighborhood where most people are not poor. Concentrated poverty is also tied to race and ethnicity: African Americans who are poor have a far higher percentage of neighbors who are also poor than do poor white Americans, with poor Latino Americans falling somewhere in between.

The concept of the urban underclass came out of research in nonsouthern cities, but many of the region's urban areas embody national trends of concentrated poverty. The concept is generally associated with research on urban poverty by William Julius Wilson, some of which dates to the 1970s, and with somewhat more recent research by Douglas Massey and colleagues on the role of racial housing segregation in producing concentrated poverty among African Americans. The concept of an underclass is a controversial one, because the concept of an underclass is seen as emphasizing cultural values and behaviors of the urban poor as a factor perpetuating their poverty. Hence, some critics of the concept of an urban underclass see it as blaming the victim, much like the earlier critiques of culture-of-poverty theory. However, a careful reading of both Wilson and Massey shows that, although they do address cultural mechanisms among the urban poor that make poverty difficult to escape when it is concentrated, both of them see the ultimate reasons for the existence of the urban underclass as structural, with the cultural features a largely inevitable result of the social and economic conditions associated with concentrated urban poverty.

Although Wilson and Massey both see the ultimate causes of urban minority concentrated poverty as structural, they disagree somewhat on the reasons why poverty is so much more concentrated among African Americans than it is among other groups. Wilson emphasizes structural changes in the American economy that have disproportionately affected central cities and African Americans; Massey emphasizes effects of racial housing segregation that make poverty more concentrated for poor African Americans than it is for poor white Americans.

According to Wilson, urban poverty became concentrated among African Americans primarily because, from the 1950s into the 1980s, good-paying jobs, often in manufacturing, departed from the central-city areas where much of the urban African American population lives. Whites and middle-class blacks could often follow the jobs to the suburbs, but poorer African Americans could not. The departure of whites and middle-class blacks from inner-city neighborhoods led to greater concentration of poverty among the poorer blacks who were left behind in these neighborhoods and eliminated much of the social and economic support needed to sustain institutions in the inner city such as retail stores, hospitals, churches, and schools. It also contributed to further erosion of employment opportunities, as additional employers followed the middle class to the suburbs.

Massey and his colleagues emphasized a different cause of concentrated poverty, but saw the consequences as much the same. They began their argument with the fact that because of a long history of racial discrimination, the poverty rate is about three times as high among the African American population as it is among the white population. A central role is attributed to racial housing segregation as a cause of concentrated poverty among urban African Americans. Massey points out that racial housing segregation as we know it today was essentially a 20th-century invention: cities at the turn of the last century were much less racially segregated than cities at mid-century and were less segregated even than most of our larger, older, racially diverse cities are today. Racial housing segregation emerged in most large U.S. cities between about 1910 and 1940 and was used by whites as a way of protecting themselves from competition from African Americans for housing, jobs, and educational opportunities. Massey argued that once this system of housing segregation was in place, an inevitable consequence was that poverty among African Americans would be much more concentrated than poverty among white Americans. The end result of the process Massey and Wilson identify is that poverty among African Americans is far more concentrated than among whites. In the five largest U.S. cities in 1970, two-thirds of poor whites lived in areas with poverty rates below 20 percent, but just 7 percent of poor whites lived in areas with poverty rates above 40 percent. In contrast, 32 percent of poor Latinos and 39 percent of poor blacks lived in areas with poverty rates above 40 percent.

When jobs disappear, the lives of the people left behind become less and less tied to work. The higher the unemployment rate, the less work is a central organizing feature in people's lives. They experience long periods of unemployment, and work opportunities are often haphazard and temporary. Thus, basic work habits such as using an alarm clock and dressing for work become less common and are less likely to be learned by young people. This lack of attachment to work is both an important characteristic of the underclass and a feature that perpetuates the chronic poverty that originated with the loss of the inner-city job base. Additionally, in a situation in which employment opportunities are few, illegitimate means frequently offer greater economic returns than legitimate ones, at least in the short term. In the short term, activities such as drug dealing, robbery, prostitution, and petty theft may offer significantly greater opportunities than any short-term, low-pay, no-benefits employment that may become available. This short-term incentive creates long-term problems, however, as many of those who engage in these activities end up in trouble with the law—producing incarceration rates far higher among the underclass than in the general population. And, finally, both the lack of employment and the turn to illegitimate sources of income that it often leads to produce major family disruptions. In inner cities, there is a severe imbalance between the number of young women and the number of potential male marriage partners available. Both unemployment and imprisonment eliminate many young inner-city black men from the pool of potential marriage partners for young urban black women, resulting in a low marriage rate and an increased proportion of births occurring outside marriage. All these characteristics of the urban underclass—detachment from work, illegal sources of income, family disruption—further exacerbate the effects of concentrated poverty, but it is important to stress that (1) the initial causes of urban concentrated poverty are larger structural conditions (inner-city job loss, out-migration of middle-class population, and housing segregation and discrimination); (2) the lack of access to employment, though tied to the factors listed above, is exacerbated by racial discrimination in hiring, which has been widely documented by recent studies; and (3) the cultural characteristics of the urban underclass, though problematic, are to a large extent inevitable consequences of situations in which large numbers of poor people are concentrated in the same geographic areas with few employment opportunities available.

Many social scientists believe that any emphasis on cultural factors as causes of continuing urban poverty may have problematic effects. These include (1) blaming the poor themselves for their problems; and (2) downplaying the structural factors that are the ultimate cause of concentrated poverty. The term "underclass" is less commonly used today than it was a decade or two ago. Evidence suggests that concentration of poverty among urban minorities decreased during the 1990s, though it is not clear whether this trend continued through the recessions following the September 11 attacks and the 2007–8 housing crisis.

The concept of the urban underclass is most tied to cities in the Midwest and the Northeast, where deindustrialization has been the greatest and the levels of racial housing segregation are the highest. The presence of a more diversified economy and lower levels of residential segregation in many southern cities has made them less prone to the structural dynamics that have produced concentrated poverty in many northern cities. The South's traditional public policy approaches that have tolerated inequalities and underfunded social welfare make, though, for a particular context for acceptance of an underclass in southern cities. Southern cities with high levels of racial housing segregation have areas of severe concentrated poverty with many of the same problems as the urban underclass in the North. Atlanta and New Orleans are perhaps the best examples, and the effects of concentrated poverty were especially evident in the racial and economic characteristics of those most victimized by Hurricane Katrina in New Orleans. Indeed, the aftermath of the hurricane laid bare the reality of concentrated poverty in American cities in a way rarely experienced by white, middle-class, suburban Americans. It was seen by some as an event that had the potential to put issues of race and poverty on the social agenda as they had not been since the 1960s, but the subsequent continued inattention to urban poverty would suggest that Hurricane Katrina was, to a large extent, a learning opportunity lost.

JOHN E. FARLEY
Southern Illinois University at Edwardsville

Chester Hartman and Gregory D. Squires, *There Is No Such Thing as a Natural Disaster: Race, Class, and Hurricane Katrina* (2006); Paul A. Jargowsky and Rebecca Yang, *Journal of Urban Affairs* (March 2006); Douglas S. Massey and Nancy Denton, *American Apartheid: Segregation and the Making of the Underclass* (1993); William Julius Wilson, *The Declining Significance of Race: Blacks and Changing American Institutions* (1978), *The Truly Disadvantaged: The Inner City, the Underclass, and Public Policy* (1987), *When Work Disappears: The New World of the Urban Poor* (1996).

Waterfront Development

In general, the story of waterfront development in the South mirrors that of urban redevelopment as a whole. It begins with federally funded urban renewal efforts of the postwar period and continues with the overall restructuring of the American economy—from manufacturing to services and the spatial shift of economic activity and people from the northern Rustbelt to the southern Sunbelt. This, combined with the concurrent movement of jobs and people from inner-city central business districts to suburban/exurban edge cities, created a situation, in many cases, of urban waterfront abandonment and dereliction. These changes, taking place nationwide, have rendered the economic viability of cities contingent on attracting and retaining geographically footloose service firms and professionals as well as equally footloose tourists/consumers. In short, cities in general have experienced a restructuring of their economic bases from productive industrial activities involving, in many cases, hard-working river ports and seaports, to activities related mostly to office-based services and consumption of both products and places. It is no wonder, given these economic and demographic shifts, that the social and built environments of southern cities have undergone a significant transformation, perhaps particularly along their diverse waterfronts.

This last point is key. Historically, in the largely agrarian South, cities that did emerge and grow were agricultural commodity transshipment points along rivers or on the Gulf or ocean coasts. Indeed, until the very recent economic restructuring of the American economy, cities in the South of any significant size were either working ports or were ones based strictly on tourist consumption of largely water-based recreational activities. As the southern economy has diversified in recent decades, the former type of city—for a dramatic example, Baltimore, but also Mobile, New Orleans, and St. Louis, as well as Tampa and others—has had to try to emulate the economic strategy and ultimate success of consumption-based places like Miami Beach, Biloxi, and Branson. This has rendered it absolutely necessary to transform their working (or, now, in many cases, increasingly nonworking) waterfronts to ones more conducive to professional and tourist consumption. Indeed, just now there is tension, particularly in Alabama, Mississippi, and Florida, concerning the perceived need to "protect" working waterfronts and the jobs associated with them from the onslaught of consumption-based service and recreational activities.

As noted, perhaps the best example of this ongoing transformation of southern waterfronts is the redevelopment of the Inner Harbor of Baltimore, which began in the 1970s. In the midst of a recession, race riots, and the loss of many port-related and relatively high-paying inner-city jobs, real estate developers, banks, and local and state governments set out to render the Inner Harbor into a tourist and recreational site. Now known by most as "Harborplace," this site includes a marine science center, a major aquarium, a convention center, a recreational marina, a festival marketplace, and a number of shopping venues, hotel rooms, and high-priced residential condominiums. Added most recently to the mix is the major new ballpark for the Baltimore Orioles—considered a model for urban redevelopment via sports—constructed on derelict train property at harbor-adjacent Camden Yards.

This dramatic transformation of Baltimore's Inner Harbor certainly brought attention to the city (its mayor was even designated the "best mayor in America" by one national magazine in 1984) and continues to serve as a model for the transition from working to leisure waterfront development. That this transformation has come at the price of the loss of higher-paying jobs in the growing sea of lower-paying tourist/service positions as well as the forced removal of lower-class, mostly black, inner-city residents as a result of high-cost, high-tax residential gentrification has been much less noticed. As a result, cities as diverse as Tampa, Mobile, Chattanooga, and St. Louis are now attempting to replicate what appears to be an overwhelmingly successful waterfront redevelopment process. Even St. Petersburg hopes one day to relocate the baseball stadium of the Tampa Bay Rays to its waterfront to shore up an aging festival pier and tottering bayside airport.

Promoting the consumption of the waterfront is thus the name of the game in the South. And this game is simply facilitated (and accelerated) by other social trends in America in the late 20th and early 21st centuries, such as the concern about the social and environmental costs of continuing urban sprawl, the renewed efforts to preserve the built heritage of cities, and the growing concern about the health of waterfront natural environments. Given this economic and social context, it is no wonder that southern cities are beginning to look quite a bit alike, both socially and spatially. Each city must have its walkways and parkland, festival marketplace, convention center, aquarium (even in relatively landlocked Atlanta), and high-priced office and condominiums on its newly open to the public (though still largely privately owned), readily accessible, pedestrian friendly, secure, safe, socially and environmentally friendly, river, bay, Gulf, or ocean waterfront.

This is true no matter what the size of the city may be. For example, Owensboro, Ky. (under 60,000 residents), just recently received over $4 million in federal funds for its waterfront development project, which will include about four acres of park and plaza space along the Ohio River. Similarly, Shallotte, N.C. (under 2,000 residents), is spending more than $60,000 in its strategic plan to revitalize the waterfront along the Shallotte River adjacent to the town's main street. For its part, Yorktown, Va. (under 20,000 residents), just recently opened a major development, Riverwalk Landing, along the York River, which features various shopping and dining venues, a performance area, and a recreational marina.

Larger cities, like Wilmington, N.C. (just under 100,000 residents), have, indeed, followed suit as the city develops, via public/private partnership, about 60 acres on the city's Cape Fear riverfront, including a convention center, hotel complex, and recreational marina. Clearly, enthusiasm runs deep for waterfront developments of this nature. At least one local politician has been quoted as saying that this project in Wilmington is really the best thing that has happened to the city since World War II. Another major riverfront project, in Knoxville, Tenn. (under 200,000 residents), is under way, to the tune of about $60 million via public/private partnership, to develop a mosaic of condominiums, greenway walks and parks, office space, multiple recreational marinas, and festival area along the city's southern Tennessee River waterfront.

Finally, of course, larger cities in the South are planning or currently undergoing similar transformations of the built and social environments along their waterfronts. Mobile (around 400,000 residents) has been quite busy sprucing up its Mobile River front, connecting its convention center with acres of publicly funded development, Mobile Landing, which includes a pedestrian promenade, a recreational marina, and a new $20 million cruise-ship terminal, along with many other amenities, among them a planned national maritime museum dedicated to the Gulf of Mexico. Tampa (also around 400,000 residents) has redeveloped a considerable portion of its traditionally heavy industrial port lands with the construction of the Florida Aquarium, the Channelside shopping and entertainment facility, a brand-new cruise ship terminal, hockey arena, and waterside convention center with several very large, high-end condominium developments in close proximity.

But perhaps the best example of trends in waterfront development in the South, and the professional and popular enthusiasm thereof, comes from the announcement of plans to revitalize a sizable stretch of Mississippi River front in New Orleans. According to planners involved, the project intends to significantly reduce what they call barriers that discourage people from enjoying the river and replace what they call decaying built structures with parks and public venues that will, undoubtedly, attract significant new private investment. Indeed, it is worth citing precise figures being thrown around to bring the plot of the present story to full completion. According to proponents, this waterfront redevelopment in New Orleans will likely trigger as much as $3 billion in private investments, add an estimated 4,500 new, permanent jobs to the city, and increase the local tax base by approximately $40 million. In the end, how could any city, no matter what size and with no matter what kind of traditional waterfront, resist such a tempting economic future?

KEVIN ARCHER
University of South Florida

Ann Breen and Dick Rigby, eds., *Waterfronts: Cities Reclaim Their Edge* (1994); David R. Goldfield, *Region, Race, and Cities: Interpreting the Urban South* (1997); Shawn Kennedy, *Architectural Record* (19 December 2007); Lawrence H. Larsen, *The Urban South: A History* (1990); Larry Sawers and William K. Tabb, eds., *Sunbelt/ Snowbelt: Urban and Regional Restructuring* (1984); Jon C. Teaford, *The Rough Road to Renaissance: Urban Revitalization in America, 1940–1985* (1990).

White Flight

The term "white flight" refers to the spatial migration of white city dwellers to the suburbs that took place throughout the United States after World War II. One of the most powerful and transformative social movements of the 20th century, white flight significantly affected the class and racial composition of cities and metropolitan areas and the distribution of a conservative postwar political ideology. In 1950, less than one-fourth of the nation's population lived in suburbs. By 1990, more than half of Americans were suburbanites. A number of factors contributed to these changes in residential geography, including federal expansion of the interstate highway system, increased automobile ownership, the availability of government-supported VA and FHA loans, and population pressures on housing and schooling produced by the postwar baby boom. But reactions to civil rights activism, fears of urban unrest, and the consequences of U.S. Supreme Court decisions, beginning with the *Brown v. Board of Education* desegregation decision, continuing with the *Swann v. Charlotte-Mecklenburg Board of Education* busing decision, and *Cisneros v. Corpus Christi ISD*, which extended the *Brown* decision to Mexican Americans, also drove white flight.

In the South, rapid growth of the suburbs, along with a simultaneous regional migration from north to south, dramatically affected economic and political power in the region. These migrations influenced the course of New South economic development and the rise of a Republican majority in the South and the nation. Unlike the overtly racist statements of some "Old South" political leaders who defended segregation as "the southern way of life," suburbanites in the second half of the 20th century were more likely to express conservative sentiments about lower taxes, neighborhood schools, less government involvement, and freedom of association than about segregationist rhetoric. But similar sentiments were shared and voiced by those who resisted desegregation. Moreover, class and racial tensions exacerbated by federal intervention in antipoverty programs, school desegregation, and voting rights legislation influenced many who moved away from central cities to racially, socially, and politically homogeneous suburbs. Some of them were white enclaves, while others were populated by racial and ethnic minorities. But most suburbanites expressed the desire to escape problems they identified with urban life and federal interventionist strategies. Many residents who fled cities during struggles over school desegregation and busing expressed hostility to the federal government, faith in free enterprise, and support for privatization of public services.

According to Kevin Kruse, modern conservatism is rooted in white flight and suburban secession, and it developed its strongest base of support in the suburban South. Leaders of the conservative revolution that took place in Congress in the 1990s were elected from the suburban South. Newt Gingrich, former congressman from metropolitan Atlanta, Speaker of the House of Representatives, and leader of the 1990s Republican Revolution, embodies the politics of the suburban South. Like many southern suburbanites, Gingrich was not a native southerner. In his home district, Gingrich's comments contrasting the work ethic of Cobb County (suburban) and the welfare-state values of Atlanta (urban) framed the political concerns of his suburban electorate without ever referring to race. In 1994, Gingrich and the Republicans announced a Contract with America, which expressed many of the economic and social principles voiced by suburbanites. In the 1994 fall elections, Republicans won a majority of seats in both houses of Congress for the first time since 1952. During a time of significant Republican gains in the United States, the suburban South experienced the greatest electoral gains in the GOP, and suburban southern leaders rose to powerful positions in Congress. House majority leader Dick Armey represented a conservative white, middle-class suburban district between Dallas and Fort Worth. Tom DeLay, the majority whip, represented a suburban district near Houston. Congressman Bob Livingston, who chaired the appropriations committee, represented a conservative white suburban district between Baton Rouge and New Orleans. Because of his seniority, Senator Trent Lott of Mississippi became the Senate majority leader, but his symbolic ties to an Old South segregationist ideology were questioned when he made controversial remarks at a birthday celebration for Senator Strom Thurmond, and the controversy contributed to calls for Lott to resign from his leadership position. Tennessee senator Bill Frist, a New South suburbanite from Nashville, replaced Lott as majority leader and served as leader for the remainder of his term in office. After the 2008 election, when a Democratic majority returned to power in both houses of Congress, southern conservatives became the base of the Republican Party and the most outspoken critics of the Obama administration's policies.

Americans in the 21st century continue to live with the legacy of white flight in political, economic, and social life. Public school enrollments reflect entrenched residential patterns of racial and class segregation. The automobile orientation of sprawling suburbs has created long commutes, traffic congestion, high levels of gasoline consumption, and air pollution, and some believe it has contributed to an epidemic of obesity. Meanwhile, strains between cities and suburbs and competition for scarce economic resources continue unabated in the midst of an economic recession.

DEDEN RUKMANA
Savannah State University

WANDA RUSHING
University of Memphis

Leslie G. Carr and Donald J. Zeigler, *Sociology of Education* (October 1990); Charles T. Clotfelter, *Journal of Policy Analysis and Management* (Spring 2001); Kyle Crowder and Scott J. South, *American Sociological Review* (October 2008); Michael O. Emerson, George Yancey, and Karen J. Chai, *American Sociological Review* (December 2001); William H. Frey, *American Sociological Review* (June 1979); Kevin M. Kruse, *White Flight: Atlanta and the Making of Modern Conservatism* (2005); Kevin M. Kruse and Thomas J. Sugrue, *The New Suburban History* (2006).

Atlanta, Georgia

From its origins as a remote railroad outpost called Terminus in the 1830s to its reincarnation as an Olympic City with international ambitions at the end of the 20th century, Atlanta has pursued an ambitious course of development throughout its history. Relying on a formula that includes equal parts transportation, commercial development, and relentless self-promotion, the city has regularly reinvented itself, becoming the "Gate City of the South" in the latter half of the 19th century, then the "City Too Busy to Hate" during the late 1950s and 1960s, and more recently the "World's Next Great City."

Though devastated by General William T. Sherman's army during the Civil War, Atlanta recovered quickly in the years thereafter, rebuilding its rail lines and welcoming thousands of new residents from Georgia's rural hinterlands. In 1866, federal authorities selected Atlanta to be the Reconstruction headquarters of the Third Military District, and two years later state legislators relocated the state capital to the city. As was the case before the war, railroads played a critical role in the city's postbellum growth, determining the course of the city's physical expansion and shaping the character of its street life and commercial development. By 1890, no fewer than 11 railroad lines passed through the city's terminal station, connecting Atlanta to markets throughout the region and beyond.

No less important than railroads to the city's growth was its penchant for self-promotion. Whether touring the northern lecture circuit or publishing editorials in the *Atlanta Constitution*, newspaperman Henry Grady set the standard for boosterism in the 1870s and 1880s. By advocating regional reconciliation and encouraging industrial development, Grady and his contemporaries lured northern investment to the city and distinguished Atlanta as the capital of the "New South." A result in large part of this tireless advocacy, a handful of skyscrapers dotted the city's skyline by the turn of the century and Atlanta boasted almost 200 different manufacturing outfits and a population of nearly 90,000.

Atlanta hosted a series of large-scale exhibitions in the late 19th century to showcase the city's accomplishments and attractions, most notably the Cotton States and International Exhibition (1895), where Booker T. Washington delivered his famous "Atlanta Compromise" address, expressing the willingness of black southerners to forfeit claims to social equality in exchange for material advancement. Similarly grand public events were less common in the 20th century, but Grady's successors were no less committed to the city's expansion. From the ranks of Atlanta's largest local firms, there developed a local commercial elite that oversaw the city's economic development and wielded tremendous influence in its political life. Imbued with "the Atlanta Spirit"—the notion that what was good for Atlanta was good for business—representatives from firms such as Coca-Cola, Rich's, and Haverty's not only grew the city's businesses but also nurtured its cultural outlets, educational institutions, and national reputation.

Atlanta's growth and development continued apace under their leadership, particularly during the 1920s, when the Chamber of Commerce–directed "Forward Atlanta" campaign helped bring more than 700 new businesses to the city.

The pressures of urban growth meanwhile revealed that, despite boosters' claims to the contrary, racial tensions still teemed beneath Atlanta's veneer of progress and prosperity. Tensions erupted in the city on 22 September 1906 when erroneous reports of assaults committed against white women by black men precipitated a violent race riot, which lasted for four days. Residential segregation only intensified in the years thereafter, and state legislators approved restrictive measures on black suffrage in 1908, ostensibly to prevent future disturbances. The specter of lawlessness was raised yet again in 1915, when a mob of angry whites lynched Leo Frank, a Jewish factory superintendent who had been convicted of assaulting and murdering Mary Phagan, a young white employee. Frank's sensational trial and subsequent lynching captured headlines nationwide, resulting in the establishment of both the Anti-Defamation League of B'nai B'rith and the modern Ku Klux Klan, which was revived on Thanksgiving Day 1915 in a ritualistic, nighttime ceremony atop Stone Mountain, some 10 miles northeast of downtown.

An influx of defense dollars and the establishment of multiple military installations during World War II delivered the city from the depths of depression and primed its economy for a period of postwar growth and development that welcomed 800 new industries to the metropolitan area during the first 10 years following the war's conclusion. Transportation remained important to the city's economy as well, particularly following the completion of the federal interstate system, which routed three interstate highways (I-20, I-75, I-85) through downtown. The 1961 expansion of Atlanta Municipal Airport, later renamed Hartsfield-Jackson Atlanta International Airport, was similarly provident, allowing the airport to become one of the world's largest and making possible, some years later, the city's claim to be the "World's Next Great City."

The abolition of the white primary and the poll tax in the 1940s altered the city's political landscape, adding tens of thousands of black residents to the city's voting rolls and signaling the coming of civil rights activism. Under the direction of the Atlanta Negro Voters League, which was formed in 1949, black voters cast their ballots for white moderates in exchange for the incremental desegregation of public facilities and spaces. The arrangement barred race-baiting segregationists from City Hall and earned Atlanta its reputation as the "City Too Busy to Hate," though the slow pace of citywide desegregation suggests that it might have been more effective at averting negative publicity than achieving racial integration. Still, with its six historically black colleges, an established black middle-class community, and relative calm, Atlanta played an important role in the civil rights movement. The city served as headquarters for a number of national organizations, including the Southern Regional Council, the Student Nonviolent Coordinating Committee, and native Atlantan Martin Luther King Jr.'s organization, the Southern Christian Leadership Conference.

During the course of the 1960s, some 60,000 whites relocated to the suburbs, producing a black majority inside the city limits by 1970. In 1973, voters elected Maynard Jackson as Atlanta's first black mayor, and African Americans have held a majority of elective and appointive offices in the years since. As mayor, Jackson established minority employment guidelines for municipal contractors and steered a larger share of city contracts to minority firms, but the demographic trends that had already begun to whittle away at the city's population worsened. From a metropolitan perspective, population growth continued unabated, increasing from 2 million in 1980 to more than 4 million in 2000. City population totals declined for much of the same period, falling from a peak of almost 500,000 in 1970 to fewer than 400,000 in 1990. Decades of unbroken geographic and demographic growth have come at considerable cost, however; daily commutes are among the longest in the nation, and the city has struggled to meet federal environmental standards. Despite their troubles, Atlanta's leaders have retained much of the "Atlanta Spirit," reinventing downtown as a convention and tourism destination and bidding successfully for the 1996 Olympic Games. Since 2000, the city has also welcomed thousands of new residents, reversing its decades-long trend of population decline and suggesting that sustained suburbanization need no longer preclude urban growth.

EDWARD A. HATFIELD
Emory University

Ronald H. Bayor, *Race and the Shaping of Twentieth-Century Atlanta* (1996); Clifford M. Kuhn, Harlon E. Joye, and E. Bernard West, *Living Atlanta: An Oral History of the City, 1914–1948* (2005); Gary M. Pomerantz, *Where Peachtree Meets Sweet Auburn: The Saga of Two Families and the Making of Atlanta* (1996); Darlene R. Roth and Andy Ambrose, *Metropolitan Frontiers: A Short History of Atlanta* (1996); James Michael Russell, *Atlanta, 1847–1890: City Building in the Old South and the New* (1988); Clarence N. Stone, *Regime Politics: Governing Atlanta, 1946–1988* (1989).

Atlanta Olympics, 1996

Atlanta beat out the cities of Athens, Belgrade, Manchester, Melbourne, and Toronto to become the host of the 1996 Summer Olympics, known officially as the Games of the XXVI Olympiad and unofficially as the Centennial Olympics. The city began its bid for the 1996 Olympics in 1987 and was awarded the position of host in 1990. Atlanta, a city exemplary of the New South economy, saw hosting the Olympics as a way to boost the local economy through tourism dollars and development.

Atlanta's bid for the Olympics was a strategy to create the image of a successful city. Because of a disparity between the city's economic capital and cultural capital, civic and government leaders were intently focused on closing that gap and saw the Olympics as, in Drew

Whitelegg's words, "a way of promoting their city through redressing its cultural deficiency rather than an old-fashioned piece of pump-priming." City leaders were particularly concerned with the cultural deficiencies in its downtown area, which depended on the convention industry because many jobs and people had left this area for the suburbs. Hosting the Olympic Games would bolster Atlanta's cultural amenities and place the city firmly on the world stage.

Atlanta's preparation for hosting the Olympics was focused on image, both physically and symbolically. Physically, the city worked toward transforming its image in building new attractions and facilities such as Centennial Park. In the process of building the park, over 1,000 homeless people were displaced, as well as 70 businesses and four homeless shelters, ameliorating city leaders' concerns about the unsavory image the area would present to Olympic visitors. Symbolically, the city worked to hide the racial tensions in its past, notably those associated with the tourist attraction Stone Mountain and the state flag. The city's presentation of the attraction left out details pertaining to its ownership by one of the highest-ranking groups in the Ku Klux Klan and connection to southern resistance.

Atlanta's reliance on image production and the media's presentation of that image to the world posed major problems in how the event was perceived and judged by critics and leaders. When things went wrong, including numerous computer glitches and transportation problems, a negative image of the city and its event management resulted.

This negative publicity could have potentially outweighed the benefits of hosting an international sporting event. One of the most well-known negative outcomes of the 1996 Olympics was the bombing that occurred in Centennial Park, which resulted in the death of one person and the injury of 111 others. The bomber, Eric Robert Rudolph, released a statement explaining the bombing as a political attack against the U.S. government.

Ultimately, the 1996 Olympics was something of a mixed bag for the city of Atlanta. This world-scale event resulted in the construction of multiple athletic facilities and provided international exposure, although it did not improve many of the impoverished areas of the city, as had been expected. The Olympics allowed for multiple athletic facilities to be repaired or built. Among the facilities built for the Olympic Games were the Georgia Tech Aquatic Center, the Georgia International Horse Park, and the Wolf Creek Shooting Complex. The 83,100-seat Olympic Stadium was built near the Atlanta–Fulton County Stadium. After the Olympics, the Olympic Stadium was later renamed Turner Stadium, and it served as the home of the Atlanta Braves, replacing the Atlanta–Fulton County Stadium as the baseball team's home. The ultimate cost for these renovations (both for new and for improved facilities) was more than $400 million. Institutions of higher learning also experienced physical growth. Residential areas built for the Olympics were later converted into residence halls for the Georgia Tech campus, with housing on the campus increasing from 6,951 to over 10,000 dormitory rooms.

Two housing projects were improved by Olympics-related preparations: the Summerhill complex was upgraded and the Techwood/Clark Howell area was established. However, although over $100 million was put toward neighborhood improvement, other impoverished areas of Atlanta were not notably improved, either before or after the Olympics. Although the Corporation for Olympic Development in Atlanta (CODA) chose 16 "Olympic Ring" neighborhoods for improvement, only a portion of those areas were improved, owing to the difficulty of obtaining private funding for neighborhoods that were less attractive for new residents because of high crime and poor schools.

The Olympic "spotlight" encouraged city improvement and focused attention on city infrastructure, such as Atlanta's aging bridges and sewer system. And, undoubtedly, Atlanta profited from tourists and visitors, but these gains were perhaps not as high as had been expected and were restricted to the immediate Olympic area, as opposed to the entire state of Georgia.

The Olympics garnered international television exposure and intensive media interest for Atlanta, although much of this attention was negative, due to numerous organizational and logistical glitches throughout the event. IBM's results service collapsed after only a few days, resulting in incorrect statistical information on competitors and even in world records not being recorded. Some individuals in the Olympic movement and observers afterward described the Games as the worst-organized in modern times.

The 1996 Olympic Games in Atlanta had both positive and negative results for the city. The Games were successful for one of the most important goals the city had in hosting the event, providing Atlanta with a new global identity. Though there were numerous organizational problems and impoverished areas were not revitalized as hoped, Atlanta gained the international exposure and recognition it sought and eased the gap between its economic capital and its cultural capital.

MARY K. LEVIE
RACHEL L. SMITH
University of Memphis

Steven P. French, *Journal of the American Planning Association* (1 July 1997); Drew Whitelegg, *International Journal of Urban and Regional Research* (December 2000).

Austin, Texas

Austin is by all accounts a very special town. It is home to a major public university, the University of Texas at Austin, as well as being the state capital. The city boasts a thriving cultural mix, which includes a nationally known music scene (including South by Southwest) and an emerging arts and entertainment industry (film production being the newest). Best of all, to many, is the environment of the city: lots of warm days, plenty of water, lovely hill country on the west, and spring-fed pools in the middle of town. The mix of culture, music, and environment creates the easy, laid-back, southern lifestyle for which Austin is known. It is widely considered one of the most desirable

Vintage postcard, 1940s, Austin, Tex. On the facing side the caption reads, "This is the main business thoroughfare of Austin. With brilliant new lights, at night it becomes a 'Great White Way,' which is very impressive to the visitor. At the 'head' of the Avenue stands the magnificent State Capitol." (Charles Reagan Wilson Collection, Center for the Study of Southern Culture, University of Mississippi)

and attractive places to live or visit in the United States today.

It began in a far more modest way, as a tiny hamlet originally called Waterloo, founded in 1839. Within a few decades, it had become both the state capital and home to the University of Texas, yet it remained for many years a backwater to other dynamic sites in the Southwest, living in the shadows of Galveston and Houston, among other Texas cities. It had a number of enterprising individuals and organizations promoting its fortunes at the time, among them Alexander Wooldridge, the first of the urban entrepreneurs to promote the city, as well as Walter E. Long, longtime director of the Austin Chamber of Commerce, and Edgar Perry, a prominent businessman. Their efforts bore no fruit until a young congressman from the hill

country outside Austin, Lyndon Baines Johnson, found himself in Washington, D.C., in the mid-1930s. With considerable know-how and great political skill, Johnson managed to get federal funds to build dams along the Colorado River. The dams, completed in the 1940s, furnished hydroelectric power and prevented the frequent flooding of Austin, and by the 1970s Austin was ready to take off as a thriving and dynamic center in the Southwest.

The university played a great role in its expansion, partly through the expertise of its faculty, especially in engineering and the sciences, and partly as a producer of some very bright young graduates, many of whom elected to stay in Austin and build their fortunes there. The most prominent, of course, was Michael Dell, a young man who dropped out of the university to start what would become an empire in the sale and distribution of new desktop and laptop computers. By 2000, Dell Computers led the computer industry in the sales of computers for homes.

But Dell is just one part of the high-tech wave that helps drive Austin's economy. Business and political elites have spent the last three decades lobbying and creating incentives for high-tech firms to locate in the city, and the economy reflects their efforts. The city is home to major tech firms such as Samsung and AMD (Advance Micro Devices) and hundreds of new start-up companies each year, and by 2008 Austin ranked eighth in the nation in high-tech employment. Along with computers, the newest ventures into the tech market are coming in shades of green — green building, energy, and transportation technology. The university, technology, and state government draw people, and since the last decades of the 20th century the city has continued to grow rapidly.

But the phenomenal growth has had a downside. As the local environment degraded and housing prices escalated, many people thought that what was special about Austin was being diminished by unplanned growth. This gave rise to another part of Austin that is nationally known: its strong, local, environmental movement. From the late 1970s until the late 1990s, Austin politics was defined by the "environmentalists vs. developers" conflict, with the city council see-sawing between growth promoters and businesspeople on the one hand and environmentalists and neighborhood

activists on the other. By the late 1990s, the environmentalists had achieved enough political power to hold on to the council for several terms. They used their power to institutionalize environmental protection by buying tens of thousands of acres of land that would remain in a natural state, preserving thousands more through private-sector mechanisms, passing policies designed to reduce energy and water use, and passing regulations governing how and where development would occur.

Though no longer the dominant political machine that it was for a decade, the environmental movement remains one of the main interest groups in town and maintains an influence on city policy today. Because of that movement, Austin has institutionalized its commitment to preserving the environment far more than most cities have. It is on the leading edge of the national Green Cities and Cool Cities movements; Austin was one of the early signatories to the U.S. Mayors' Climate Protection Agreement in June 2006 and created its own Climate Protection Plan in 2007. That plan details how the city will use green technology to reduce its carbon footprint in transportation, energy systems, and buildings. Austin is regularly ranked in the top 10 Green Cities in the nation.

Richard Florida, author of the book *The Rise of the Creative Class*, places Austin very high on the list of cities with great creativity and, as a result, high tolerance for diverse and interesting lifestyles. The environment, technology, and the arts scene, along with state government and education, have helped to inspire and shape this creative class and to make Austin the singular place that it is today.

ANTHONY ORUM
University of Illinois at Chicago
SCOTT SWEARINGEN
Austin, Texas

Richard Florida, *The Rise of the Creative Class* (2003); Anthony M. Orum, *Power, Money, and the People* (2002); Scott Swearingen, *Environmental City: People, Place, Politics, and the Meaning of Modern Austin* (2010).

Birmingham, Alabama

Surveying Jones Valley in Jefferson County in 1860, John T. Milner, later a key Birmingham founder, viewed it as "one vast garden as far as the eye could reach." "It was, on the whole," he later wrote, "a quiet, easy-going, well farmed, well framed, and well regulated civilization."

Life in the region was never quite so perfect, but whatever tranquility existed was shattered forever after 1861. The Civil War dramatically changed this "vast garden" and brought railroads and the iron industry to the region for the first time. Birmingham was founded in 1871 for the express purpose of creating an industrial city in the heart of Alabama's mineral district. Coal, iron ore, and limestone—three critical ingredients needed for iron and, later, steel production—were abundant within a 50-mile radius of the new town, and new railroads were being built to intersect at its very center. The speculative entrepreneurs who founded Birmingham called it the "Magic City" and grandly predicted that it would become the "El

Dorado of the iron masters" and the "manufacturing center of the habitable globe."

Birmingham never fulfilled that lofty prophecy and initially struggled through a cholera epidemic and a full-scale national depression before the founders' vision was compelling enough to attract major investors by 1880. Within two decades, this cadre of New South industrialists, led by Henry Fairchild DeBardeleben, James W. Sloss, and Enoch Ensley, had constructed 28 furnaces, sunk numerous mines into the rich seams of coal and iron ore nearby, and constructed railroads and mining towns throughout the mineral district, with Birmingham at its center. Due primarily to the development of resources around Birmingham, coal production in Alabama increased from only 17,000 tons in 1872 to 8 million tons in 1900, and pig iron production exploded from just 11,000 tons to more than 1 million tons in the same period. By 1898, Birmingham was the single largest exporter of pig iron in the United States and the third largest in the world. It also had gained a new nickname: the "Pittsburgh of the South."

With economic prosperity came new challenges. Birmingham did not achieve dominance as the industrial center of the district without competition. First, the industrial village of Ensley sought the title, followed in 1887 by the upstart "Marvel City" of Bessemer. In both cases, the aspirations of these towns were thwarted by the consolidation of most of the companies into one large and dominant company, the Tennessee Coal, Iron, and Railroad Company, or TCI, as it was generally known. In 1907, during another national financial crisis, a debt-ridden TCI was consolidated when J. P. Morgan engineered its purchase by United States Steel at a bargain-basement price. From that time forward, the industrial destiny of the Birmingham District was virtually controlled in a colonial fashion by corporate leaders in Pittsburgh, backed by investment bankers in New York City.

Nonetheless, Birmingham became a symbol of the New South—bustling, dynamic, and forward looking, downplaying its lingering ties to the antebellum South of plantations and slavery. A diverse and complex urban-regional system evolved. Although this urban system was based primarily on industry, it also performed regional transportation and commercial activities and financial functions, developing varied sources for wealth and growth. Along with native-born whites and newly arrived immigrants, the first generation of free blacks had streamed into the district beginning in the 1880s. Their numbers grew, until blacks constituted nearly 40 percent of Birmingham's population, ranking it first among cities of its size nationally for the proportion of its black population. By 1900, whites had fully consolidated political power in Alabama, and in Birmingham they duly instituted one of the most stringent Jim Crow regimes anywhere in the South.

Birmingham and its environs experienced economic booms and busts consistent with a heavy reliance on the economically sensitive iron and steel industries. When times were good, they could be very good; when they were bad, it could be nearly disastrous. Overall, the city grew and prospered, and by 1920 the Birmingham metropolitan area was the third largest in the South, surpassed only by New Orleans and Atlanta. As the editors of the *Age-Herald* declared in 1922, "Birmingham lives in the present, not in the past, and builds for the future." Despite its prosperity, Birmingham suffered during the Great Depression, but the federal "Lend Lease" policy during World War II eventually provided a stimulus to the dormant steel industry.

During the 1950s, Birmingham's rigid, unyielding adherence to Jim Crow segregation provoked Rev. Fred L. Shuttlesworth to form the Alabama Christian Movement for Human Rights and to mount a vigorous, nonviolent challenge to the dominant white commercial civic elite, the so-called Big Mules. In response, Ku Klux Klan terrorism increased, until violence against Freedom Riders in 1961 finally awakened the white elite to the reality that Jim Crow's days were numbered. However, an entirely new city government to oust Eugene "Bull" Connor and massive demonstrations led by Shuttlesworth and Dr. Martin Luther King Jr. in spring 1963 were both required before modest levels of desegregation could be achieved. In September, the tragic deaths of four young girls in the Klan bombing of the 16th Street Baptist Church served as catalyst for even harder work for racial peace. Better relations between blacks and whites progressed slowly, but mostly outside forces—federal court decisions and the passage of the Civil Rights Act of 1964 and the Voting Rights Act of 1965—created the main impetus for change.

Since the mid-1960s, Birmingham has experienced a major political transformation. The exclusive power of the white economic and commercial elite has been replaced by much more diverse political leadership. In 1979, Richard Arrington became the first African American to be elected mayor of Birmingham, and he was reelected by large margins in four successive elections, serving a total of 20 years as mayor. He has been followed in office by three other African American mayors, William Bell (acting mayor), Bernard Kincaid, and Larry Langford. The Birmingham City Council meantime has had a black majority since 1989. In addition, blacks have been elected mayor in two other municipalities in the region, Fairfield and Bessemer. Two African Americans have served on the Jefferson County Commission since five-member district elections were instituted by an agreement to settle a voting rights case in 1986. Finally, in 1992, an African American was elected to the U.S. Congress from one of the two Birmingham area districts for the first time since Reconstruction.

Birmingham's economic transition from its dependence on the steel industry has been equally transformative. The city's economic life is centered now on the educational and research enterprise at the University of Alabama at Birmingham (UAB) and its world-renowned medical center. UAB has become Alabama's largest employer, with more than 18,000 faculty and staff working at the university and in the UAB health system. An Urban Land Institute study named UAB "the city center's single most important growth and job generator." More recently, *Southern Business Development* magazine ranked UAB among the top 10 universities in the South that are instrumental to its region's economic development because of the scope of its research and development activity.

From its origins at a rail crossing in a cornfield nearly 140 years ago, Birmingham in the last three decades has been transformed from a gritty and smoky iron and steel center into a modern metropolis with a diverse economy and a rich cultural heritage.

ROBERT G. CORLEY
University of Alabama at Birmingham

Leah Rawls Atkins, *The Valley and the Hills: An Illustrated History of Birmingham and Jefferson County* (1981); Lynne B. Feldman, *A Sense of Place: Birmingham's Black Middle-Class Community, 1890–1930* (1999); John C. Henley, *This Is Birmingham: The Story of the Founding and Growth of an American City* (1963); Marjorie Longenecker White, *The Birmingham District: An Industrial History and Guide* (1981); Bobby M. Wilson, *America's Johannesburg: Industrialization and Racial Transformation in Birmingham* (2000), *Race and Place in Birmingham: The Civil Rights and Neighborhood Movements* (2000).

Busch Gardens, Tampa, Florida

Busch Gardens Tampa, one of several Florida theme parks, is Tampa's most popular tourist attraction and a leading example of urban-based amusement venues in the South. When Busch Gardens opened in 1959, it encompassed 15 acres of vegetation, birds, and limited amusements adjacent to a brewery, which tourists and locals could visit at no charge. The original gardens evolved into an elaborate African-themed park, which attracted more than 4 million visitors annually at the height of its popularity.

August A. Busch Jr., the chairman of the board and president of Anheuser-Busch, sought a southeastern location for a brewery. Busch was familiar with the Tampa area because the St. Louis Cardinals, the major league baseball team that he owned, held its spring training in St. Petersburg. Busch initially purchased 152 acres and expanded to 265 acres in late 1965 and eventually to its present size of 335 acres. During its first several years, Busch Gardens attracted about 1.5 million visitors annually, more than any other attraction in Florida. It included a hospitality house overlooking a lagoon where visitors could enjoy complementary glasses of Budweiser.

Busch Gardens opened a monorail in 1966 to carry passengers above its newly created Wild Animal Kingdom, re-creating the African veldt. The area included several animal species found in Africa—chimps, lions, rhinos, cheetahs, and elephants. In 1970, when Disney was about to open its Orlando facility, Busch decided to compete. He announced that he would expand Busch Gardens and charge admission for the first time.

Busch Gardens added several different sections, including Nairobi, Serengeti, Stanleyville, Congo, and Tim-

buktu. The park also included a large amphitheater and a movie theater. In late 1975, advertising for Busch Gardens emphasized the African theme and branded the park as "The Dark Continent." Advertisements included such headlines as "The Best Part of a Florida Vacation Is Spending a Day in Africa" and "Instead of a Zoo, We Created a Continent." According to the general manager, the "Dark Continent" offered visitors "a place where the entire family can step back in time and relive the misery, intrigue and adventure associated with big game, native folklore and classic feature films made on location in Africa." Eventually, "The Dark Continent" was dropped and the name Bush Gardens Tampa Bay was adopted. Starting in 2006, visitors entered Busch Gardens Africa, a brand introduced to correspond with the Anheuser-Busch park in Williamsburg, Va., whose name was changed to Busch Gardens Europe.

In addition to its rides, animals, elaborate vegetation, and variety of shows, Busch Gardens offers roller coasters. Its first roller coaster, the Python, opened in 1976. The Scorpion followed in the Timbuktu area in 1980. Kumba opened in 1993, claiming to be the largest steel roller coaster in the Southeast. Montu, an Egyptian-themed coaster, opened in 1996. Gwazi, the "Southeast's largest and fastest double wooden coaster," was completed in 1999. SheiKra was introduced in 2005, billed as North America's first dive coaster.

Busch Gardens has been positively reviewed by theme park analysts and aficionados. *Forbes* magazine recognized it in 2005 as among the world's top 10 amusement parks. In 2000, *Forbes* reported that frequent riders of steel roller coasters voted Montu as their second favorite, and the Golden Ticket Awards presented by *Amusement Today* have several times recognized Montu as one of the country's top 10 steel roller coasters. Busch Gardens has also won several awards from the International Association of Amusement Parks and Attractions, including prizes for the quality of its entertainment and its landscaping.

Busch Gardens has played a significant role in Tampa's economy, consistently rated as the most important draw for tourists and a major employment generator. During the 1980s, it ranked in the top 10 private-sector employers in Hillsborough County. The Busch brewery in Tampa closed in 1995. In mid-2008, Belgian brewer InBev NV acquired Anheuser-Busch, and the acquisition included the 10 Anheuser-Busch theme parks. In 2009, InBev sold all Busch properties to the Blackstone Group, which removed the last remaining traces of Anheuser-Busch ownership other than the name.

ROBERT KERSTEIN
University of Tampa

Dana Anderson, *Journal of Popular Culture* (Fall 1999); Ken Breslauer, *Roadside Paradise: The Golden Age of Florida's Tourist Attractions, 1929–1971* (2000); Mark Gottdiener, *The Theming of America: Dreams, Media Fantasies, and Themed Environments* (2001); Karen Haymon Long, *Tampa Tribune* (27 January 2002); Gary Mormino, *Land of Sunshine, State of Dreams: A Social History of Modern Florida* (2005).

Charleston, South Carolina

Charleston, or Charles Town as it was originally known, was the first major settlement in the new Restoration colony of Carolina. Founded in 1670 at Albemarle Point on the Ashley River by settlers from England and Barbados, it moved to its current location on the peninsula between the Ashley and Cooper rivers in 1679–80. By the middle of the 18th century, the town was growing in wealth, thanks to the growth of rice and indigo cash crops. Charles Town became substantial enough to warrant a protective wall, the only one for any British city in what became the United States. It also became the colonial capital of South Carolina when the state split from the northern section in 1719. Charles Town developed a sophisticated urbane culture with a library, theater, newspaper, and various societies and clubs and what became the College of Charleston, the oldest municipal university in the country. The city retained a Caribbean connection both in its architecture and in the fact that most of its population was African and African American slaves. For most of the 18th century, and in the early part of the 19th, it was the major slave port in mainland North America.

Although dominated by planters, the city developed a burgeoning merchant and artisan class. There was major opposition to the Stamp Act in the 1760s, and the town became a target for the British during the American Revolution, eventually falling to their forces in 1780. After the British evacuated in 1782 and the Treaty of Paris ended the war in 1783, the city incorporated as Charleston. The growing white population farther inland forced Charleston to give up its status as capital to Columbia in 1790. The city remained important economically, however, shipping most of the state's cotton crop. City authorities showed some vision in supporting what became the South Carolina Railroad in the early 1830s, which linked the city with Hamburg on the Savannah River (near Augusta, Ga.).

The city was generally disdainful of industry, however, and fell far behind many in the northern states. Even in the South, Charleston had lost its prominence. Despite the presence of some Whig sympathizers among the merchant class, fiery proslavery advocates such as Robert Barnwell Rhett and his mouthpiece, the *Charleston Mercury*, came to symbolize the city to the rest of the nation. Charleston cemented this view when the South Carolina convention passed and signed the secession ordinance there in December 1860, and the Civil War started in the harbor the following April. The city paid for its secessionism with a blockade and siege by Union forces, which included serious bombardment from 1863 onward.

When the city fell to Union forces in February 1865, it was in very poor physical and economic shape. Like most of South Carolina, the Reconstruction experience in Charleston was tumultuous, but its people showed more willingness for negotiation than was true in other parts of the state. The city's large immigrant population and the politically active local African American population promoted compromise on occasions. Nonetheless, white Charles-

ton eventually helped end Reconstruction and seemed to embrace the "New South creed," at the expense of equality for African Americans. Despite the growth of a phosphate industry in the 1870s, the city languished economically and was also hit by hurricanes and, in 1886, an earthquake. As late as 1900, the city's economy remained in the doldrums.

The opening of the Charleston Navy Yard in 1901 and new, more progressive mayors such as John Patrick Grace (1911–15, 1919–23) and Thomas P. Stoney (1923–31) pushed economic development like never before. Grace forced the railroad companies to sell the docks to the city (later taken over by the State Ports Authority in 1942), and Stoney pushed tourism, encouraging the construction of hotels and gas stations in the 1920s. He was also, however, a friend of the Society for the Protection of Old Dwellings (SPOD), founded in 1920, and established Charleston's and the country's first historic district in 1931, which was supervised by a Board of Architectural Review. Also in the 1920s the city experienced an outburst of cultural activity known as the "Charleston Renaissance." Writers such as DuBose Heyward and Josephine Pinckney and artists such as Alice Ravenel Huger Smith and Elizabeth O'Neill Verner tried to reconcile the old with the new, establishing a somewhat anachronistic and exotic view of the city.

The preservation efforts and the nostalgic nature of the renaissance made Charleston a tourist attraction, but many parts of the city remained in the condition they had been in since the antebellum era. In the 1930s, Mayor Burnet Maybank, a strong supporter of the New Deal, pursued vigorous "urban renewal." As a result, however, a lot of inner-city African Americans were moved farther up the peninsula, making Charleston more segregated residentially than it had ever been in its history. Maybank became governor of the state and was elected to the U.S. Senate. With the help of the senator he replaced, a key Roosevelt administration member, Charleston native James F. "Jimmy" Byrnes, Maybank made sure that a lot of federal largesse went to the Charleston naval base during World War II. After the war, federal money continued to flow into the naval yard as the United States went into the Cold War, and this continued funding eased some of the economic dislocation of demobilization.

The postwar period, however, brought political turmoil as the city's African American population sought to overthrow the Jim Crow system. Local leaders such as Septima Clark of the NAACP put pressure on city authorities to integrate the public work roll and public facilities. Despite widespread and deep opposition from local whites, the city hired black policemen in the 1950s and in 1960 integrated the public golf course, the first municipal institution desegregated in the state of South Carolina. Black activists continued to pressure the city with marches and sit-ins, and, in general, the mayor and police responded in a more restrained way than those in other cities throughout the state and region. Nonetheless, racism in employment remained, triggering the Nurses Strike of 1969 when

local hospitals fired black union organizers.

By the 1970s, black Charlestonians were making their voices heard at the ballot box as well. In 1975, they played a major role in electing Irish American Joseph P. "Joe" Riley mayor. Riley explicitly acknowledged that African Americans, despite the removal of legal obstacles, had not been recognized in Charleston's history. During his administrations (as of 2009 he was in his ninth term), he has sought to correct that imbalance through everything from establishing an African American arts festival in 1979 to hiring a black police chief in 1982. Riley has also been a major booster for the city, encouraging economic development through new hotels, larger hospitals, a larger College of Charleston, support for the port, and the establishment of the major arts festival, Spoleto Festival USA.

Together, Riley and the city council have tried to preserve the city's historical heritage. Hurricane Hugo in 1989 and the closure of the naval base in 1995 hurt the city, but its tax base has rebounded thanks to the revitalization of the historic district and its spread up the peninsula. Although hemmed in on its north side by the city of North Charleston (incorporated in 1972) and east of the Cooper River by the city of Mount Pleasant, the city continues to spread west of the Ashley River. The move across this river to West Ashley began in 1959, but Riley has been an aggressive annexationist there and on various islands, now linked by bridges, near the city. In the 21st century, Charleston still tries to preserve the past while embracing the future. Property development remains a major political issue. Many economic disparities remain, however, and the city is very dependent on the hospitality industry, something that can be easily hurt by economic downturns and the ever-present danger of another hurricane or earthquake. Thus, Charleston remains very much the way writer Allen Tate once described the South, marching into the future but always with "a backward glance."

DAVID GLEESON
College of Charleston

Walter J. Fraser, *Charleston! Charleston!: The History of a Southern City* (1989); James M. Hutchisson and Harlan Greene, *Renaissance in Charleston: Art and Life in the Carolina Lowcountry, 1900–1940* (2003); Maurie McInnis, *The Politics of Taste in Antebellum Charleston* (2005); Michael O'Brien and David Moltke-Hansen, eds., *Intellectual Life in Antebellum Charleston* (1986); Bernard Powers, *Black Charlestonians: A Social History, 1822–1885* (1994); George C. Rogers Jr., *Charleston in the Age of the Pinckneys* (1969); Stephanie Yuhl, *Through a Golden Haze of Memory: The Making of Historic Charleston* (2005).

Charlotte, North Carolina

Located in the rolling hills of the Piedmont near the border of South Carolina, Charlotte is the largest city in both Carolinas and one of the nation's top banking centers. The Queen City has come a long way from the "trifling place" that visitor George Washington noted in his diary two centuries ago.

Charlotte's heritage as a trading city dates back before European settlement. Catawba Indians walked two trading paths that crossed on a hilltop, today the main streets of Tryon and Trade at the heart of the center city. Scots-Irish settlers began arriving via the port of Philadelphia and Virginia's Great Wagon Road in the mid-18th century, and by 1768 there were enough people to incorporate the courthouse village as Charlottetown. The name honored King George's wife, Queen Charlotte, and the surrounding county became Mecklenburg in memory of her German birthplace.

For most of its first century, Charlotte remained a tiny backcountry farm town limited by the lack of navigable waterways. Local farmers cherished their independence, in May 1775 signing the Mecklenburg Resolves disputing royal power and, according to local tradition, also signing a Mecklenburg Declaration of Independence. British general Lord Cornwallis stormed through late in the Revolution and was quickly run off, calling Charlotte a "hornets nest" of rebellion. After the war, small farmers dominated the landscape, with less than a handful of plantations owning as many as two dozen slaves. Small gold mines enlivened the economy beginning in 1799 when North America's first gold discovery was made some 25 miles to the east. In 1837, a U.S. Mint began coining gold pieces, eclipsed after 1849 by the California gold rush.

Charlotte's growth took off during the New South era of the late 19th century. Railroads built beginning in the 1850s coalesced into the Southern Railway mainline, the "Main Street of the South." Local promoter D. A. Tompkins helped launch a Cotton Mill

Campaign that saw the South overtake New England in the textile industry by the 1920s. Notable firms in the vicinity included Cannon, the world's leading producer of towels, and Springs, known for Springmaid sheets. James B. Duke's Duke Power dammed the area's rocky rivers to produce inexpensive hydroelectric power. Families streamed off farms to find work in the cotton factories. Charlotte became the mill region's banking and wholesaling hub, and city population surged from less than 4,000 in the 1860s to 80,000 by the late 1920s.

Though always notably intent on moneymaking, Charlotte has nonetheless made important contributions to American culture. Evangelist Billy Graham grew up on a dairy farm just outside town, and today the Billy Graham Library is a major tourist attraction. From the 1920s to the 1940s, Charlotte rivaled Nashville as a country and gospel recording center, where bluegrass pioneer Bill Monroe cut his first discs. NASCAR, the National Association for Stock Car Auto Racing, held its initial "strictly stock" race at a Charlotte dirt track in 1949; today the engineering shops of many NASCAR teams dot the Charlotte metro area and the NASCAR Hall of Fame attracts fans to the center city. In civil rights, Charlotte experienced less violence and thus garnered fewer headlines than some other southern cities, but struggles were no less profound. The Supreme Court's 1971 landmark ruling in *Swann v. Charlotte-Mecklenburg Schools* made Charlotte the national test case for court-ordered busing to promote racial integration. Charlotte's growth, ever-increasing

since the 1850s, entered a new phase at the end of the 20th century. Textile factories left for cheaper labor overseas, but that barely affected Charlotte's diverse economy of wholesalers, regional offices, and financial services. In 1982, local bank NCNB searched out legal loopholes that allowed it to acquire a bank in Florida, kicking off the U.S. interstate banking revolution. By the beginning of the 21st century, Charlotte boasted the headquarters of two of America's top four banks—Bank of America (formerly NCNB) and Wachovia (formerly First Union)—and the city ranked second only to New York as a national financial center. Even Wachovia's acquisition by San Francisco–based Wells Fargo in the 2008 U.S. financial crisis could not topple Charlotte from that number-two spot.

Economic success spurred growth of civic institutions. Professional sports teams arrived, led by the Carolina Panthers (1995) of the National Football League and the Charlotte Bobcats (2004) of the National Basketball Association. A bustling hub airport for U.S. Airways regularly ranked among the country's dozen busiest. In the city's eastern suburbs, the University of North Carolina at Charlotte emerged as a full-fledged research university. Downtown, new facilities for the Mint Museums (art and craft), Discovery Place (science), ImaginOn (children's theater and library), Levine Museum of the New South (history), Bechtler Museum (modern art), and the Harvey Gantt Center for African American Arts and Culture clustered near the 2007 LYNX light-rail line.

New residents poured in from across the country and around the globe. A Brookings Institution study identified Charlotte among America's top four Latino "hypergrowth" cities from 1990 to 2000, and other sizable immigrant groups arrived from Southeast Asia, India, and Eastern Europe. In the center city, old buildings disappeared as a new skyline arose. Suburbs sprawled outward, with Mecklenburg County population projected to pass 1 million during the 2010s.

TOM HANCHETT
Levine Museum of the New South

Frye Gaillard, *The Dream Long Deferred: The Landmark Struggle for Desegregation in Charlotte, North Carolina* (2006); Janette Greenwood, *Bittersweet Legacy: The Black and White "Better Classes" in Charlotte, 1850–1910* (1994); Thomas Hanchett, *Sorting Out the New South City: Race, Class, and Urban Development in Charlotte, 1870s–1970s* (1998); Mary Kratt, *Charlotte: Spirit of the New South* (1992); Matthew Lassiter, *The Silent Majority: Suburban Politics in the Sunbelt South* (2006); Ross Yockey, *McColl: The Man with America's Money* (1999).

Chattanooga, Tennessee

Southeast Tennessee's Lookout Mountain presents a towering barrier to the Tennessee River, bending the river's north-south course to the west, a bend said to resemble an Indian's moccasin. Before construction in the early 20th century of the now-destroyed Hales Bar Lock and Dam, the moccasin bend was the last easily navigable water before the treacherous shallows and rapids known as the Suck.

The Creek were early inhabitants of the bend. The Cherokees pushed out the Creek, and used the river as their gateway through the mountains. Cherokee trading trails stretched from the moccasin bend south into Georgia and to the north over the Cumberland Plateau into Kentucky.

In the mid-1500s, Spanish explorers passed through the area. The French followed the Spanish, and the Scots-Irish followed the French. Scotsman John McDonald married a Cherokee. Their daughter Molly married Daniel Ross, another Scot. Molly and Daniel's son John became a tribal chief, and he and his brother opened a trading station at the Moccasin Bend ferry landing, astride the north-south trade routes. Chief Ross's Cherokees remained in control of the region until they, in turn, were driven out by land-hungry whites, many of whom were Scots-Irish who themselves had been cleared from the highlands of Scotland.

After the controversial 1835 Treaty of New Echota, white settlers moved in, and in 1837 the white families living around Ross's Landing laid out city plots and changed the name of their new village from Ross's Landing to Chattanooga. Within the year, the former Ross's Landing became one of the major assembly camps for the removal of the Cherokee—a starting point for the infamous Trail of Tears. If the former highland Scots saw irony in a forced clearance of the Cherokees, that record no longer exists.

Twenty-five years after the Cherokee removal, northern warriors brought the next major change—an end to the re-

Chattanooga, Tenn., on the Moccasin Bend of the Tennessee River from Lookout Mountain. The original site of the city, Ross's Landing, is around the bend in the river hidden behind the tall buildings of the city. (Photograph courtesy of Kittrell Rushing)

gion's slave-based economy. In November 1863, Confederate general Braxton Bragg's army retreated from Chattanooga, opening the doorway for General Sherman's Union Army to advance through Atlanta to the Georgia coast.

After the war, many victorious Union soldiers remained in the area. They joined in business with remnants of the defeated Confederates to lay a foundation for an industrial economy that lasted almost 100 years. The northern entrepreneurial spirit bonded with the remaining vestiges of southern class and society to create an industrial city touted as the Dynamo of Dixie. Ideally situated in the Moccasin Bend's gateway to the South and served by river, rail, and highways, Chattanooga became a 20th-century city of foundries, rolling mills, manufacturing, insurance, and railroads, which together fueled the flames of commerce and, as a side effect, created one of the most polluted cities in the United States.

In the last third of the 20th century, the region's economic foundation began to dissolve as production and jobs migrated from the old U.S. industrial centers. According to *Forbes* magazine, Chattanooga lost 10 percent of its population in the 1980s, as the foundation on which the economy had rested for more than a century disappeared. One by one, the foundries and mills shut down, passenger rail service ended, air service declined, and Chattanooga once again experienced a change of cultures. During the last decade of the 20th century, Chattanooga began to clean up its environment and modernize its economic base. The transformation resulted in Chattanooga becoming one of the few U.S. cities in the early 21st century to experience an economic resurgence. The city focused on making itself a pleasant place to live and work. With a multimillion-dollar aquarium as an anchor, the once-blighted downtown filled with restaurants, boutiques, and condominiums. Abandoned industrial sites were turned into parks. The city's population rebounded, employment increased, and the city's economic foundation grew stronger.

In 2002, Chattanooga's Chamber of Commerce adopted a long-range plan to attract target industries to replace the collapsed heavy industry. The plan targeted business and information services, food and beverage manufacturing, insurance services, and plastics manufacturing. Tourism-related businesses became increasingly important to the economy. Transportation surged with the development and modernization of freight centers. The University of Tennessee at Chattanooga's National Center for Computational Engineering, coupled with a business-friendly location and an increasingly environmentally conscious community, proved inviting to modern, high-tech industry and business. A noteworthy success in the strategy was Volkswagen's 2008 decision to locate its major U.S. factory in Chattanooga.

In 2008, in spite of a weakening national economy, the city's ability to change its economic base resulted in financial analysts describing the city's economy as evidence of a vibrant business climate. One analyst cited Chattanooga's economy as diverse and strong with potential for growth. The city's high fund balance was described as flexible enough to counter the country's economic downturn. In its assessment

of Chattanooga's budget, Standard & Poor's raised the city's debt rating from AA to AA-plus, praising Chattanooga's "continued economic growth and diversification, consistently strong financial position and well embedded management policies."

According to the U.S. Bureau of the Census, the population of Chattanooga–Hamilton County, Tenn., in 2007 was more than 330,000, and the population of the metropolitan statistical area (MSA) was more than 514,000. With its location on the Moccasin Bend, its interstate highway system, the railroads, river traffic, and environment friendly policies, modern Chattanooga, like its historic progenitor Ross's Landing, maintains itself as a gateway of commerce, trade, and lifestyle.

KITTRELL RUSHING
University of Tennessee at Chattanooga

Zella Armstrong, *The History of Hamilton County and Chattanooga, Tennessee* (1931); Dave Flessner, "S&P Upgrades City's Bond Rating," *Chattanooga Times Free Press* (6 December 2008); James W. Livingood, *Chattanooga: An Illustrated History* (1980); Henry Saxon, *Wall Street Journal* (2 December 2006); Jim Webb, *Born Fighting: How the Scots-Irish Shaped America* (2004); John Wilson, *Chattanooga's Story* (1980).

Church of God in Christ and Annual Convocation

The Church of God in Christ, commonly referred to as COGIC, is a predominantly African American religious denomination established in 1907. Memphis has long been the headquarters for this organization, the largest

Pentecostal Church body in the United States, and has hosted its annual convocation for one week each fall. An estimated 70,000 church members, known as saints, gathered in Memphis for the COGIC Convocation Centennial in 2007.

COGIC traces its origins to the 19th-century Holiness Movement. Although baptismal services were given under the name of Churches of God in Christ as early as 1897, COGIC really emerged 10 years later. In 1907, church founders Charles Price Jones and Charles Harrison Mason traveled to Los Angeles to attend the Azusa Street Revival, a meeting characterized by speaking in tongues and ecstatic worship. When they returned to Memphis, the two church leaders split over the fundamental issue of speaking in tongues, or "glossolalia." Jones did not consider the experience of baptism through glossolalia as scripturally sanctioned, but Mason, based on his own experiences at the Azusa Street Revival, believed that baptism accompanied by glossolalia was proof of sanctification. The two men

parted company, and Mason became the unchallenged head of the Churches of God in Christ.

What began as a regional organization, with churches in rural Mississippi, Arkansas, and Tennessee, spread throughout the United States during the Great Migration. During this period of American history, roughly 1910–30, millions of African Americans moved away from the South to seek greater economic opportunity and improved quality of life in the North, Midwest, and West. With this migration of COGIC members to urban areas outside the region, churches sprang up in St. Louis, Chicago, Detroit, and other locations. COGIC women, called church "mothers," took charge of policing the spiritual and secular lives of migrants, who faced new temptations in an urban environment. Through an autonomous organization, COGIC's Women's Department, women who took the lead in establishing rural southern religious practices in diverse urban settings also became responsible for "planting" churches throughout the United States.

One prominent church mother, Lillian Brooks Coffey, founded 11 congregations and is credited with being the first COGIC official to establish churches north of the Mason-Dixon line.

The COGIC has played an important role in African American civic life and has been associated with significant events in the civil rights movement. In 1955, when 14-year-old Emmett Till left Chicago to visit his family in Money, Miss., he stayed at the home of his great-uncle, Moses "Preacher" Wright, pastor of a local COGIC church. After Emmett Till's murder and the recovery of his mutilated and disfigured body, Till's mother had his body shipped to Chicago for funeral services at the Roberts Temple COGIC. For four days, thousands of mourners filed through the church to view Till's body. In 1965, the funeral of Malcolm X was held at Faith Temple COGIC in Harlem. In 1968, Mason Temple, the church's international headquarters in Memphis, was the site of Martin Luther King Jr.'s delivery of his final "I've Been to the Mountaintop" speech. He was fatally shot the next day.

Since the church's founding in 1907, COGIC has had enormous influence in both the secular and the religious spheres and claims more than 6.5 million members worldwide in more than 50 countries. The COGIC remains the largest Pentecostal church in North America, as well as the fastest-growing religious denomination in the United States.

KATHERINE A. WARREN
WANDA RUSHING
University of Memphis

Edith L. Blumhofer, *Restoring the Faith: The Assemblies of God, Pentecostalism, and American Culture* (1993); Anthea D. Butler, *Women in the Church of God in Christ: Making a Sanctified World* (2007); COGIC Publishing Board, *The Story of Bishop C. H. Mason and the Development of the Church of God in Christ* (video recording, 1993); James Dowd, *Memphis Commercial Appeal* (1 November 2008); Charles H. Pleas, *A Period in History of the Church of God in Christ* (1991); Stephen J. Whitfield, *A Death in the Delta* (1988).

CNN (Cable News Network)

Founded by former billboard magnate, accomplished yachtsman, and successful buffalo rancher Ted Turner, Atlanta-based Cable News Network (CNN) has established a worldwide and somewhat controversial media presence. Second only to the BBC in terms of sheer scale, it engendered the 24-hour television news revolution, giving rise to the "CNN effect."

A resident of Georgia since the age of nine, Turner has come to bear the nickname the "mouth of the South," for his ability to make hyperbolic statements and because his entire media empire was conceived and born in the region. From the relatively humble beginning of buying Atlanta's Channel 17, Turner had gradually gained access to satellite broadcasting by 1976. Four years later, CNN was created, retaining Turner's geographic base in Georgia but breaking entirely with the traditional format of news found on the dominant New York, Los Angeles, and international television networks.

A southern location, far from hampering Turner with any kind of provincialism, allowed him to innovate a new form of news media and to take advantage of the era of burgeoning satellite-based communications. His idea for CNN was simple: 24 hours of airtime were to be filled with "rolling" (repeating) news stories, and breaking news would be covered without delay. It was to be a "stop the presses" news organization, premised upon immediacy but with none of the physical impracticalities of print. By contrast, America's dominant television networks—CBS, ABC, and NBC—had dedicated news shows, filling the rest of their time with varied programming.

A system designed for flexibility paid off immediately when, on its inaugural day of 1 June 1980, CNN alone showed viewers Jimmy Carter's visit to Vernon Jordan, a civil rights leader hospitalized owing to a white supremacist assassination attempt. CNN again had the scoop in 1981 as the only live station broadcasting the address by President Reagan in the Washington Hilton, which ended with his being shot in the chest upon leaving the venue. In 1986, another major live event followed when CNN was the only station covering the launch of the *Challenger* space shuttle, when, 73 seconds after liftoff, it exploded, killing all seven crew members. The biggest scoop of all came in 1991, when CNN was initially the only news station to broadcast President George H. W. Bush's Gulf War from "within the trenches" (or at least atop the al-Rashid Hotel in Baghdad).

CNN's coverage in Iraq brought international attention to the new format of uninterrupted news broadcasts. The gap between a situation arising and images thereof being distributed was essentially destroyed, even if editorial mediation still took place. The immediacy of images of missiles raining down upon the Fertile Crescent had spectacular force. When French theorist Jean Baudrillard declared that the Gulf War did not take place and thus debated what "war" means in a remote control, computerized age, CNN in part helped to dispute his statement. The "war" had been broadcast live; it must therefore have taken place. The "CNN effect" of 24-hour live coverage impacted policy-making and its presentation. In Iraq, an old political tactic of gunboat diplomacy was transformed by CNN from a shadowy event reported several hours, even days later, into a Hollywood-like spectacle.

This unrelenting dispersal of information and images is CNN's legacy. Ted Turner's format has become so dominant that few major news-media groups are willing to forgo it, be it the BBC, al Jazeera, Bill Gates's MSNBC, or Turner's nemesis, Rupert Murdoch and his Fox News and Sky News stations. Turner always envisaged grandiose possibilities for the Atlanta-based CNN, however. Summarizing his original mission for the channel, with his trademark bombast, he stated shortly before its launch: "We won't be signing off until the world ends. We'll be on, and we will cover the end of the world, live, and that will be our last event."

JOHN GULLICK
University of Nottingham

Jean Baudrillard, *The Gulf War Did Not Take Place* (1995); Richard Hack, *Clash of the Titans: How the Unbridled Ambition of Ted Turner and Rupert Murdoch Has Created Global Empires That Control What We Read and Watch* (2003); Hank Whittemore, CNN: *The Inside Story* (1990).

Colonial Williamsburg, Virginia

Williamsburg, Va., has had two periods of urbanization since its founding. Both periods resulted from its being the late-colonial-period seat of government in England's largest and most prosperous colony.

In 1633, the House of Burgesses in Jamestown, 12 miles distant, encouraged the settlement and growth of what was then called Middle Plantation. The town grew in population as the cultivation of tobacco became more prosperous and colonists looked for better land than the mosquito-ridden swamps that nearly encircled Jamestown.

Williamsburg became a center for education in 1693 when the College of William and Mary was founded, and the seat of government moved from Jamestown in 1699 after the House of Burgesses building burned in 1698. Upon settlement, Middle Plantation was renamed Williamsburg in honor of King William III and served as the colonial capital during a period of rapid population, territorial, and economic growth. Legislators such as Thomas Jefferson, George Washington, Patrick Henry, and James Mason played central roles in the town's political events leading up to and during the America Revolution.

The town's population, never more than 2,000 permanent residents, grew exponentially when the House of Burgesses was in session. Many in government built their own houses, although most lodged and dined in the taverns. Local shops provided luxuries that were often not otherwise available in the largely rural colony. The college—and later the first psychiatric hospital established in the English colonies—added to the local economy.

Once chosen as the new capital, Williamsburg was formally surveyed and planned with wide avenues and, it has been argued, zoning of separate areas for residential and government/merchant sections of town. The original survey map shows it to be 220 acres in size. The classical architectural style, which favored geometry, symmetry, and formality, dominated the colonial era buildings; the George Wythe House and the Wren Building exemplify this style. Three hundred years later, 48 percent of modern Williamsburg is controlled by strict building codes that maintain the classical architecture.

After Governor Thomas Jefferson moved the capital to the village of Richmond in 1780, Williamsburg entered a period of accelerated economic decline, referred to as the "Rip Van Winkle" period. The faded town provoked one writer to note in 1816, "Indeed, if it weren't for the College, the Court, and the Lunatics, I don't know what would become of it." Even the college closed its doors between 1881 and 1888.

When the celebration of the tercentennial of Jamestown's founding in 1907 generated interest in historic preservation of the old capital, Williamsburg experienced its second period of urbanization. Rev. William Goodwin of Brewton Parish in Williamsburg successfully lobbied John D. Rockefeller to bankroll his vision of re-creating the 18th-century capital, a partnership that led to the creation of Colonial Williamsburg.

Today, the Colonial Williamsburg Foundation owns over 300 acres, including the original 220 acres that lie at the heart of the modern city. Since the late 1920s, almost 130 period buildings have been meticulously restored and numerous others have been rebuilt, establishing Colonial Williamsburg as a popular tourist destination and open-air classroom. In 2008, Colonial Williamsburg drew over 280,000 visitors, and the daily population in the city grows by as much as three times during the warm months. The small, historical, college-town quality of life has attracted a flood of new residents to the area, yet between 1990 and 2006 the city of Williamsburg's population increased by only 263 to 11,793. James City County, however, which borders Williamsburg on three sides, increased by 24,889, or 58 percent, over the same period.

The city is now 9.2 square miles. Strict building codes control 48 percent of the town, and another 39.5 percent is mandated as green space. Because of the limited amount of developable land, there is a lack of affordable housing within city limits, but efforts are currently under way to address this problem.

The economic foundations of present-day Williamsburg parallel its days as a capital city. Much of its 18th-century economy depended on visitors coming for the legislative session—living in rented rooms, dining in taverns, and buying things not available in the countryside. Today, tourism is Williamsburg's chief industry, followed by hospitality and retail. Over 9,300 hotel rooms exist within the Williamsburg area—almost one room for every resident. The Colonial Williamsburg Foundation manages hotels, restaurants, and City Center, the largest retail and dining area in town. Even with the surrounding counties growing quickly, through sound town planning, Williamsburg has largely insulated itself from the problems that stem from rapid growth.

WILLIAM S. BURDELL III
St. Simons Island, Georgia

Rhys Isaac, *The Transformation of Virginia, 1740–1790* (1999); Robert P. Maccubbin, *Williamsburg, Virginia: A City before the State, 1699–1999* (2000); Marcus Whiffen, *The Public Buildings of Williamsburg, Colonial Capital of Virginia: An Architectural History* (1958); George Humphrey Yetter, *Williamsburg Before and After: The Rebirth of Virginia's Colonial Capital* (1988).

Dallas, Texas

The city of Dallas is the seat of Dallas County in north-central Texas. The city's 385 square miles are divided northwest to southeast by the Trinity River, and several rail lines and major highways—I-20, I-30, I-35E, and I-45/U.S. 75—pass through Dallas, making it a hub for regional transportation and logistics. In addition, two airports (Dallas–Fort Worth, home of American Airlines, and Love Field, home of

Southwest Airlines) provide area residents with regional, national, and international service.

Founded in 1841 by John Neely Bryan at a crossing on the Trinity River, Dallas had fewer than 700 residents by 1860, but by 1890 it had grown to become — for the only time in its history — the largest city in Texas, with more than 38,000 citizens. Despite suffering the ravages of the national economic depression during the 1890s and a serious flood in 1908, Dallas reached a population of 92,104 in 1910.

Dallas cemented its role as a regional center when, in 1914, it became the site for a new federal reserve bank. When oil was discovered in east Texas in 1930, Dallas bankers expanded into petroleum financing. During the Depression, Dallas retained its role as a center for banking, insurance, textiles, and commerce. In 1931, the Highland Park Village became the nation's first shopping center.

During and after World War II, local defense-related industries stimulated regional economic growth. By 1950, Dallas's population reached 434,462, and its suburbs — which in earlier decades had been independent communities serving the surrounding farming areas — expanded in size and population along major highways out of the city. Banking, insurance, commerce, and textiles were joined by technology and real estate as key elements in the regional economy. Dallas's image suffered enormously when, on 22 November 1963, President John F. Kennedy was assassinated during a visit to the city.

Opening the Dallas–Fort Worth International Airport in 1974 marked the beginning of another era of economic expansion. Dallas's 1970 population of 844,401 grew to 1,007,618 by 1990 and was estimated to be 1,300,350 at the beginning of 2008. The city of Dallas contains more than half of the 2,451,800 residents of Dallas County and is the largest city in the 16-county metropolitan area (population 6,538,850). As a city, Dallas is ranked the ninth largest in the United States and is the major city in a metropolitan area with more than 6 million residents — the nation's fourth largest.

Dallas is economically heterogeneous, with both affluent neighborhoods (for example, the Park Cities and Preston Hollow) and poor (for example, the Fair Park area, South Dallas, and South Oak Cliff). Overall, the cost of living in Dallas is less than the national average, but so is the estimated median household income (about $42,000 versus the Texas state average of $48,000). Dallas is noteworthy for its wide range of shopping centers and high-end stores, especially Neiman-Marcus, founded in Dallas in 1907.

The city of Dallas is an ethnically diverse "majority minority" community, with 36 percent Latino (most of whom are of Mexican origin), 35 percent white non-Latino, 26 percent black, about 3 percent of Asian origin (especially from India, Korea, and Vietnam), and less than 1 percent American Indian. Dallas often is characterized as a place where the "haves" live north of the Trinity and the "have-nots" to the south. This is too simplistic a model for the city and region but does reflect histori-

A postcard from Dallas, Tex., with images depicting the city's urban landscape (Charles Reagan Wilson Collection, Center for the Study of Southern Culture, University of Mississippi)

cal prejudices grounded in old racial politics and uneven economic development between north and south Dallas.

Ethnic and class segregation permeate not only the city's neighborhoods but also its religious makeup—Dallas is not exempt from Martin Luther King's remark that "the most segregated hour" in Dallas is at 11:00 A.M. on Sundays. Sometimes called the "Buckle of the Bible Belt," Dallas long has been home to large Episcopal, Pentecostal, Presbyterian, and Baptist congregations, as well as to nondenominational megachurches (for example, the Potter's House). The Dallas diocese of the Catholic Church has more than 600,000 adherents, many of whom are recently arrived, Spanish-speaking immigrants. In recent years, the important role of "non-Western" immigrants has resulted in the construction of numerous mosques, temples, and similar worship centers.

Sports represent another "religion" for many Dallas inhabitants. The Dallas Cowboys (now located in a new stadium in suburban Arlington), the Texas Rangers (also located in Arlington), the Dallas Mavericks and the Dallas Stars (both in the American Airlines Center near downtown Dallas), and FC Dallas (with its home in suburban Frisco) represent the sports of football, baseball, basketball, hockey, and soccer, respectively. College sports are not a vital part of the Dallas sports scene, with only Southern Methodist University competing in NCAA Division I.

The city's educational system has felt the impact of ethnicity and religion. Very few schools in the Dallas Independent School District have student populations in proportion to the city's overall population. This is mainly a result of the unequal distribution of ethnic groups throughout the city but also reflects the preference of many Anglo parents to send their children to private, often church-operated, schools. As a result, in several areas of the city, the schools are more than 90 percent Latino.

Self-proclaimed as the "City That Works: Diverse, Vibrant, and Progressive," Dallas is the largest American city using the city manager/city council form of government. The city's leaders have developed master plans at several points over the past century, especially after the disastrous Flood of 1908. The current comprehensive plan, "Forward-Dallas!"—in effect since June 2006—focuses on education, public safety, the environment, transportation, and quality of life. In these and other areas, Dallas faces many problems, from improving the infrastructure of streets and schools to dealing with more than 6,000 homeless persons living in or near the central business district. As of 2009, no planning issue was as controversial as the project to construct bridges, roads, and parks in and around the Trinity River just west of downtown Dallas. In the wake of Hurricane Katrina, many Dallasites wonder about the wisdom of disturbing the current levee system.

The Trinity Project is the most recent effort by politicians and corporate leaders to demonstrate the "can-do" spirit of Dallas's 19th-century founders and 20th-century builders. Moving forward into the 21st century is proving to be as challenging as dealing with the 1908 Flood, the 1954 *Brown v. Board of Education* decision, and the 1963 assassination of President Kennedy. Even today, these historical events are still part of the fabric of life in Dallas.

ROBERT V. KEMPER
Southern Methodist University

Robert B. Fairbanks, *For the City as a Whole: Planning, Politics, and the Public Interest in Dallas, Texas, 1900–1965* (1998); Royce Hanson, *Civic Culture and Urban Change: Governing Dallas* (2003); Michael V. Hazel, *Dallas* (1997); Patricia Evridge Hill, *Dallas: The Making of a Modern City* (1996); Robert V. Kemper, ed., *Urban Anthropology and Studies of Cultural Systems and World Economic Development* (Summer/Fall 2005); Warren Leslie, *Dallas Public and Private: Aspects of an American City* (1964); Darwin Payne, *Big D: Triumphs and Troubles of an American Supercity in the 20th Century* (1994); Michael Phillips, *White Metropolis: Race, Ethnicity, and Religion in Dallas, 1841–2001* (2005).

Dollywood

Dollywood is located in the Great Smoky Mountains, nestled in the small town of Pigeon Forge, Tenn., in Sevier County. The Greater Pigeon Forge area is the third-largest destination for visitors to Tennessee. Dollywood mixes amusement rides with regional culture to provide a uniquely situated rural theme park in an urbanizing area. Although the park is named for its co-owner, Dolly Parton, this more-than-four-decades-old site was known in previous incarnations as the Rebel Railroad, Goldrush Junction, and Silver Dollar City.

Dollywood features 40 recurring attractions. Besides the obvious variety in these exhibits and rides—the different rides are marketed toward children, adults, or the whole family or are designed for water park or thrill ride situations—these attractions focus primarily on Dollywood's surrounding wildlife and geography, as evidenced by the Beaver Creek, Busy Bees, Calico Falls Schoolhouse, and the Thunderhead (Gap) rides. The names of several rides are also a nod to local culture, with sites such as the Robert F. Thomas Chapel (named after a beloved Sevierville doctor and where church services are performed) and the Smoky Mountain Home (a replica of Dolly Parton's childhood "Tennessee Mountain" house).

Beyond park rides and year-round attractions, Dollywood has diversified its activities, focusing on specific and special events. Dollywood's four most notable festivals, Smoky Mountain Christmas, National Gospel and Harvest Celebration, Kids Fest, and Festival of Nations, capitalize either on regional identification or the national/global worldview.

Smoky Mountain Christmas gathers together various secular and religious customs—local representations of southern traditions such as "Dolly's Christmas Chapel" and "Appalachian Christmas" festivities. The fall National Gospel and Harvest Celebration promises "four weeks featuring more than 250 free concerts" as well as traditional harvest offerings, such as autumn-oriented arts and crafts. Kids Fest, fulfilling childhood theme park wishes of pets and pictures, adds more animal displays and provides for more photo opportunities with "roving characters" like Miss Penny and Patches the Scarecrow. The spring Festival of Nations brings globe-spanning offerings to the rural park, presenting dance and vocal groups like Ecuador's Atahualpa band and the Zambia Vocal Group.

Dollywood was part of an economic tourist boom in Pigeon Forge beginning in the mid-1980s, which initially increased the town's revenue but eventually led to skyrocketing land prices and property taxes, which local farmers and other citizens who make their living off

working in the tourist industry could no longer afford. Nevertheless, the park is the largest employer in the area, providing approximately 1,000 jobs in peak season and half a billion dollars in payroll. Many of the park's employees are from Sevier County and surrounding areas. Some of the employees are "work campers"—retirees who travel and live in RVs, working in different parts of the country throughout the year.

As a result of Dollywood's ability to attract workers from surrounding counties, Sevierville, the Sevier County seat, which is approximately 13 minutes away from Pigeon Forge, now qualifies as an "urban cluster," while Sevier County is considered a "micropolitan" statistical area. Sevier County has a reciprocal relationship with the Knoxville metropolitan area. In 2003, while Sevier County had 6,522 citizens who worked in Knox County, it also had 1,634 in-county workers from Knox County.

Sevier County has increased in population in recent years, from 71,707 in 2000 to 84,835 in 2008 (Sevierville increased from 11,757 to over 13,000 during this period). According to the Sevier County Economic Development Council, the county is one of the fastest growing in Tennessee. Through the jobs offered at and because of Dollywood, such as tourist shops and local restaurants, Sevierville and Sevier County are both growing in importance and interdependence within the local region. Specifically, Sevierville, whose motels and hotels have occupancy for over 40,000 people, is clearly a locale geared toward tourism. Great Smoky Mountains attractions like Dollywood have seemingly provided the catalyst for the area's jump into urbanization. Eastern Tennessee has commodified its rural culture into touristic success, with both positive (more jobs) and negative (higher taxes) results for the region's residents.

RACHEL L. SMITH
MARY K. LEVIE
University of Memphis

Houston, Texas

Founded shortly after the Texas Revolution in 1836, Houston successfully marketed itself to gain regional, then national, economic and political dominance. The effort of city leaders to capitalize on the city's resources throughout Houston's lifetime has created opportunities that consistently pull a variety of people into the city, changing its culture and landscape.

During the 19th century, the fledgling town, built on Buffalo Bayou, became a commercial center as the 17 railroad lines that connected the city to the nation transported cotton, rice, and timber. White southerners and slaves (and freedmen after emancipation) primarily composed the city's population. Affluent citizens lived near the heart of the city and the poor lived in boardinghouses or on the fringes. Houstonians began altering Buffalo Bayou almost immediately, making it more navigable for trade. By 1915, the Ship Channel, Houston's inland deepwater port, was completed.

After the Civil War, with population topping 9,000, Houston's government turned its attention to solving urban problems such as epidemics, population growth, and new industries. This created a need for infrastructure, such as water systems, streets, streetcars, and electricity. Although clean drinking water was initially a challenge, Houston discovered it was atop one of the largest aquifers in the United States. Eventually, new infrastructure helped attract citizens and improve urban life. Unfortunately, the city did not find a satisfactory solution for floodwaters from the tropical storms and hurricanes that constantly plagued the city, a problem that continues today.

In 1901, the oil gusher Spindletop announced the massive east Texas oil fields, which quickly became the most important resource to the city. Production, refining, and the petrochemical industry drastically increased the number of people and businesses in Houston, changing the landscape and demographics. The oil rush also attracted new city leaders who contributed billions of dollars to cultural, medical, and educational institutions. These became important city centers, such as the Medical Center, the arts community, NASA, and all the universities in the city. Not until after the economic devastation of the oil glut in the 1980s did Houstonians begin to realize how important these secondary industries were to the diversity of Houston's economy.

After World War II, two major changes drove the postwar population boom: the petrochemical industry and air-conditioning. In the second half of the century, the population grew by almost a million and a half and the city limits extended to encompass over 600 square miles. Changes in infrastructure and government in the 19th century had provided Houston with mechanisms to cope with the boom, but the growth of highways made it possible for large numbers of people to migrate to the city and live in new suburban communities, which prevented overcrowding but caused sprawl. During the postwar housing boom that built the suburbs, builders began to build homes with air-conditioning. Air-conditioning opened up the South to many people who would not have migrated without it. Although the first suburb appeared at the beginning of the 20th century, it was not until after World War II that suburbs became so prevalent as to overtake the rice and cotton fields that provided the commerce on which Houston had initially gained regional economic power.

The influx of population combined with suburban building drastically altered Houston's landscape; the result was an escalation of existing infrastructure problems, annexation wars, pollution, and increased vulnerability to disaster, since Houstonians depended on electricity and air-conditioning to maintain their lifestyles. The loss of trees to suburban building deprived the city of important water-absorbing capacity and much-needed shade. Acres of new pavement increased flooding problems that sewers could not handle and provided a breeding ground for insects.

Postwar urbanization trends altered old communities and created new ones. After emancipation, Houston's African American community built a neighborhood to the northwest of town just south of the bayou. Freedman's Town became the center of the African American community until the 1940s and 1950s, when white flight and aggressive integration opened other housing options. It dissolved when the city built a major road through the remaining community. After World War II, Houston's gay, lesbian, bisexual, and transgender community began to emerge in a blighted neighborhood west of downtown among Houston's thriving art community in the Montrose neighborhood. Over the century, the neighborhood was transformed into one of the most sought-after urban communities in the city.

As the oil industry became international, so did Houston's population. Over the 20th century, people from all over the world came to Houston, and immigrant populations often settled in concentrations throughout the city. During the 1970s and 1980s, Midtown, just west of downtown, became the center of a thriving Vietnamese community. In the southwestern part of town (commonly called Uptown), one can find the most densely populated and highly diverse communities. Indian restaurants, home-style pizza places, sari stores, and Asian malls are crammed in with hundreds of apartment communities. Houstonians' ability to capitalize on what is available has attracted people and commerce and created networks of suburbs contributing to the urbanization of Texas's Gulf Coast.

STEPHANIE FUGLAAR
University of Houston

Marguerite Johnston, *Houston: The Unknown City, 1836–1946* (1991); David G. McComb, *Houston: A History* (1981); Martin V. Melosi and Joseph A. Pratt, *Energy Metropolis: An Environmental History of Houston and the Gulf Coast (2007); Harold L. Platt, *City Building in the New South* (1983); Robert D. Thomas and Richard W. Murray, *Progrowth Politics: Change and Governance in Houston* (1991).

Little Rock, Arkansas

In 1940, Little Rock, the capital city of Arkansas, had a population of 88,039, of which 25 percent was African American. At the turn of the 21st century, the city had a population of 183,133, of which 40 percent was African American. Little Rock's postwar growth and its racial makeup are two intertwined stories that have profoundly shaped the city's identity. As the African American population has grown, the city has become more geographically segregated along racial lines. In 1940, a study by the Greater Little Rock branch of the National Urban League noted, "While Negroes predominate in certain sections . . . in Little Rock there are . . . no widespread . . . 'Negro sections' [of residence]." In 1992, a study by Little Rock's Racial and Cultural Diversity Task Force noted that over 70 percent of the city's population lived "in either an area of white or African American isolation." African American neighborhoods predominated in the eastern and central areas of the city, while white neighborhoods predominated to the west and beyond into sprawling suburbs.

A catalyst for the racialization of Little Rock's residential patterns was the Housing Act of 1949 and its provision for slum clearance and urban renewal. As B. Finley Vinson, head of the Little Rock Housing Authority and its slum clearance and urban renewal director, put it, "The city of Little Rock through its various agencies . . . systematically worked to continue segregation." This became clear as African American neighborhoods were targeted for clearance and renewal as much for their racial composition as their slum status. Compounding the impact of these policies was the Interstate Highway Act of 1956. In the 1960s, this act led to the construction of Interstate 30, which formed a barrier between Little Rock's downtown and the African American east end of the city. The construction of an east-west expressway formed a barrier between African American and white working-class areas in the south of the city and the more affluent, exclusively white middle- and upper-class districts in the north and west. It also demolished part of Little Rock's downtown West Ninth Street, the historic African American business district, and cut it off from the city's African American Philander Smith College and its surrounding African American middle-class residential area.

The integration of Central High School in September 1957 led to conflict and crisis, which was only resolved when President Eisenhower federalized National Guard troops and sent in federal soldiers to escort nine African American students into the school.

In the 1960s and 1970s, 41,000 whites moved from east to west Little Rock, while 17,000 African Americans moved—or were moved—in the opposite direction. Schools have continued to provide a key indicator of racial trends. After the U.S. Supreme Court's 1971

The Little Rock, Ark., skyline (Photograph courtesy of the Department of Parks and Tourism, State Capitol, Little Rock, Ark.)

Swann v. Charlotte-Mecklenburg Board of Education decision permitted busing and race-based school assignments to combat the effects of white flight, the private Pulaski Academy in the white western suburbs was built for those, its patron William F. Rector said, who "don't like busing." By the 1990s, four out of 10 students in the white western suburbs attended private schools. A tipping point was finally reached in 2003 when the *Arkansas Democrat-Gazette* reported, "Little Rock has become a city of mostly black public schools and mostly white private schools."

Recent events have opened up a new chapter in the city's history. In 1996, the River Market District development began to revitalize the downtown area. The headquarters of the charity foundation Heifer International and the

William Jefferson Clinton Presidential Library are located nearby. The presidential library was caught up in the controversy over city planning when the original architects' plans seemed to have the building turning its back on downtown and African American neighborhoods. The architects eventually rotated the plans for the building 90 degrees to address the problem. How the latest surge of renewal and regeneration plays out promises to shape the city's development and race relations into the 21st century.

JOHN A. KIRK
Royal Holloway, University of London

Ben F. Johnson III, *Arkansas in Modern America, 1930–1999* (2000), in *An Epitaph for Little Rock: A Fiftieth Anniversary Retrospective on the Central High Crisis*, ed. John A. Kirk (2008); John A. Kirk, *Beyond*

Little Rock: The Origins and Legacies of the Central High Crisis (2007), *Redefining the Color Line: Black Activism in Little Rock, Arkansas, 1940–1970* (2002); University Task Force on the Little Rock School District, *Plain Talk: The Future of Little Rock's Public Schools* (1997); Works Project Administration, *Survey of Negroes in Little Rock and North Little Rock, Compiled by the Writers' Program of the Work Project Administration in the States of Arkansas* (1941).

Little Rock Nine

The "Little Rock Nine" is the collective term used to describe nine African American students who desegregated Central High School in Little Rock, Ark., in September 1957, thus helping to define the civil rights movement. Their efforts to test the 1954 *Brown v. Board of Education* U.S. Supreme Court decision led to federal soldiers being sent to the city to protect the students. Federal intervention at Little Rock dealt a blow to "massive resistance" campaigns opposing desegregation. The episode, covered on American television, made international news headlines at the time and remains a symbol of racial conflict and reconciliation. At the 40th anniversary in 1997, President Bill Clinton, former governor of Arkansas, recognized the significance of the event for the state and the nation and celebrated the Little Rock Nine. The nine students were Ernest Green, at 17 the only senior in the group; Minnijean Brown and Thelma Mothershed, both 16; Elizabeth Ann Eckford, Melba Pattillo, Gloria Ray, Terrance Roberts, and Jefferson Thomas, all 15; and Carlotta Walls, 14.

The nine students were chosen to integrate Central High by Little Rock superintendent of schools Virgil T. Blossom. After the court ruling, Blossom formulated a plan for minimum compliance with the law. Part of this plan involved building new high schools to reflect the increasingly racially separate African American and white residential areas in the city. Horace Mann High School was built in the African American east end of the city, and Hall High School was built in the affluent white suburbs of the west. Downtown Central High School was chosen as the sole school to integrate in September 1957. Dismayed by the perceived reluctance to implement a desegregation program immediately, the local NAACP branch filed suit, in *Aaron v. Cooper* (1956). The courts upheld Little Rock's desegregation plan on the grounds that it operated within the "with all deliberate speed" guidelines issued by the U.S. Supreme Court in May 1955.

By the time that Blossom had submitted around 200 African American applicants to desegregate to a rigorous selection process, either forcing candidates to withdraw or persuading them to withdraw voluntarily, only nine African American students remained. President of the Arkansas NAACP state conference of branches Daisy Bates acted as their mentor and liaison with the NAACP's national office. The day before Central High was due to desegregate, Governor Orval Faubus surrounded the school with National Guard troops. Although Faubus claimed this was simply to preserve the peace, when the African American students tried to enter Central High the state troops stopped them. Faubus was finally persuaded to remove the soldiers by President Dwight D. Eisenhower. However, when the soldiers left, a white mob gathered that forced school officials to remove the African American students from the school for their own safety. Eisenhower then federalized the National Guard and sent in federal soldiers to escort the nine students into Central High.

An armed escort for the students remained in place throughout the school year. The attention of segregationists turned to forcing the nine students to withdraw from the school voluntarily. Over the ensuing weeks, the NAACP noted, they were subject to "threatening notes, verbal insults and threats, crowding, bumping and jostling in the halls." On 17 December 1957, Minnijean Brown was expelled for reacting to the torments of white students. No white students were ever expelled for their actions. With the help of the NAACP's national office and African American psychologist Kenneth B. Clark, Brown received a scholarship to attend New Lincoln High School in New York. The eight remaining students survived the school year, and in May 1958 Ernest Green became the first African American to graduate from Central High. The following year, Faubus closed all of the city's schools to prevent integration. Only when the city's white professional elite mobilized to take control of the school board did the city's schools open on a token integrated basis, in August 1959.

In 1958, the Little Rock Nine and Daisy Bates won the NAACP's Spingarn Medal. In 1999, the Little Rock Nine were awarded the Congressional Gold Medal. In 2007, the United States Mint made a commemorative silver dollar as a tribute to the courage displayed by the nine.

The 50th anniversary in 2007 demonstrated the mixed legacy of the Central High crisis. A monthlong commemoration program culminated in a speech by former U.S. president Bill Clinton on the steps of Central High. This underscored the political transformations in the South and the nation that had taken place since 1957. However, earlier that same year, the courts finally declared the Little Rock School District unitary and released it from their oversight and monitoring for the first time since 1957. During the intervening years, largely because of white flight from the city, the school district's population has been transformed from a 25 percent African American minority to a 24 percent white minority. There are still clearly defined African American and white schools in the city. All–African American and all-white classes are still taught inside Central High School. Despite the political changes that have taken place, in practical terms Little Rock schools remain racially divided.

The Little Rock Nine helped to define Little Rock's image for a generation. Their experiences affected how other southern urban areas approached school desegregation, influencing some school boards to desegregate to avoid violence. By contrast, many rural and small-town public schools in the South did not integrate until the early 1970s.

JOHN A. KIRK
Royal Holloway, University of London

Daisy Bates, *The Long Shadow of Little Rock: A Memoir* (1962); Melba Pattillo Beals, *Warriors Don't Cry: A Searing Memoir of the Battle to Integrate Little Rock's Central High* (1994); Virgil T. Blossom, *It Has Happened Here* (1959); Wiley A. Branton, *Journal of Negro Education* (Summer 1983); Tony A. Freyer, *Little Rock on Trial: Cooper v. Aaron and School Desegregation* (2007); Elizabeth Jacoway, *Turn Away Thy Son: Little Rock, the Crisis That Shocked the Nation* (2007); Elizabeth Jacoway and C. Fred Williams, eds., *Understanding the Little Rock Crisis: An Exercise in Remembrance and Reconciliation* (1999); John A. Kirk, *Beyond Little Rock: The Origins and Legacies of the Central High Crisis* (2007), *Redefining the Color Line: Black Activism in Little Rock, Arkansas, 1940–1970* (2002); John A. Kirk, ed., *An Epitaph for Little Rock: A Fiftieth Anniversary Retrospective on the Central High Crisis* (2008); Catherine M. Lewis and J. Richard Lewis, eds., *Race, Politics, and Memory: A Documentary History of the Little Rock School Crisis* (2007); Brent Renaud and Craig Renaud, directors, *Little Rock Central High: 50 Years Later* (HBO Home Video, 2007); Rob Thompson, director, *Journey to Little Rock: The Untold Story of Minnijean Brown Trickey* (Ottawa, Canada: North-East Productions, 2001).

Louisville, Kentucky

Founded in 1778 by George Rogers Clark, Louisville quickly became a bustling settlement primarily because of its proximity to the Ohio River. However, cultural city institutions were slow to take root. For example, when the University of Louisville opened in 1837, the first public school had just been launched a few years earlier, in 1829. As Clyde F. Crews states, "The earliest priorities of Louisville were commercial and political."

Although the arts and education were not initial priorities for the city, clearly present-day Louisville prides itself on cultivating the cultural side of urban life, with its focus on higher education and artistic affairs. Because of its higher learning institutions, Louisville has a college student population of more than 40,000 people, and organizations and foundations such as the Kentucky Opera, Louisville Ballet, Kentucky Center for the Arts, and the Bach Society have prominence on the city's downtown scene.

The Kentucky Derby is Louisville's best-known sports event and cultural institution. The event, held the first Saturday in May at the Churchill Downs racetrack, is a thoroughbred horse race, the first leg of the U.S. Triple Crown of Thoroughbred Racing. It is often referred to nationally as "The Fastest Two Minutes in Sports." The Kentucky Derby festival is held two weeks prior to the event, culminating in the race, and is the largest single annual event in the city. The race is enjoyed by individuals from all backgrounds, including those who buy general admission for the infield spectator area and those who watch the race from "Millionaire's Row," the expensive box seats for the rich and powerful. Since the 1920s, Stephen Foster's "My Old Kentucky Home" has been sung when the horses are led to the post parade.

The local economy first developed in the shipping and cargo industries because of Louisville's geographic location in the central United States and its proximity to the Falls of the Ohio, the only natural obstacle in the Ohio River. Shipping is also important in the present-day economy—United Parcel Service (UPS) has a global hub at the Louisville International Airport. More recently the local economy has developed in the health-care industries, making important contributions to heart and hand surgeries and cancer treatments. Humana, one of the largest health insurance companies in the country, is headquartered in Louisville. The city is also the producer of one-third of the world's bourbon whiskey.

Louisville consolidated its city and county governments in 2003, merging the former city of Louisville with Jefferson County. Consolidation was largely supported because voters believed it would positively affect the economy, based on perceptions of what had occurred in the neighboring cities of Nashville, Jacksonville, and Indianapolis after consolidation. This city-county consolidation was the first large one to occur in an American city in 30 years and has attracted much national interest. The city government consists of the Louisville Metro Council, a 26-seat legislative body, and the mayor of Louisville Metro. Current mayor Jerry Abramson had served as mayor of the city before the consolidation and is a big promoter of the benefits it has brought to the city, including streamlining services, forging more effective partnerships, saving money, and fostering "bigger-picture" planning and thinking.

The population of the consolidated city and county of Louisville as of the 2000 census was 693,604 people; the population of the city of Louisville before the consolidation was 245,315. The racial breakdown of the consolidated population is 77.38 percent white, 18.88 percent African American, 1.78 percent Latino, 0.22 percent American Indian, 1.39 percent Asian, 0.04 percent Pacific Islander, 0.68 percent from other races, and 1.42 percent from two or more races.

Louisville is ranked one of the safest cities in the country, reporting the fifth-lowest crime rate in the United States. The city has less total crime and violent crime than other cities its size. Like urban areas in many former border states, Louisville has had a complex relationship with racial inequality, slavery, and segregation. During the 1840s, both slave sales and abolition meetings took place at the courthouse, a striking example of Louisville's border status. Although Union forces essentially occupied Kentucky during the Civil War, the city demonstrated Confederate sympathies. Beginning in the late 1880s, Louisville policies and sympathies increasingly matched other southern states, which included a whites-only city library system until 1950 and segregated, unequal housing policies until 1960.

Some scholars argue that the Great Migration played an important part in Louisville's development in the early part of the 20th century. Luther Adams argued that "though the city was something of a 'way-station' to the North for some migrants, Louisville became a final destination for many African Americans." In fact, according to Adams, because of Louisville's border state location and a higher black population than in other areas of Kentucky, the African American migration urbanization experience is perhaps more complex than previously thought: for many black people, the move to Louisville (from a southern rural area or from another southern city) was confusing and exciting, frightening and joyful.

African Americans have gained significant economic and political power in present-day Louisville, although there are still many who live in poverty and the city is highly segregated. There has been extensive effort within the city to desegregate the public schools system, but with high levels of residential segregation this process continues to be difficult. Louisville's journey from rural lakeside settlement to thriving urban center has been heavily influenced by the Ohio River, which serves as the border between the North and the South.

MARY K. LEVIE
RACHEL L. SMITH
University of Memphis

Luther Adams, *Journal of Social History* (Winter 2006); Clyde F. Crews, in *Spirited City: Essays in Louisville History* (1995); H. V. Savitch, Takashi Tsukamoto, and Ronald K. Vogel, *Journal of Urban Affairs* (Number 4, 2008).

Mardi Gras

Mardi Gras, literally "Fat Tuesday," is a pre-Lenten holiday celebrated in February or March before Ash Wednesday. Coastal Gulf cities, originally settled by French and Spanish Catholics, were the first cities in the United States to celebrate Mardi Gras, with parades, private parties, and masking. These 18th-century celebrations evolved into impromptu street processions and organized societies that, by the prosperous antebellum era, became sponsored parades and exclusive balls. It is the most prominent urban festival in the South.

In 1830, businessmen in Mobile, Ala., organized the Cowbellion de Rakin Society as a masked parading club. The Cowbellions introduced mule-drawn floats in 1840, a tradition that lasted throughout the region until the introduction of tractors and electric lighting in the 1950s. In 1857, transplants from Mobile established a parading society in New Orleans named the Krewe of Comus (from the Greek *komos*, meaning "revelers"). The term "krewe" remains popular and reflects the mythical themes often depicted by floats. New Orleans quickly received the bulk of national publicity, given its large population, the reach of Mississippi River traffic, and the emergence of extravagant krewes such as Rex, Momus, and Proteus in the 1870s and 1880s.

Suspended during the Civil War, Mardi Gras celebrations revived by the late 1860s, as parade societies ridiculed Republican officials and Reconstruction. Joe Cain rekindled festivities in Mobile. The oldest surviving organization in Mobile is the Order of Myths, established in 1867. The emergence of Carnival royalty in Mobile and New Orleans, with each organization usually selecting a king, queen, and dukes, suggested white racial purity and the persistence of white supremacy. Parades also advertised the economic resilience of postwar southern cities. Galveston, Memphis, and other cities in the South developed Mardi Gras celebrations to capitalize on the festival, although most survived only a few years. The Mobile, Galveston, and, particularly, New Orleans Carnivals emerged as major tourist events.

As Prohibition threatened Carnival hedonism and as automobiles made travel easier, New Orleans boosters during the 1920s democratized the festivities by encouraging masking at costume contests and public balls, exploiting new film and radio technologies and fostering new krewes that extended the parading season to a week before Mardi Gras. Organizations began throwing glass beads to encourage interaction within the crowd. Aluminum doubloons, introduced in the 1960s, and, from the 1970s, plastic beads and cups became standard throws. In Mobile, parade throws include Moon Pies (southern snacks), as well as candies, beads, and trinkets.

Three megakrewes hosting prominent national celebrities—Endymion (founded 1966), Bacchus (founded 1968), and Orpheus (founded 1993)—now dominate weekend festivities before Mardi Gras. Smaller cities, including Mobile, Biloxi, and Galveston, foster a more community-oriented, family-atmosphere Mardi Gras celebration than that of New Orleans, which is more permissive of public drinking and nudity within the city proper. Allegedly inspired by Buffalo Bill's Wild West show during the 1880s, working-class blacks in New Orleans created neighborhood-oriented "tribes" that pay homage to Indians' resistance to white authority as well as the mingling of Indian and African bloodlines. Today, these tribes, numbering over 20, include the Wild Tchoupitoulas and Creole Wild West. A Big Chief heads each hierarchical tribe. On Mardi Gras, the tribes don feathered and beaded outfits reminiscent of Indian dress. The suits are handcrafted in the months leading up to the holiday. The tribes conduct an informal parade, with dancing, singing in a call-and-response format, and the shouting of stock phrases like "iko iko" and "jockomo feena nay." Founded in 1909, the Krewe of Zulu, which began parading in 1914, is the oldest African American krewe. Formed from the black middle class, they parody stereotypes of Africans as primitive by wearing blackface, donning grass skirts, and tossing decorated coconuts.

Since the civil rights movement of the 1960s, organizations have largely abandoned discriminatory membership policies targeting blacks and Jews in order to receive public parade permits. Gays have become increasingly visible as well. Although organizations remain predominantly black, white, or divided by sex, Mardi Gras today represents the greater openness and diversity of the urban South.

ANTHONY J. STANONIS
Queen's University Belfast

Kevin Fox Gotham, *Authentic New Orleans: Tourism, Culture, and Race in the Big Easy* (2007); Samuel Kinser, *Carnival, American Style: Mardi Gras at New Orleans and Mobile* (1990); Reid Mitchell, *All on a Mardi Gras Day: Episodes in the History of New Orleans Carnival* (1995); Ann Pond, "The Ritualized Construction of Status: The Men Who Made Mardi Gras, 1830–1900" (Ph.D.

diss., University of Southern Mississippi, 2006); Mark Souther, *New Orleans on Parade: Tourism and the Transformation of the Crescent City* (2006); Anthony J. Stanonis, *Creating the Big Easy: New Orleans and the Emergence of Modern Tourism, 1918–1945* (2006), *Southern Cultures* (Summer 2008); Robert Tallant, *Mardi Gras* (1949).

Memphis, Tennessee

Memphis, founded in 1819 on the east bank of the Mississippi River, is located in the southwest corner of Tennessee. Historically, the city's advantageous riverfront location on the Fourth Chickasaw Bluff was controlled first by the Chickasaws, then occupied by Spanish soldiers, and then by U.S. soldiers. It was then ceded to the United States and opened as a gateway for western expansion. Andrew Jackson, James Winchester, and John Overton founded the city of Memphis on 5,000 acres they had purchased in the 1790s. The bluff city, where the state boundaries of Tennessee, Arkansas, and Mississippi converge, developed as a center of transportation and distribution in the Mid-South. Midway between New Orleans and St. Louis, the city supplied thousands of towns and plantations in a multistate delta region including the Mississippi Delta, the Arkansas Delta, the Louisiana Delta, the Missouri Bootheel, and western Tennessee. As a center of cotton production and trade, Memphis became the home of the largest cotton warehouses in the world, the largest inland cotton market in the world, the largest producer of cottonseed products in the world, the largest hardwood market in the United States, and the nation's second-largest pharmaceutical market and third-largest grocery market. Today, as the headquarters of Federal Express and home of the busiest cargo airport in the world, Memphis occupies a unique status as a distribution center in the global economy. But the city is also identified with innovative popular music—blues, rock and roll, and soul—as well as racial tensions and bitter conflicts associated with the 1968 Sanitation Workers Strike and the assassination of civil rights leader Dr. Martin Luther King Jr.

The city's central east-west geographic location in the continental United States and its north-south location equidistant between Toronto, Canada, and Monterrey, Mexico, have been enhanced by nearly 200 years of investment in the city's transportation infrastructure. A confluence of transportation routes—river, rail, interstate, and air—connects Memphis and its concentration of logistics industry providers to global markets. The port of Memphis, the largest still-water harbor on the Mississippi River and the fourth-largest inland port in the United States, serves as a vital link in the 2,600-mile inland waterway connecting the United States to Mexico via the Mississippi River and the Gulf of Mexico. The city is the third-largest rail center in the United States and operates as a hub for five U.S. Class I railroads: Burlington Northern–Santa Fe, Canadian National, CSX, Union Pacific, and Norfolk Southern. All major truck lines operate in Memphis. The Bluff City now claims the title of North America's Distribution Center.

The entrance to AutoZone Park in downtown Memphis, Tenn., the home of the Memphis Redbirds
(Photograph courtesy of David Wharton)

The incorporated city of Memphis, with its population of 672,277, ranks as the 17th-largest city in the United States and the largest city in Tennessee. The city's 63 percent African American population is conspicuously different from a Tennessee state population that is 80 percent white. Beyond the city's incorporated boundaries, the Memphis Metropolitan Statistical Area (MSA) is the second largest in Tennessee, behind first-ranked Nashville-Davidson. As of 2005, the Memphis MSA population of 1,260,905 was 45 percent African American. The Memphis MSA ranked fifth nationally in percentage of population that is African American. According to census projections, in the near future metropolitan Memphis will become the first large metropolitan area in the United States populated by an African American majority.

It has been said that no other city in the South "derives its sustenance and character so completely or from such a large area of farm lands and little towns." Yet, remarkably, the music rural migrants brought with them, as transformed by urban experiences and technology, became the global popular music of the mid-20th century. Elvis Presley, Johnny Cash, Rufus Thomas, B. B. King, Isaac Hayes, Otis Redding, and the Staples singers are but a few of the world-renowned musicians who came through Memphis. Elvis Presley's home, Graceland, as well as Beale Street, Sun Studio, Stax, and other landmarks attract millions of tourists to the city. The city is also identified with the 21st-century cultural innovation of rap artists and filmmakers, including Academy Award winners Three Six Mafia and Craig Brewer.

Beale Street and downtown Memphis suffered after the 1968 assassination of Dr. Martin Luther King Jr. at the Lorraine Motel during the Sanitation Workers Strike. More than 40 years later, following years of conflict, urban renewal, and white flight, progress has been made toward community reconciliation. The National Civil Rights Museum, built on the site of the Lorraine Motel, commemorates the civil rights movement and honors the struggle for human rights around the world. A downtown resurgence of residences, restaurants, hotels, art galleries, nightspots, and sports arenas welcomes residents and visitors to a revitalized downtown. An emerging biotechnology industry also is centered downtown and supported by the city's transportation and logistics infrastructure. Participants and supporters include the University of Tennessee Health Science Center, the University of Memphis, Baptist Memorial Health Care, Methodist Le Bonheur Healthcare, Veterans Hospital, Campbell Clinic, FedEx, AutoZone, St. Jude Children's Research Hospital, Hyde Family Foundations, Plough Foundation, and biomedical device manufacturers Smith, & Nephew, Wright Medical, and Medtronic Sofamor Danek.

WANDA RUSHING
University of Memphis

Robert Gordon, *It Came from Memphis* (1995); Peter Hall, *Cities in Civilization: Culture, Innovation, and Urban Order* (1998); Shields McIlwaine, *Memphis Down in Dixie* (1948); Wanda Rushing, *Memphis and the Paradox of Place: Globalization in the American South* (2009); U.S. Census Bureau, *County and City Data Book: 2007,* Table C-1, 728, and Table D-2, 844; U.S. Census Bureau, *State and Metropolitan Area Data Book: 2006,* Table C-1, 197, Table B-1, 123, and Tables E-14, E-19.

Miami, Florida

Miami is the central city in a three-county south Florida metropolitan area of 5.4 million people that stretches more than 100 miles along the Atlantic coastline. The city of Miami itself is a relatively small and compact urban center of 410,000 people, a small fraction of Miami–Dade County's population of 2.4 million. The city traces its origins to the 1890s, when land speculators and urban boosters, primarily business magnate Henry M. Flagler, began promoting tourism in southern Florida. Essentially a 20th-century city, Miami began as a distant frontier outpost, emerged quickly as a tourist and vacation paradise, and eventually morphed into a vibrant Sunbelt metropolis and then, by the end of the century, into a multicultural global city. More than most American cities, Miami has been continuously transformed over time by powerful forces for change, including depression, war, race, internal migration, immigration, technology, environmentalism, and government policy. Rarely out of the national spotlight, Miami has maintained its allure in good times and bad.

Flagler, a millionaire oilman and railroad builder, completed his Florida East Coast Railway from Jacksonville to Miami in 1896. Within months, he established a newspaper, calling it the *Miami Metropolis*, and then poured money into streets, utilities, port facilities, and luxurious hotels, subsidizing the transformation of the south Florida frontier. Other builders, boosters, and promoters followed in the 1910s and 1920s, pushing Miami and the nearby communities of Miami Beach, Coral Gables, and Hialeah into boom conditions. Real estate speculation peaked in 1926, after which the south Florida boom fizzled for a few years, but Miami's image as a sunny winter retreat had been firmly embedded in the national consciousness. Building on its essential natural resources of sunshine, seashore, and subtropical climate and despite the Great Depression, Miami emerged as one of the fastest-growing metropolitan areas in the nation between 1920 and 1940. Miami always has had a sizable black population, including large numbers of black immigrants from the Bahamas, and the African American population increases kept pace with the white population through most of the 20th century.

World War II brought significant change to Miami, pushing the local economy beyond tourism, service industries, and regional agriculture. The federal government established numerous military bases and training facilities in the Miami area, investing heavily as well in new infrastructure, including vast expansion of Miami's airport and seaport facilities. Service and construction jobs attracted thousands of civilian workers, and after the war they were joined by additional thousands of veterans who had trained in the Miami area and now returned as permanent residents. As the city's population grew, real estate developers subdivided and built up the urban periphery. The rising affluence of Americans, monthly social security checks for retirees, the postwar expansion of air travel, and the widespread adoption of air-conditioning in the 1950s strengthened Miami's place as a retirement haven and the nation's top tourist destination. Miami–Dade County's 1960 population of 935,000 doubled the 1950 total.

By the 1950s, northern migration to Miami and Miami Beach left big demographic change in its wake. The Miami area's Jewish population rose dramatically, from 8,000 in 1940 to 140,000 in 1960. Liberal Jews challenged Miami's entrenched pattern of racial segregation. They worked with black activists in civil rights organizations such as the NAACP and the Congress of Racial Equality in voter-registration campaigns and lunch-counter sit-ins. Miami's postwar demographic transformation also contributed reformist energy to the creation of a powerful metropolitan government for Miami–Dade County in 1957. The first of its kind in the nation and still in existence at the beginning of the 21st century, this two-tier municipal system diminished the political influence of the city of Miami but promised, and mostly delivered, effective government to Miami–Dade County.

The half-century after 1960 brought still greater change and bigger challenges to Miami. Race relations, never very good in the days of segregation, bubbled to the surface in several racial disturbances in 1968, 1980, and the 1990s. A massive exodus to the United States of almost 1 million Cuban exiles and refugees between 1959 and 2000, most of whom settled in the Miami area, permanently altered the city's character and culture. They built an enclave economy and eventually came to dominate city and county politics. Other Latino exile and immigrant groups followed, including Nicaraguans, Colombians, Dominicans, and others. As of 2007, Latinos made up 69 percent of the city of Miami's population and 62 percent of Miami–Dade County's population. At 20 percent of the total, metro Miami's black population has also grown rapidly through the arrival of several hundred thousand Haitian exiles and black immigrants from all over the Caribbean. By 1990, non-Latino whites had become a minority in the Miami metro population, and that demographic revolution intensified in subsequent decades. In 2007, non-Latino whites in Miami–Dade County made up 18 percent of total population. More than 70 percent of the county's residents spoke a language other than English at home, mostly Spanish.

As Cuban, Caribbean, and Latin American exiles and immigrants poured into the Miami area after 1960, the city emerged as the business and cultural capital of the entire Caribbean basin, finally fulfilling the booster claims of the 1920s and 1930s that Miami was the "gateway to Latin America." Miami became a major center of international trade and banking by the 1980s. As air cargo and container-laden freighters headed south with American products, foreign investment flowed into Miami, along with the profits of a lucrative illegal drug trade. New skyscraper development in the central business district and high-rise waterfront condominiums dominate the city's 21st-century skyline. Miami no longer attracts many vacationers from the rest of the United States, but greater numbers of European and Latin American tourists have been flocking to south Florida's beaches, golf courses, nightclubs, and shopping malls. In its relatively short history, powerful currents of change have buffeted Miami. From its early tourist beginnings in the 1890s, Miami has become a 21st-century global city, shaped by its distinctive geographical location and marked by vibrant international networks, diverse immigrant connections, and a worldwide image as glamorous multicultural metropolis. Needless to say, Miami has always been an anomaly in the American South.

RAYMOND A. MOHL
University of Alabama at Birmingham

Marvin Dunn, *Black Miami in the Twentieth Century* (1997); Maria Cristina Garcia, *Havana USA: Cuban Exiles and Cuban Americans in South Florida, 1959–1994* (1996); David B. Longbrake and Woodrow W. Nichols Jr., *Sunshine and Shadows in Metropolitan Miami* (1976); Raymond A. Mohl, *South of the South: Jewish Activists and the Civil Rights Movement in Miami, 1945–1960* (2004); Deborah Dash Moore, *To the Golden Cities: Pursuing the American Jewish Dream in Miami and L.A.* (1994); Alejandro Portes and Alex Stepick, *City on the Edge: The Transformation of Miami* (1993); Melanie Shell-Weiss, *Coming to Miami: A Social History* (2009); Edward Sofen, *The Miami Metropolitan Experiment* (1966).

Mobile, Alabama

Founded by the French in 1702, Mobile is Alabama's oldest city and only port. The city's history has been inextricably tied to the development of its port facilities and the economic prosperity of the adjoining hinterland. For three centuries, precious cargo from northern Alabama and Mississippi has traveled through Mobile.

Colonial Mobile was a city of limited size and potential, due in no small part to the stagnant economic prospects of the French, and later Spanish, settlements in the New World. By the time Mobile became an American city in 1813, its population had already become multicultural, a trait that would distinguish it throughout history. Yet American investment provided Mobile with much-needed capital to make improvements and strengthened its economic standing. New building projects began, and by the 1820s the city was established as an exporting center for Alabama and the South to markets in the Northeast and Europe. Cotton proved to be the most profitable export of antebellum Mobile, and the city's economic fortunes prospered, along with the wealthy plantations of the interior region.

The Civil War brought an end to Mobile's prosperity as a federal blockade stifled foreign trade. The city was spared the devastation of southern ports like Charleston and New Orleans, but in late May 1865 a waterfront armory with 200 tons of ordinance exploded, killing 300 workers and devastating the waterfront facilities. The city was forced to rebuild a large portion of its port, which slowed its postwar recovery.

The early years of the New South were unkind to Alabama's port city. The population decreased as the cotton-dependent economy languished in a postwar malaise. In 1879, the Alabama legislature repealed the city's charter to save the area from economic ruin. The repeal lasted until 1886, by which time timber had replaced cotton as the chief export and municipal improvements signaled that the city was recovering. As Mobile prepared for the 20th century, it increased its imports of bananas from South America and made plans to deepen its shipping channel.

A combination of Progressive era politics and Victorian morality contributed to Mobile's development in the early 20th century. Streetcar and telephone service expanded, and the city adopted the commission form of government in 1911. Numerous saloons and brothels closed as religious citizens applied Christian ethics to the city's social problems by spreading the Social Gospel. Yet progress was again hampered by war, and when the British government recalled its ships for wartime service, Mobile's port once again grew stagnant. American entry into World War I provided jobs in Mobile's shipbuilding facilities. Yet the need for wartime industrialization exposed a major problem of the city's industrial development. Following the war, Mobile's wealthy businessmen invested heavily in port improvements and lobbied for the creation of the Alabama State Docks.

Mobilization during World War II transformed Mobile into a shipbuilding city. The city quickly became the most crowded city in America, and tensions rose as workers, white and black, fought over contested space and jobs. In 1941, the U.S. Army opened Brookley Field, an air supply depot that would be the city's largest postwar employer for two decades. The closure of the base in the 1960s contributed to Mobile's stagnating economy.

Mobile was spared the violent protests of its northern neighbors Montgomery, Birmingham, and Selma during the civil rights movement. In Mobile, two local grassroots organizations, the Non-Partisan Voters' League and later the Neighborhood Organized Workers, exerted influence on city politics. The league initiated several important legal suits, including *Bolden v. Mobile*, which held that the at-large election of representatives was inherently discriminatory to minorities, and the desegregation suit for Mobile's public schools, which was one of the longest-running cases of its kind. Throughout the 20th century, Mobile maintained a carefully cultivated aura of respectability and was home to such cultural rituals as the Azalea Trail, the American Junior Miss Pageant, and Mardi Gras. Mobile's Mardi Gras, the first in North America, continues to be a deeply segregated event with only a smattering of integrated mystic societies.

In recent years, large industrial development has characterized the area around Mobile, including the Tennessee-Tombigbee Waterway and natural gas platforms along the coast. In 2007, the German steel corporation Thyssen-Krupp announced plans to build a $3 billion facility north of the city, the largest single investment in the United States in that year. Mobile continues to be dependent upon the port facility for the majority of its economic prosperity and is fueled by a sense of optimism not seen since the heady days of the antebellum cotton boom.

SCOTTY E. KIRKLAND
University of South Alabama

Harriet E. Amos, *Cotton City: Urban Development in Antebellum Mobile* (1985); Michael W. Fitzgerald, *Urban Emancipation: Popular Politics in Reconstruction Mobile, 1860–1890* (2002); Richard A. Pride, *The Political Use of Racial Narratives: School Desegregation in Mobile, Alabama, 1954–1997* (2002); Michael V. R. Thomason, ed., *Mobile: The New History of Alabama's First City* (2001).

Montgomery, Alabama

Located in the traditional plantation Black Belt, Montgomery sprawls away from a high red bluff overlooking an oxbow bend in the Alabama River, just below the fall line and the end of the Appalachians. It was both the "Cradle of the Confederacy" and the birthplace of the civil rights movement.

Hernando de Soto and his soldiers were the first white men to see the area near present-day Montgomery, stopping at the Indian village of Tawasa on 8 September 1540. For more than 200 years, Spain, France, and Great Britain struggled for empire there, but Americans finally gained the territory in 1814. Montgomery was founded in 1819 on the site of the Alibamo village of Ecanchata. The frontier village grew as a transportation center for cotton, and in 1846 the state capital was moved there from Tuscaloosa. Montgomery became

State capitol, Montgomery, Ala., constructed in 1851 (Ann Rayburn Paper Americana Collection, Archives and Special Collections, University of Mississippi Library, Oxford)

a political center and a stronghold of the growing southern states' rights movement. The Deep South states selected Montgomery as the site for their secession convention, and they organized the Confederate States of America in Alabama's Capitol, where Jefferson Davis was inaugurated president on 18 February 1861. The Confederate capital was moved to Richmond later in 1861. After Confederate defeat and Reconstruction, recovery occurred slowly, but Montgomery recovered faster than some Old South cities because of its continuing importance in government, agriculture, transportation, and some light industry.

In 1917, World War I gave Montgomery another economic boost with establishment of four military installations, the largest of which was Camp Sheridan, where Lieutenant F. Scott Fitzgerald courted debutante Zelda Sayre at the Montgomery Country Club. On the plantation site where de Soto had camped and where the Wright Brothers had run the nation's first civilian pilot-training school in 1910, the War Department established an aviation installation, Maxwell Field, now one of the four oldest U.S. Air Force bases in the country. The Air Corps Tactical School moved there in 1931 and developed the strategic bombardment doctrine later employed in World War II. After that war, Air University, the U.S. Air Force's professional educational center, was placed at Maxwell Air Force Base. In the late 1920s, Mayor William A. Gunter pioneered in building America's first planned municipal airport, which is now Maxwell Gunter Annex, the air force's data systems computer and cyberspace center.

In 1955, Montgomery again found itself in the vortex of change with the beginning of the Montgomery bus boycott. A painful 15-year period followed, including the 1961 Freedom Bus Riders' beatings, the Selma-to-Montgomery March of 1965, and eventually desegregation.

Cattle and soybeans long ago unseated King Cotton on Montgomery's old plantation lands. Now there are the $1.4 billion Hyundai automobile factory, some light industry, insurance, banking, and finance. However, Montgomery's economic success depends on government at all levels, involving both civilian and military positions. Nearly one out of five residents is connected, either directly or indirectly, with the military. There are three public and two denominational institutions of higher learning—traditionally black Alabama State University, Auburn Montgomery, Troy Montgomery, Methodist-affiliated Huntingdon College, and the Churches of Christ's Faulkner University—as well as the air force's colleges and schools of Air University. The 2008 Montgomery population numbered 202,000, and the tri-county River Region numbered 362,000.

Montgomery high society maintains its complex circles and hierarchies of elitism, based on an older South. These circles have been revitalized by new people bringing in talent, energy, and new wealth. The Alabama Shakespeare Festival Theater, along with the Montgomery Museum of Fine Arts, has made Montgomery a cultural center. Meanwhile, the city's historic preservation group, the Landmarks Foundation of Montgomery, guards "the Cradle's" visible past, restoring its historic buildings and attracting many tourists. Folk culture has its shrine at Hank Williams's grave.

Downtown Montgomery struggled for three decades. Suburbs and office parks marched relentlessly east along Interstate 85 toward Macon County. In recent years, downtown Montgomery has focused on redeveloping its riverfront. On Ecanchata, the High Red Bluff, the 1898 Union Station now operates as the Visitors' Center. Its restored Train Shed, one of three still standing in the United States, is a venue for public entertainment, as is the adjacent new Riverfront Amphitheater. The new Riverwalk Baseball Stadium is home to the professional Class AA Montgomery Biscuits. A luxurious new five-star hotel, spa, and convention center and other new hotels are luring back large business and professional conventions, mystic society balls, businessmen, and tourists. There is a scenic riverwalk trail, a paddle-wheel riverboat provides cruises and onboard entertainment, and there are chic shops and sidewalk cafes. Motorized trolleys shuttle tourists and office workers downtown. Old warehouses are being converted into loft apartments.

Whereas the attractions of many cities are scattered, most of Montgomery's are downtown and within walking distance. They include the magnificent 1849 Alabama State Capitol, the First White House of the Confederacy, the Dexter Avenue King Memorial Baptist Church and Parsonage, the Maya Lin–designed Civil Rights Memorial, the Rosa Parks Museum, the Hank Williams Museum, the Children's Museum, and the Alabama Cattlemens' Mooseum. Downriver two miles, Maxwell Air Force Base's officer education systems continue to expand at the U.S. Air Force's intellectual and doctrinal center, Air University.

JOHN HAWKINS NAPIER III
CAMERON FREEMAN NAPIER
Montgomery, Alabama

J. Wayne Flynt, *Montgomery: An Illustrated History* (1980); Wayne Greenhaw, *Montgomery: The Portrait of a City* (1993); Beth Taylor Muskat and Mary Ann Neeley, *The Way It Was, 1850–1930* (1985); Society of Pioneers of Montgomery, *A History of Montgomery in Pictures* (1958); Clanton Ware Williams, *The Early History of Montgomery* (1979).

Nashville, Tennessee

Situated on the Cumberland River at the confluence of three major interstates (I-24, I-40, and I-65), Nashville is a southern city whose form and politics reflect recent economic and social changes as well as historical cultural and political practices. The state capital of Tennessee and the country music capital of the world, Nashville is a center of publishing and of health care and home to new arrivals from across the United States and around the world.

Nashville was settled in 1779 and became the state capital in 1843. It was the first major Confederate city to fall in the Civil War, after which both the city's racial segregation and economy grew. By the 1890s, Nashville was experiencing sustained urbanization, which lasted through the 1930s, as white and black rural migrants were drawn to its employment opportunities. Nashville never fully industrialized, however, positioning itself instead as the cultural "Athens of the South," primarily because of the colleges and universities in the area. These include public and private universities such as Vanderbilt, Fisk, Belmont, Lipscomb, Meharry Medical College, and others. Despite some growth, it remained a regional city through the mid-20th century, with limited national visibility and political and social linkages.

In the 20th century's closing decades, Nashville began to change. Automotive manufacturing came to communities around Nashville, with Nissan, headquartered in nearby Franklin, opening in Smyrna in 1983 and Saturn in Spring Hill in 1990. In 1999, Dell established production, sales, and call centers in Middle Tennessee. Although the company has experienced recent layoffs and its desktop production shut down in January 2009, Dell at times has had more than 3,000 workers and remains a key employer in Middle Tennessee.

By the late 1990s, Nashville's service economy was also taking off, and surrounding counties were experiencing rapid population growth and a construction boom. According to 2007 estimates, Nashville's Davidson County has approximately 614,000 residents, with 1.5 million in the greater metropolitan area. Within Nashville, population growth has been especially strong

The Music Row area of Nashville, Tenn., with the famed Ryman Auditorium and other music venues in the foreground beneath towering hotels and office buildings (Photograph courtesy of David Wharton)

among the foreign-born, who constitute approximately 10 percent of Davidson County's population. Nashville has one of the largest Kurdish communities in the United States, a large population from Latin America, and refugees from various global hot spots. Nashville is, thus, a multicultural southern city at the same time as it continues to be shaped by a racial binary.

Located in Middle Tennessee between a Democratic West and a conservative Republican East, Nashville's political image vis-à-vis race relations and urban politics has been one of moderation and is often contrasted with that of Memphis. Nashville's history of political activism, however, should not be overlooked. During the civil rights movement, for example, a series of student-led sit-ins were held in Nashville to challenge segregated downtown lunch counters. These 1960 sit-ins, which garnered national attention and included many future civil rights leaders, sparked protests in other cities and led to Nashville's being the first large southern city to begin desegregation of such sites.

Along the same lines, although Nashville's urban development and renewal did not generate the large-scale unrest seen elsewhere in the United States, the building of the interstate system through the city produced protest and resistance across African American neighborhoods, which were disproportionately affected by interstate construction and urban renewal. Similarly, the 1962 establishment of Nashville's metropolitan government, while putting the city on the map for innovative urban governance, precipitated community organizing on both sides of the debate. In the 1960s and 1970s,

Nashville's busing plan, too, generated a range of activism, ultimately leading to white flight from Davidson County into surrounding communities like Franklin, the creation of private academies around Nashville, and a busing policy that lasted well into the late 1990s.

Central to these debates in Nashville has been the city's residential geography itself. With historically black neighborhoods and institutions like Fisk University in north Nashville, white working-class, and now immigrant, neighborhoods in southeastern Davidson County, predominantly white, middle-class neighborhoods in west Nashville, and gentrifying neighborhoods in east Nashville, Nashville has been and remains a racially and economically segregated city. The task that Nashville faces, thus, is balancing the needs and strengths of these different areas and constituencies. As Nashville comes to grips with the challenges and opportunities its newest arrivals and industries bring while addressing the ongoing demands and contributions its longtime residents and businesses make, the city's path will have to encompass all these facets of its place at the crossroads of region, economy, and history.

JAMIE WINDERS
Syracuse University

Donald Doyle, *Nashville since the 1920s* (1985); Louis Kyriakoudes, *The Social Origins of the Urban South: Race, Gender, and Migration in Nashville and Middle Tennessee, 1890–1930* (2003); Bobby Lovett, *The Civil Rights Movement in Tennessee: A Narrative History* (2005); Richard A. Pride and J. David Woodard, *The Burden of Busing: The Politics of Desegregation in Nashville,* *Tennessee* (1985); Jamie Winders, in *Latinos in the New South: Transformations of Place,* ed. Heather A. Smith and Owen J. Furuseth (2006), *Social and Cultural Geography* 7 (3) (2006).

Natchez, Mississippi

Today a small city of less than 20,000 inhabitants, Natchez is one of Mississippi's oldest cities, once its capital, and arguably its best-known urban place. Visitors come from around the country—and the world—to tour its famed antebellum mansions during its fall and spring pilgrimages and to visit its many historic sites. Although in many respects a typical small southern city of strip malls, modest industry, and quiet neighborhoods, Natchez stands out, in the estimation of the National Trust for Historic Preservation in 2003, as "one of America's most distinctive destinations." What gives Natchez its distinctiveness is its ongoing, and ever-evolving, connection to the past.

That human past began long ago (A.D. 800–1400) with indigenous mound-building cultures and their modern ancestors, the Nachee, or Natchez Indians. Like all the continent's native inhabitants, the Natchez people were dramatically affected by the arrival of European imperial powers, the French (1699–1763), the British (1763–79), and the Spanish (1779–98). Each left its mark on the Natchez people, who were nearly completely destroyed during these colonial-era struggles, and on the subsequent city named in their memory. Most notable, perhaps, was the Spanish-era plan that laid out the fledgling city's roads in a distinct grid pat-

Longwood, at Natchez, Miss., built in the 1850s (Photograph courtesy of Natchez Pilgrimage Garden Club)

tern on a magnificent bluff overlooking the Mississippi River, providing Natchez its distinct and enduring urban geography.

By the time that the young United States eventually took control of the Natchez district in 1798, technological innovation and market demand were poised to bring tremendous change to the city and its vast economic hinterland. The recent invention of the cotton gin and the development of a more resistant, hybrid cotton strain combined with the increasing demand for that crop in distant textile mills to lure thousands to both Mississippi and its territorial, and then state, capital. Although Natchez soon lost the seat of state government to Jackson as population

shifted north and east, it remained the region's cultural and economic capital.

Natchez's status as a vital urban center in antebellum America was the result, in no small measure, of its enduring prestige as the place for the area's wealthy planters to establish their homes. With vast holdings throughout the lower Mississippi Valley, this class formed a remarkably tight social group, which might have held competing ideas on politics and especially the question of secession but one that shared prosperity unmatched throughout the South. At the pinnacle of this exceptional planter class was Stephen Duncan, who, far from being a prototypical paternalistic slave master, was more of a modern master of capitalism. His nine plantations and more than 2,000 slaves, when combined with other investments, brought him unprecedented wealth.

Planters such as Duncan could only take advantage of the booming cotton market—and thereby enable their opulent lifestyle—by investing heavily in the labor necessary for the crop's intensive cultivation. Not coincidentally, a dynamic slave market sprang up in Natchez, at the "Forks of the Road," which was outpaced only by New Orleans as the busiest in the antebellum South. Until recently, very few remains of the "Forks of the Road" site could be identified, apart from the roads that marked its intersection. That has changed with the determined efforts of African American preservation activists and historians who have sought to expand the concept of historic preservation in this deeply historically conscious city.

That historical consciousness might have been first triggered by the antebellum planters themselves, who frequently created colossal estates based on hazy notions of Greek Revival as the style most appropriate for a cotton baron. But equally important was the active promotion of these landscapes as embodiments of a sentimental notion of the Old South. Beginning in the early 1930s and continuing today, the city's two garden clubs—the Natchez Garden Club and the Pilgrimage Garden Club—have been extremely influential in restoring the city's antebellum homes and in making these landscapes "mustsee" tourist destinations. With more than 40 plantation homes and antebellum mansions, 6 historic districts, the

Natchez National Historic Park, and 110 properties listed on the National Register of Historic Places, heritage tourism in Natchez has expanded well beyond the two relatively short pilgrimage seasons to become the year-round staple of the economy. Natchez—the city "Where the Old South Still Lives," as a 1930s-era tourist promotion campaign put it—is an intriguing site from which to view both the landscapes of the past and the changing interpretations of it.

STEVEN HOELSCHER
University of Texas at Austin

Jim Barnett and H. Clark Burkett, *Journal of Mississippi History* (Fall 2001); Martha Jane Brazy, *An American Planter: Stephen Duncan of Antebellum Natchez and New York* (2006); Jack E. Davis, *Race against Time: Culture and Separation in Natchez since 1930* (2001); Ronald L. F. Davis, *Good and Faithful Labor: From Slavery to Sharecropping in the Natchez District, 1860–1890* (1982); Steven Hoelscher, *Annals of the Association of American Geographers* (September 2003); Anthony E. Kaye, *Joining Places: Slave Neighborhoods in the Old South* (2007).

New Orleans, Louisiana

New Orleans is a multiracial, multiethnic, largely Catholic city located on the fringes of the Bible Belt. Founded by Jean-Baptiste Le Moyne, Sieur de Bienville, in 1718 as a French fortification near the mouth of the Mississippi River, the original city (now the French Quarter or Vieux Carré) was modeled after La Rochelle in France. The central town square in this area originally was called the place d'armes but was renamed Jackson Square in 1849. The mosquito-infested, disease-ridden site combined with French neglect to retard growth and make New Orleans an economic liability for much of the French reign. Ceded to Spain in 1762–63, the city prospered as its new administrators spurred colonization and permitted British and American settlers into the region. Spain ceded New Orleans and the rest of the Louisiana Territory back to France only to see Napoleon sell it to the United States in 1803. The Anglo-American occupation of New Orleans not only brought democratic forms of government to a majority nonwhite, Creole town, but found that a virtually new city, a distinctive mix of Spanish and French architecture, had arisen from the ashes of a devastating 1788 fire.

The antebellum era was a golden age for New Orleans. By 1860 it was the largest city in the South (population 168,675) and the fifth-largest city in the United States. The War of 1812 brought cooperation between Americans and Creoles against the British, and afterward the city became an even more important trade center. It remained a predominantly French-speaking city throughout the period, although a large influx of Americans, bolstered by German and Irish immigration, made an already cosmopolitan population more heterogeneous. The first modern Mardi Gras parade was in 1857, and the parade soon became a symbol of the New Orleans spirit. New Orleans was occupied by federal forces in 1862, but its white majority resisted Reconstruction by electing Democratic mayors who were determined not to share power with African Americans, whether free or freed. In the Gilded Age, the city

stagnated economically and saw its race relations devolve into violence (a politically driven massacre at the Mechanics' Institute in 1866 and the Robert Charles riot in 1900 framed the period). The city finally sought to restore order by imposing and defending segregation against Homer Plessy's famous 1896 challenge before the U.S. Supreme Court. It was this charged racial atmosphere that greeted yet another immigrant addition to New Orleans's polyglot population at the end of the 19th century. Thousands of Sicilians arrived and became the focal point of an international incident when 11 were lynched in the Orleans Parish Prison following the murder of police chief David Hennessy in 1891. Sanitation problems promoted recurrent outbreaks of cholera and, especially, yellow fever into the 20th century. Despite this troubled context, New Orleans demonstrated its cultural vitality by developing jazz as a popular art form and producing artists such as Louis Armstrong.

In the 20th century, New Orleans possessed one of the South's rare urban political machines, which dominated the city from 1904 until its defeat by De Lesseps S. "Chep" Morrison in 1946. Although New Orleans lagged behind its more dynamic Sunbelt competitors after World War II (it ranked no higher economically than fifth among cities of the Old South in 1980), oil and tourism bolstered an occasionally reinvigorated economy. A busy but declining port better represented long-term trends. The Voting Rights Act of 1965 transferred political power to a growing black population by the 1970s, which elected progressive white mayors such

The famous French Quarter in New Orleans, La. (the Vieux Carré), the city's oldest neighborhood
(Photograph courtesy of David Wharton)

as Moon Landrieu in 1970 and then Ernest N. "Dutch" Morial, the city's first black mayor, in 1978. Such political breakthroughs reflected new demographic realities. By 1980, eight out of every 10 metropolitan area blacks lived in what had become a majority-black city while seven out of 10 whites had taken up residence in the suburbs.

New Orleans has continued to fill a distinctive cultural niche, as it has throughout most of southern history. St. Louis Cathedral, completed in 1794, is the oldest one of its kind in the United States. The city was an early center of opera with its St. Charles Theater. The French Quarter, Bourbon Street, and Mardi Gras all evoke images of joyous entertainment and celebration. The Storyville district, a center for prostitution and gambling around the turn of the 20th century, reinforced a less

than savory reputation. Modern New Orleans has built on such foundations, opening Harrah's Casino and filling spring and summer months with a succession of festivals (most notably, its now justly famous Jazz and Heritage Festival and French Quarter Festival) that acknowledge its Creole culture and the unique excellence of its music and food.

The city's attempt to retain its "major league" status is finally reflected in its efforts to develop as a home to big-time professional sports. A national center for prize fighting and horse racing in the 19th century, New Orleans now hosts the annual Sugar Bowl and "Bayou" college football classics in the world-famous Louisiana Superdome and houses the professional New Orleans Saints football team in that same publicly constructed and supported structure. The New Orleans Hornets represent the National Basketball Association (NBA) in a companion public arena next door to the Superdome, and baseball is played by the Zephyrs, a Triple A (AAA) minor league franchise that is domiciled in yet another new, publicly supported stadium in suburban Jefferson Parish. Singular events, such as Super Bowls, college basketball Final Fours, and even a 1984 World's Fair (held to celebrate the centennial of the 1884 World's Cotton Exposition), have also been used to keep New Orleans before the world as a haven for tourists.

Hurricane Katrina, which devastated the city on 29 August 2005, however, raises questions about the city's future as a major urban center. Claiming roughly 1,200 lives in the metropolitan area, Katrina placed nearly 80 percent of the city under water (only 40 of its 180 square miles escaped inundation) for several weeks and left New Orleans a task of recovery. Three years after the catastrophe, its population remained reduced (to approximately 300,000, down from a pre-Katrina total of nearly 500,000) and racially polarized. If New Orleans is to rise yet again, it will be on what remains of its resilient, and still unique, local culture.

ARNOLD R. HIRSCH
University of New Orleans

Caryn Cosse Bell, *Revolution, Romanticism, and the Afro-Creole Protest Tradition in Louisiana, 1718–1868* (1998); Kent B. Germany, *New Orleans after the Promises: Poverty, Citizenship, and the Search for the Great Society* (2007); Jed Horne, *Breach of Faith: Hurricane Katrina and the Near Death of a Great American City* (2006); Ari Kelman, *A River and Its City: The Nature of Landscape in New Orleans* (2003).

Orlando, Florida

Orlando has undergone dramatic changes in recent years. It has sprawled tremendously, with its built environment taking up an ever-widening swath of central Florida territory in honeycomb fashion as ever-more residential communities intersperse with ever-more entertainment/tourist venues loosely connected by an ever-increasing number of highways and byways. The population has also thoroughly changed its makeup, from predominantly yet spatially separate black and white communities to a veritable mosaic of shades in between, as a result of the rapid increases in Latino residents over the last few decades (1,500 percent Latino growth in the metropolitan area from 1980 to 2007). There is very little left of what used to be the social and spatial characteristics of the city of Orlando of 1970—that is, before Disney arrived. The metropolitan area has exploded, socially and spatially, since then, with a 289 percent population increase between 1970 and 2007.

Although there is a traditional downtown to the City of Orlando, the metropolitan region is, in fact, a series of downtowns spread over four counties in central Florida—Lake, Orange, Osceola, and Seminole—and, because of the ever-growing need for affordable housing, the area is a main commuter hub for many other counties. This explosion of the metropolitan region took place rapidly on what was nearly a featureless economic plain. Before

1970, Orlando was essentially a small, traditional, southern agricultural and transportation crossroads town in the middle of citrus groves and cattle ranches. Some important changes were afoot even then, however, portending what was soon to come. During World War II, the military located bases to the east and south of downtown Orlando, and after the war this activity, particularly air base–related, was expanded and combined with that of NASA on what is now called the Space Coast of Florida. This military activity began the territorial stretch of Orlando away from downtown, as military/NASA activity, personnel, and families located near the bases.

The military/NASA presence also played a role in the next phase of Orlando's metropolitan transformation. When Walt Disney was considering the area for the location of his eastern theme park, it did not hurt that it had a strong military/patriotic atmosphere. After all, one of the major reasons that Disney was considering a new park was because he thought that he had the answer to the growing social ills of the nation's cities in the 1960s. Military discipline was just the sort of thing that would help ensure the success of his planned, residential, Experimental Prototype City of Tomorrow—Epcot. It also helped that the Cold War space race was on, with all that that meant for higher-tech experimentation à la Tomorrow Land. Disney's top secret arrangements to purchase some 42 square miles of territory in the area as a location for his eastern "World" concerned a location over 20 miles south and west

of the traditional city center, thereby ensuring the sociospatial stretch of the metropolitan region in quite the other direction.

The arrival of Disney World played the largest role in making Orlando what it is today. It served as a powerful agglomerative magnet for additional major tourist/entertainment attractions, such as Universal Studios and Sea World, as well as untold numbers of smaller "worlds," hotel/motels, and T-shirt–knick-knackity–gator-themed shops lining the edges of roads leading every which way and catering to every kind of tourist from everywhere imaginable. Orlando became a global tourist attraction, actively advertised as the "happiest place on earth," safe and sanitized, leading to the latest phase of metropolitan explosion in central Florida.

Orlando has become a major tourist town with an ever-increasing number of jobs in the mostly low-wage, few-benefit service sector filled with people ever on the verge of financial ruin. That they continually arrive seeking affordable homes in a metropolitan area of ever-increasing property values, at least in the major, diversely located areas of central attraction, has led directly to sprawl—not so much of suburban wealth but of verging poverty and, as mentioned, of increasing color, as Disney pioneered job recruitment in Latin America and the Caribbean and as its competitors followed suit.

Arguably, however, the Disney magic remains. It has been clear for some time that a metropolitan economy based on low-wage, mostly dead-end tourist and entertainment jobs eventually leads to more problems than not. Yet two things portend well for metropolitan Orlando's future. First, changes in the entertainment/tourist sector itself, where simulation and virtuality now abound, have led to an increasing need for high-skilled, professional workers in the field. Second, there remains in most people's minds a Disneyesque image of Orlando as clean, safe, and fun, rather than the reality of increasingly high crime rates. In the hyperglobalized, spatially footloose world of the service-information economy, this renders an attractive advantage to Orlando in relation to other cities, like Tampa to the west, which actually experienced an industrial phase with lasting built and social remainders. Orlando is a quintessential postindustrial city for a postindustrial age, precisely because it produced postindustrialism on a relatively empty economic plain. No wonder, as the latest statistics bear witness, that it now appears that the metropolitan economy is actually bimodal, with nearly as many jobs in the higher end of the information-technology/business services sector as in the tourist/entertainment sectors.

KEVIN ARCHER
University of South Florida

Kevin Archer, *Economic Geography* (1997), in *Growth, Technology, Planning, and Geographic Education in Central Florida: Images and Encounters*, ed. R. Oldakowski, L. Molina, and B. Purdum (1997); Douglas Frantz and Catherine Collins, *Celebration U.S.A.: Living in Disney's Brave New Town* (1999); Andrew Ross, *The Celebration Chronicles: Life, Liberty, and the Pursuit of Property Value in Disney's New Town* (1999).

Piedmont Urban Crescent

North Carolina's Piedmont Urban Crescent extends from Raleigh to Charlotte (Map 1). The curved band of cities and towns connects the state's three largest urban regions and includes two-thirds of the state's total population. The three urban regions are metropolitan Charlotte, the Triad (Winston-Salem, Greensboro, and High Point), and the Research Triangle (Raleigh, Durham, and Chapel Hill). The crescent-shaped pattern of urban development began with American Indian trading paths, followed by early colonial settlements. But the North Carolina Railroad, built in the 1850s to connect the small towns of Raleigh, Hillsborough, Greensboro, and Charlotte and to move cotton and tobacco, influenced development and defined the urbanizing region by the early 20th century. Today, the cities are connected by I-85, a section of I-40, and U.S. 70, and the state's largest airports are located at Raleigh/Durham, Greensboro/Winston-Salem/High Point, and Charlotte.

The Charlotte-Gastonia-Concord metropolitan statistical area (MSA) is the state's largest city, with a population of 1.5 million. The Raleigh-Cary MSA (which excludes Durham) is the second-largest city, with a population of 1.1 million, and the Greensboro–High Point MSA (excluding Winston-Salem) ranks third. In recent years, Charlotte and Raleigh have experienced the greatest increases in population and economic growth, but in 2009, Raleigh-Cary became the fastest-growing metropolitan area in the country, surpassing Austin, Tex.

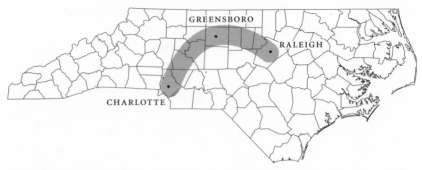

MAP 1. *Piedmont Urban Crescent*

Raleigh's population and economy are closely tied to the Research Triangle's high-technology and biotechnology industries and the state capital. Changes in housing and financial markets have had a greater impact on Charlotte employment and growth rates, both positive and negative, because of Charlotte's role as the nation's second-largest banking center. The Triad cities have been more closely connected to the state's traditional industries, including textiles, furniture, and tobacco. These cities have suffered in recent years as textile and furniture manufacturers have moved abroad and tobacco markets have shifted. But the loss of job opportunities for farmers and textile workers has been surpassed by gains in white-collar employment, particularly for workers in the "knowledge economy." Rob Christensen notes that by the end of the 20th century, "more people worked at computer giant IBM's facility in the Research Triangle Park than grew tobacco in North Carolina." Today, the Piedmont Urban Crescent has a higher proportion of high school and college graduates, a higher median income, and a higher rate of economic growth than other parts of the state. Trends indicate that cities in the Urban Piedmont Crescent are expected to continue growing, albeit at a slower rate. Within the three urban concentrations, cities and towns are growing together, a product of expansion and sprawl.

Residents of cities in the region enjoy the benefits of superior colleges and universities. The Research Triangle Park was founded in 1959 as a collaboration involving state government, private businesses, and three research universities—the University of North Carolina at Chapel Hill, North Carolina State University, and Duke University—but the Triangle area includes additional universities and colleges. The University of North Carolina at Greensboro, North Carolina A&T, Greensboro College, Elon University, Bennett College, and Wake Forest University are vital to the Triad. The University of North Carolina at Charlotte, Davidson College, and Queens College are a few schools located in the Charlotte area.

WANDA RUSHING
University of Memphis

Rob Christensen, *The Paradox of Tar Heel Politics: The Personalities, Elections, and Events That Shaped Modern North Carolina* (2008); Kristin Collins, "Raleigh-Cary Area Tops Nation in Growth," *Raleigh News & Observer* (19 March 2009); Allen W. Trelease, *The North Carolina Railroad, 1849–1871, and the Modernization of North Carolina* (1991).

Richmond, Virginia

Richmond began as a small trading port in colonial Virginia and evolved into the state capital, a major industrial city, the second capital of the Confederate States of America, and eventually a modern city in the New South. The settlement rose in the falls region of the James River, once a borderland between the Tidewater's Powhatan Confederation and the Monacan Indians to the west. Virginia's Indians shared the resources of the falls, mining the rock outcroppings for tools and harvesting the runs of migrating shad. An inland trade developed first with native groups and eventually with European and enslaved African settlers. The colonial settlement was chartered in 1742, supposedly named for Richmond upon Thames in England. As with many such settlements, growth occurred slowly due to the dominance of plantation-based tobacco agriculture.

The successful conclusion of the Revolutionary War brought new life to the city, which grew from 3,761 residents in 1790 to 9,735 in 1810, when it was the 12th-largest city in the United States. A rising industrial center and now state capital, the city saw an influx of mer-chants, government functionaries, enslaved workers, free blacks, and craftsmen, many working on Richmond's first building of major architectural significance—the Virginia State Capitol designed by Thomas Jefferson.

The Richmond economy faltered in the 1820s and 1830s, exacerbated by the national economic downturn of 1837. The 1840s saw renewed activity, and late antebellum industrial leaders included the Tredegar Iron Works, the Gallego Flour Mills, and a number of major factories in the suitably named town of Manchester directly across the James River from Richmond. Major canal projects and five railroads converged on the city by 1861. The domestic slave trade became one of the most dynamic sectors of the city's economy, as the Upper South exported many thousands of men, women, and children into the bourgeoning Cotton South.

After secession, the Confederate capital was moved from Montgomery, Ala., to Richmond, in May 1861, placing it only about 100 miles from the federal seat of government. Despite its close proximity to Union lines and arms, the city offered the Confederacy a substantial railroad network, a powerful arms-making industry, and a venerable political heritage that helped legitimate the new nation's claim as the true heirs of the American Revolution. It is estimated that the city tripled in population as workers, government functionaries, soldiers, and often their families converged on the new capital. The social disruption wrought by war led to dramatic scenes: a bread riot led by the city's women in 1863, an explosion in the Confederate cartridge-making shops, which killed many women workers, and high mortality among Union prisoners confined to the Belle Isle Prison in the James River. The Evacuation Fire (2–3 April 1865) brought widespread destruction to Richmond at war's end.

Virginia's Reconstruction lasted until 1870, when a new state constitution was adopted. Thirty-three African Americans served Jackson Ward on Richmond's city council from 1871 to 1902, when the new state constitution effectively disenfranchised most African Americans. The post–Civil War period also saw the development of Confederate memorial movements and the rise of the Lost Cause ideology, as seen in the Hollywood Memorial Association's monument to the Confederate dead at Hollywood Cemetery and in equestrian statues of Robert E. Lee (1890), James Ewell Brown ("Jeb") Stuart (1907), and Stonewall Jackson (1919), on Richmond's Monument Avenue.

The 1902 state constitution disenfranchised most blacks, and de facto separation in some public accommodations was quickly replaced by de jure segregation in almost all aspects of life. The segregation of streetcars inspired a boycott by African American residents in 1904, which failed after a protracted battle, and soon neighborhoods and all public facilities were strictly segregated. Exacerbating this trend was the determined march of white middle-class residents outward from the central city, aided by the introduction of electric streetcars in 1888, the first operational system in the United States. Developers soon recognized the potential of the lines and began building new suburbs such as Ginter Park, Lakeside, and Woodland Heights and also created popular amusement centers such as Forest Hill Park, which featured a midway, a carousel, and popular rides. Most black residents remained in segregated downtown communities such as Randolph and Jackson Ward.

Challenges faced Richmond's economy in the early 20th century. The grain milling business, long a mainstay, waned due to the opening of the American Midwest and competition from abroad. Richmond's port could not accommodate the larger draught of newer ships, and oceangoing trade shifted toward the Hampton Roads area. The largest metalworking firms did not participate in the production of steel on a large basis and faded in significance. One continued area of growth was the manufacturing of tobacco, especially cigarettes. The American Tobacco Company, Liggett and Myers, Larus Brothers, Lorillard, and latecomer Philip Morris all operated plants in the city.

Major changes in post–World War II Richmond resulted from the Bartholomew Plan in 1946, which advocated zoning enforcement, housing rehabilitation, and other measures to stem flight from the city center. Unfortunately, the city seemed to favor demolition rather than rehabilitation, knocking down many downtown neighborhoods that provided homes for low-income people. Likewise, new interstate and expressway projects ripped through black and white working-class communities. These actions stirred a nascent historic preservation movement, and activists such as Mary Wingfield Scott of the William Byrd Chapter of the Association for the Preservation of Virginia Antiquities made common cause with neighborhood associations.

Economic transformation also affected the city landscape in major ways. Richmond's famed Tobacco Row of major manufacturers stood empty by the late 1980s, the neighborhood now housing downtown apartments for young urban professionals. The move from manufacturing to a knowledge and service economy saw the dramatic growth of Virginia Commonwealth University (1969) and of the private University of Richmond. Other Richmond institutions of higher learning include Virginia Union University (1865), a historically black Baptist school, Union Theological Seminary in Virginia (1812), and the Presbyterian School of Christian Education (1914). Richmond also has a strong banking and financial services community, anchored by the Federal Reserve Bank of Richmond, founded as one of 12 regional centers by the Federal Reserve Act of 1913.

Postwar reform changed the face of city government. A modified city charter did away with the elected mayor and bicameral city council in favor of a city manager and nine-member council, with a relatively weak mayor elected from within the council. The policy of massive resistance to integration in the 1950s followed by state leaders and some local officials prevented meaningful integration of Richmond schools until the late 1960s. By that time, flight to the suburbs had largely resegregated the

schools. In 1960, the major downtown department stores, Miller and Rhoads and Thalhimers, and other Broad Street accommodations were integrated through sit-ins. Richmond annexed a large swath of Chesterfield County in 1970 after lengthy litigation, again greatly expanding the city and bringing in white suburbanites as well as their taxes and votes. More recently, Richmond's population has declined from a high of 249,621 in 1970 to less than 200,000 in 2009 as the city continues to lose population to the growing suburbs of the surrounding counties.

Richmond continues to struggle with the legacy of Jim Crow segregation and urban decline. The failure of major downtown projects such as Sixth Street Marketplace and the flight of retail to suburban malls, a high per-capita murder rate, a declining population, and constant battles over historical memory have plagued the city. The placing of a statue of tennis legend and author Arthur Ashe on Richmond's Monument Avenue drew a wide range of reactions. Some African Americans expressed dismay that a black hero would share space with Confederate traitors, while Confederate heritage groups protested the defiling of their sacred avenue. The majority, especially most of the many newcomers to the city, voiced embarrassment at the negative national press coverage and wondered why so many natives could not get over a war that occurred more than 130 years ago. Only time will tell if changes in governance, attempts at racial reconciliation, and recent public projects, such as the new convention center, the redevelopment of the city's riverfront, and a proposed performing arts center, can revitalize downtown and unify the city.

GREGG KIMBALL
Library of Virginia

Gregg D. Kimball, *American City, Southern Place: A Cultural History of Antebellum Richmond* (2000); John T. O'Brien, *From Bondage to Citizenship: The Richmond Black Community, 1865–1867* (1990); Robert A. Pratt, *The Color of Their Skin: Education and Race in Richmond, Virginia, 1954–1989* (1992); Christopher Silver, *Twentieth-Century Richmond: Planning, Politics, and Race* (1984); Emory M. Thomas, *The Confederate State of Richmond: A Biography of the Capital* (1971); Marie Tyler-McGraw, *At the Falls: Richmond, Virginia, and Its People* (1994); Marie Tyler-McGraw and Gregg D. Kimball, *In Bondage and Freedom: Antebellum Black Life in Richmond, Virginia* (1988).

St. Jude Children's Research Hospital

St. Jude Children's Research Hospital in Memphis, Tenn., was founded by the late entertainer Danny Thomas. The hospital, which opened in 1962, is the realization of a promise Thomas made as a struggling actor years before to St. Jude Thaddeus, the patron saint of hopeless causes. Thomas had vowed, "Show me my way in life, and I will build you a shrine."

In the 1950s, Thomas consulted friends about what form this vow might take, and he decided to build a children's hospital devoted to finding cures for catastrophic childhood diseases, in Memphis. The city was centrally located and had a large medical community and an established medical school at the University of Tennessee. Supporters came together across racial, ethnic, religious, regional, and national divisions to alleviate the suffering of children from leukemia, sickle cell anemia, and other diseases. Support for St. Jude also helped build powerful coalitions between the business and research economies and undermined local segregation practices. Construction of the St. Jude campus began in the 1950s and was completed in the 1960s at a time when Memphis hospitals and other public accommodations were racially segregated and city residents were ambivalent about the treatment of indigent patients coming to Memphis from the rural countryside. But St. Jude's commitment to medical treatment without regard for race, religion, income, or residence positively influenced practices in the city of Memphis and in other southern cities.

Thomas and his wife, Rose Marie, traveled all over the United States raising money to build the hospital. He then turned to his fellow Americans of Arabic-speaking heritage, and in 1957 they founded the American Lebanese Syrian Associated Charities (ALSAC) as a way to show thanks to the United States for providing freedom and opportunity to their parents. ALSAC became the fund-raising organization of St. Jude Children's Research Hospital and exists today solely to raise the funds necessary to operate and maintain the hospital. The daily operating cost of St. Jude is nearly $1.4 million dollars.

The mission of St. Jude is to find cures for children with cancer and other catastrophic diseases through research and treatment. St. Jude treats upward of 250 patients per day—on average, more than 5,400 children annually—most on an outpatient basis. The hospital maintains 78 beds for patients who require hospitalization. St. Jude is the only pediatric cancer research center where families never pay for treatment not covered by insurance. No child is ever denied treatment because of the family's inability to pay. Patients come from all 50 states and from around the world. Patients and a family member are provided airfare to and from Memphis and are housed free of charge.

The current research at St. Jude includes work in gene therapy, chemotherapy, radiation treatment, hereditary and blood diseases, pediatric AIDS, and the psychological effects of catastrophic illnesses. St. Jude has developed protocols that have helped push overall survival rates for childhood cancers from less than 20 percent when the hospital opened in 1962 to more than 70 percent. It has one of the largest pediatric sickle cell disease programs in the country, which built upon the early efforts of researcher and pathologist Lemuel Diggs at the University of Tennessee in Memphis. The scientific discoveries are shared freely with medical communities throughout the world, and teams of doctors come to St. Jude to study and learn protocols, which they can take back home. St. Jude is the only pediatric cancer center to be designated as a Comprehensive Cancer Center by the National Cancer Institute.

The location of St. Jude has helped create a vibrant neighborhood in a previously marginalized area of low-income housing projects and has become part of the historic urban fabric of Memphis. Recent construction more than doubled the size of the campus, creating jobs and providing a substantial employment and residential base in downtown Memphis and revitalizing the local urban infrastructure. St. Jude now has more than 20 buildings and 2.5 million square feet of research, clinical, and administrative space dedicated to finding cures and saving children.

The campus is close to downtown, one of the most diverse areas of Memphis, which includes governmental, medical, cultural, commercial, sports, and entertainment services and agencies. The hospital campus is a close neighbor of Uptown, a resurgent historic 100-block neighborhood that is a private-public revitalization by downtown development pioneers Henry Turley and Jack Belz, along with the city of Memphis.

St. Jude Children's Research Hospital was the first hospital in Memphis to be integrated. Dr. Diggs, one of the original members of the St. Jude Board of Governors, wrote an impassioned letter to ALSAC CEO Mike Tamer on the issue of integration. Dr. Diggs detailed how one of his lab technicians had just lost his son to leukemia and how in addition to that terrible loss, the family also had $20,000 in medical bills. "The petty matters of race pale into unimportance in the face of catastrophes of this type," Diggs wrote.

In addition to being the first integrated hospital in Memphis, St. Jude played a key role in the integration of Memphis area hotels. When the hotel that St. Jude had contracted with to house patients and their families refused to provide rooms for African American families, St. Jude director Dr. Donald Pinkel issued an ultimatum: If the hotel refused to accept African American children being treated at St. Jude, their services would not be used for any patient being treated at St. Jude.

PALLAS PIDGEON
Memphis, Tennessee

Wanda Rushing, *Memphis and the Paradox of Place: Globalization in the American South* (2009); Keith Wailoo, *Dying in the City of the Blues: Sickle Cell Anemia and the Politics of Race and Health* (2001).

Savannah, Georgia

Founded on a bluff overlooking the Savannah River, the city of Savannah developed with deliberation and planning and has had continuing cultural importance since its initial establishment by James Oglethorpe in 1733. Influenced by the neighborhood developments of late 17th-century London, Oglethorpe envisioned and planned a city of symmetrical squares, gardens, and broad avenues. Even as the military purposes of the Georgia colony gave way to the rice and cotton economy of the 18th century, Savannah retained the charm of its origins. British occupation during the Revolution and repeated difficulties with epidemics such as yellow fever, as well as major fires in the 1790s and again in the 1820s, limited the early growth of the city.

During the 19th century, Savannah joined other southern cities in an active boosterism to enlarge its trade and commercial activity. A modest success resulted, and Savannah emerged as an important cotton and timber port for the Georgia and South Carolina Piedmont. The building of the Central of Georgia Railway to Macon contributed to this role, and on the eve of the Civil War Savannah's population of 22,292 made it the largest city in Georgia and large by southern urban standards. During the war years, General William Sherman targeted Savannah as his destination for the March to the Sea, and the city fell to Union forces in December 1864. The war-related destruction was substantial. After the war, the influx of newly freed slaves influenced the postwar city developments. The city, however, quickly recovered its prewar fortunes, extended rail lines, and expanded cotton and timber exporting. By 1880, the city could still boast the gardenlike charm of its origin and a population of 30,709.

In the late 19th and early 20th centuries, Savannah joined with the state of Georgia in a gradual diversification of economic patterns. The slowness of that transformation dampened Savannah's population growth but indirectly contributed to the preservation of the original plan and many of its historic structures. Cotton diminished in importance after the 1890s, but timber, particularly pulpwood and turpentine products, remained strong. This pattern continued into and through the 20th century, and Savannah in the early 21st century remains one of the leading foreign trade ports between Baltimore and New Orleans, with a continuing importance of timber products and a high volume of containerized shipping. The city census of 2000 showed 131,510 residents, but the three-country metropolitan area had nearly 300,000 in population. As is typical of cities throughout the nation, the population of Savannah itself has declined slightly in recent decades, including in the early 21st century. The larger region has, however, increased in population.

As with other southern cities, the demographic portrait of Savannah is one in which there has long been a significant African American population. Before the Civil War, there was both a significant slave population and a population of freed African Americans. Typical of such populations, urban slaves and freedmen were craftsmen, laborers, seamstresses, household servants, and workers. In the 20th century, large African American populations continued to shape the city. In the 21st century, the city itself has a majority African American population (57 percent), while the metropolitan statistical area maintains a ratio of white to African American that is not dissimilar from 19th-century Savannah (61.2 percent white, 34.9 percent African American).

The commercial development of Savannah is not its most important contribution to the urbanization patterns of the South. Savannah's principal role is that of the preservation of its own history. That importance is heralded today by the fact that its top industry is tourism, which is centered on the city's own history. Since 1839, the city has been home to the Georgia Historical Society, a major center for the study of southern history. Telfair Academy of Arts and Sciences, founded in 1920, serves as a museum of decorative arts, costumes, paintings, and sculpture. As the leading population center of coastal Georgia, Savannah has a historical black college, Savannah State University, and what was once a junior college but is now a baccalaureate- and master's degree–granting institution, Armstrong Atlantic State University, both of which are part of the University System of Georgia. The Savannah School of Art and Design, founded in the late 1970s, has emerged as a major educational force for the city and the region and has taken a particularly important role in the preservation of Savannah's historic built environment, including its commercial and cultural properties as well as its residential neighborhoods. Even though there was significant loss of historic property in the years before World War II, the 75 years since have made Savannah (through the Historic Savannah Foundation, founded in 1955) a source of both preservation and pride for the entire region. The restoration of old Savannah is one of the most complete of all American cities. Through that restoration one can still witness the plans of James Oglethorpe, the restored architecture of William Jay, Charles Clusky, and W. G. Preston, and the distinctive use of wrought iron, gardens, and the Oglethorpe squares. Domestic historic preservation has been accompanied by work on public buildings and commercial districts, including the city hall, the Factor's Walk, the Cotton Exchange Building, the Telfair Academy, and a number of architecturally significant churches representing both historically white and historically African American congregations.

The restored charm of Savannah is what drives the 21st-century economy, as the city is host to numerous small conventions even as it is an inspiration for the restoration of other cities and a continuing symbol of the importance and beauty of urban planning in a southern setting. The commerce of the city, although still influenced by historic patterns of the river and the port as well as manufacturing, is dominated by the retail and accommodations industry. The largest number of employees is in those areas, a decided shift from the late 19th and early 20th centuries.

THOMAS F. ARMSTRONG
Louisiana State University at Alexandria

Federal Writers' Project, WPA, *Savannah* (1937); Richard Haunton, "Savannah in the 1850s" (Ph.D. diss., Emory University, 1968).

Spartanburg, South Carolina

Spartanburg County was founded in 1785, and the town of Spartanburg was incorporated in 1831. The population of the town is estimated at slightly below 40,000, and the county at approximately 254,000 (2000 Census). Spartanburg gets its name from the Spartan Rifles, a Revolutionary War unit that fought in the Battle of Cowpens (1781), located slightly northeast from present-day Spartanburg.

Prior to the arrival of Europeans during the 1700s, the Spartanburg area was the traditional home for the Piedmont Cherokees and Catawbas. With the coming of the Revolutionary and antebellum eras, the region also received groups of Scots-Irish, German, African American, and English settlers.

An archetypal New South town, Spartanburg grew and prospered with railroads and industry, particularly textiles. The roots of the local textile industries reach back to the 1810s. During the antebellum era, textiles gradually replaced ironworks as the most important manufacturing operations in the region. By the coming of the Civil War, Spartanburg was one of the leading textile manufacturing towns in the southern Piedmont.

After the Civil War and Reconstruction, Spartanburg continued its growth as a textile town. With the abundance of cheap labor, raw materials, and waterpower and railroads that connected Spartanburg to New York and New Orleans, the town was well positioned for an industrial future. Local capital formation was supplemented by northern textile industrialists, who steadily continued to increase their investments and presence in the region, continuing all the way to the post–World War II years. Many of the town's most notable textile families and industrialists, such as the Converses and Roger Milliken, originate from the Northeast.

From the 1870s to the 1970s, Spartanburg was an important center of the southern Piedmont's textile belt, which stretched from southern Virginia to northern Alabama. Spartanburg's biggest mills, including the Spartan, Pacolet, Inman, Converse, and Saxon Mills, dominated the town economically and culturally, warranting the nickname favored by local boosters: the "Lowell [Mass.] of the South."

With the arrival of World War II, Camp Croft, a large training base, opened in Spartanburg County. Between 65,000 and 75,000 soldiers moved through Camp Croft every year. The base closed soon after the war's end.

During the 1950s and 1960s, Spartanburg began to achieve even international fame as an important center of foreign manufacturing in the South. With the looming decline of the textile industries, the CEO of the Greater Spartanburg Chamber of Commerce, Richard Ellery (Dick) Tukey, began to systematically recruit foreign manufacturers to the town. By the 1970s, Spartanburg hosted a number of foreign factories, ranging from German chemical industry giant Hoechst to French tire company Michelin. The globalization of the Spartanburg economy culminated with the 1991 arrival of the German auto manufacturer BMW.

Spartanburg has made a largely successful transition to the post-textile era. The town continues to be an important industrial center in the Anderson-Greenville-Spartanburg metropolitan area, alongside the Interstate 85 "boom belt."

Spartanburg County is the home of Wofford and Converse Colleges, Spartanburg Methodist College, and several other institutions of higher learning. The town also has an active cultural life.

MARKO MAUNULA
Clayton State University

David Carlton, *Mill and Town in South Carolina, 1880–1920* (1982); Vernon Foster, *Spartanburg: Facts, Reminiscences, Folklore* (1998); Bryant Simon, *A Fabric of Defeat: The Politics of South Carolina Millhands, 1910–1948* (1998); Betsy Wakefield Teter, ed., *Textile Town: Spartanburg, South Carolina* (2002); Federal Writers' Project, WPA, *A History of Spartanburg County* (1940, 1977).

Tampa, Florida

The village of Tampa originated as a civilian settlement adjacent to Fort Brooke, an army post established in 1824 near Tampa Bay on Florida's Gulf Coast. Tampa grew slowly and prospered in the 1850s as a commercial center with a port that dominated the area's cattle trade to Cuba. The town's white population of some 500 people overwhelmingly supported the Confederacy.

After several decades of decline, Tampa's population expanded during the 1880s from 720 to 5,532 as a result of the arrival of the cigar industry. Spanish- and Cuban-born entrepreneurs who had fled war-torn Cuba were attracted to Tampa by its port and rail facilities and its proximity to Cuban sources of clear Havana tobacco, which was used to make luxury, hand-rolled cigars. The skilled labor force was composed of Cubans and Spaniards, who were later joined by Italian immigrants. The cigar industry started in the company town of Ybor City, which was annexed by Tampa in 1887. In the 1890s, the industry spread to West Tampa, a new community that was incorporated into Tampa in 1925.

By 1910, Tampa had become the

capital of domestically produced clear Havana cigars, and 45 percent of its residents were first- or second-generation immigrants. Separated from both the native Anglo and African American communities, the Latin population lived in Ybor City and West Tampa, where mutual aid societies and foreign-language newspapers thrived. The cigar city continued to prosper through the 1920s, when its population exceeded 100,000.

The Great Depression nearly destroyed Tampa's economy, which was based on a luxury product that never regained its former popularity. Moreover, the city's image was sullied by its reputation for political corruption, crime, and vigilante violence directed at immigrants, radicals, and African Americans.

After World War II, Tampa broadened its economic base by taking advantage of its location. Military expenditures at MacDill Field stimulated the economy, as did phosphate shipments that made Tampa one of the nation's busiest ports. With the city's population largely stagnant, Tampa turned to annexation of unincorporated suburbs to increase its population and tax base. Through annexation in the 1950s, the city more than doubled its population, reaching 275,000 in 1960. Additional incorporation of fast-growing suburban areas in the 1980s and 1990s helped push the city's population to over 300,000 in 2000, but many more people still lived in nearby unincorporated suburbs. Tampa, St. Petersburg, and Clearwater together form the hub of the third-largest metropolitan area in the southeastern United States.

In the decades after World War II, Tampa gradually overcame its reputation for rampant corruption and organized crime. Its new image as a progressive city was advanced by achieving desegregation peacefully in the 1960s. City politics became more inclusive with the election of several women to the city council in the 1970s and the election of women mayors in 1987 and 2003. The first African American to serve on the city council since 1887 was elected in 1983, and blacks (constituting some 25 percent of the city's population) have gradually increased their influence in local politics, symbolized by their success in getting the Confederate flag removed from the county seal in 1994.

In recent decades, Tampa leaders have successfully attracted new businesses, largely related to services, such as banks, insurance companies, and customer service centers. In addition to offering a variety of subsidies, Tampa provides businesses with an attractive location and a relatively low-wage workforce.

Tampa's emergence as a leading Sunbelt city was marked by the creation of new educational and cultural institutions. The University of South Florida was established by the state legislature in 1956, and a public community college began operating in 1968. The city also has a private college, the University of Tampa (1931). Cultural institutions established since the 1970s include an art museum, a performing arts center, and a museum of science and industry. Since opening in 1959, Busch Gardens has become one of Florida's busiest tourist attractions, and Tampa's recent efforts to expand tourism include construction of an aquarium and a convention center. The city has also gained prominence as the home of a professional football team, the Tampa Bay Buccaneers, and a professional hockey team, the Tampa Bay Lightning, both of which have won league championships.

Although originally a southern city with a Latin flavor, Tampa has been "Americanized" and homogenized to the point where today neither its population nor its culture is distinctively southern.

ROBERT P. INGALLS
University of South Florida

Robert P. Ingalls, *Urban Vigilantism in the New South: Tampa, 1882–1936* (1993); Robert Kerstein, *Politics and Growth in Twentieth-Century Tampa* (2001).

INDEX OF CONTRIBUTORS

INDEX

Page numbers in boldface refer to articles.

erism, 25, 126, 177; city planning, 32, 33; civic clubs, 35; and crunk, 41; education, 48, 49; expressways, 54, 55, 56, 57, 58, 165; farmers markets, 59; gentrification, 68; and globalization, 75; health conditions, 82; homelessness, 90; leadership, 97, 98, 99, 100; medical centers, 105; megachurches, 107; politics, 125; population change, 130, 131, 140; redevelopment, 139, 141, 142; segregation, 149, 150, 178; suburbanization, 156; and CNN, 197–98

Atlanta Braves, 152, 180
Atlanta Constitution, 24, 177
Atlanta Falcons, 152
Atlanta Life Insurance Company, 22
Atlanta Negro Voters League, 178
Atlanta Olympics (1996), **179–81**
Atlanta University, 22
Auburn Montgomery, 223
Augusta, Ga., 71, 72
Austin, Tex., 78, 79, 81, 107, 128, 165, **181–84**, 233
Automated teller machines, 19
Automobiles, 9, 46, 54–58, 74, 163, 164–65, 175

Badin, N.C., 72
Baltimore, Md., 70, 96, 124, 153; crime, 9; city planning, 32; suburban sprawl, 56, 79; gangs, 62, 66; redevelopment, 140, 142; waterfront development, 170–71
Baltimore Orioles, 170
Bank Holding Company Act of 1970, 18
Banking industry, **17–20**, 192
Bank Merger Act of 1960, 18
Bank of America, 20, 68, 162, 192
Barber, Bryan, 7, 43
Barbour, Haley, 123
Barksdale, Jim, 123
Bartholomew, Harland, 36, 55
Bates, Daisy, 209, 210
Baton Rouge, La., 52
Baudrillard, Jean, 198
Beale Street Caravan, 6

Bean v. Southwestern Waste Management, 50, 52
Behrman, Martin, 99, 126
Bell, William, 186
Belmont, N.C., 68
Belmont University, 224
Belz, Jack, 239
Bennett College, 234
Bentonville, Ark., 12
Bessemer, Ala., 72, 184, 186
Billy Graham Library, 192
Biloxi, Miss., 5, 6, 123, 129, 170, 213
Birmingham, Ala., 4, 14, 68, 72, 74, **184–86**, 221; knowledge economy, 11; banking, 17; boosterism, 25; city planning, 33; education, 48, 50; expressways, 54, 56, 57, 58; growth, 76; health conditions, 82; medical centers, 106; megachurches, 107; politics, 125, 127; segregation, 147; suburbanization, 156; transportation, 163, 164
Black middle class, **21–23**. *See also* African Americans
Blacksburg, Va., 78
Bland, Theodorick, 31
Blossom, Virgil T., 209
BMW, 243
Bolden v. Mobile, 221
Boosterism, 10, 12, **23–27**, 35–36, 124, 125, 126, 177, 240
Boston, Mass., 48, 49
Bradenton, Fla., 78
Bragg, Braxton, 194
Branson, Mo., 170
Brevard County, Fla., 29
Brewer, Craig, 7, 43, 216
Breyer, Stephen, 148
Briggs v. Elliott, 146
British American Tobacco, 72
Brookley Field, 221
Brooklyn Dodgers, 153
Brooks, Garth, 6
Brown, Minnijean, 209, 210
Brown and Williamson Tobacco Company, 72

Brownell, Blaine A., 125
Brownsville, Tex., 79
Brown v. Board of Education, 48, 146–47, 173, 203, 209
Bryan, John Neely, 201
Buchanan v. Warley, 33, 146
Buffalo, N.Y., 49
Bullard, Robert, 51, 52
Bureau of Public Roads, 54, 55
Burlington Northern–Santa Fe Railroad, 215
Busch, August A., Jr., 187
Busch Gardens, 12, **186–88**, 244
Bush, George H. W., 198
Bush, George W., 93, 158
Business improvement districts, 141
Business progressivism, 98–99
Bynum, N.C., 68
Byrnes, James F. "Jimmy," 190

Cain, Joe, 213
California, 45, 47, 64, 107, 130
Camp Croft, 243
Camp Sheridan, 222
Canada, 74
Canadian National Railroad, 215
Candler, Warren A., 48
Cape Canaveral, Fla., 13
Cape Town, South Africa, 59
Carnival, 213–14
Carolina Panthers, 192
Carter, Jimmy, 198
Carter Family, 6
Cash, Johnny, 216
Cash, W. J., 5
Celebration, Fla., 30–31, 34, 123
Center for Health, Environment, and Justice, 52
Centering Pregnancy program, 102
Centers for Disease Control and Prevention (CDC), 13, 101, 102, 103, 105
Central Arkansas, University of, 7
Central Florida, Disneyfication of, **28–31**
Central High School (Little Rock), 207, 209–10

Certified Local Government, 87
Chapel Hill, N.C., 11, 68, 75, 233, 234
Charleston, S.C., 4, 13, 70, 74, **188–91**; boosterism, 27; city planning, 32, 33, 34; gentrification, 68, 69; historic preservation in, 84, 189; leadership, 96, 97, 98, 99; and New Urbanism, 122; segregation, 150
Charleston Mercury, 189
Charlotte, N.C., 4, 153, 162, **191–93**, 233, 234; transportation, 9, 54, 164, 165; banking, 11, 17, 192; city planning, 32, 33; education, 48, 49; expressways, 57; farmers markets, 59; gentrification, 68; growth, 78, 142; megachurches, 107; population change, 131, 140; redevelopment, 141; suburbanization, 156
Charlotte Bobcats, 192
Charlottesville, Va., 32
Chattanooga, Tenn., 74, 171, **193–95**
Cherokee, 193
Chesterfield County, Va., 237
Chicago, Ill., 44, 48, 49, 64, 65, 130, 149, 196, 197
Chicopee, Ga., 32
China, 72
Christensen, Rob, 234
Church of God in Christ (COGIC), 12–13, **195–97**
Cigarettes, 72
Cisneros v. Corpus Christi ISD, 173
Citicorp, 19
City planning, **31–34**, 35–37
Civic clubs, 35
Civil Rights Act of 1964, 185
Civil rights movement, 4, 127, 147, 164, 221; in Atlanta, 8, 178; and churches, 13, 197; and expressway construction, 57; and suburbanization, 156; in Memphis, 217; in Nashville, 225
Civil War, 4, 24, 62, 189, 194, 220, 235–36, 240
Clark, George Rogers, 211
Clark, Kenneth B., 210
Clark, Septima, 190

U.S. Mayors' Climate Protection Agreement, 183
United States Steel, 185
Universal Studios, 28, 232
Urban, Keith, 6
Urban Development Action Grant, 10, 139
Urban redevelopment, 9, **138–42**, 169
Urban renewal, 33, 138, 139, 169, 190, 207, 217, 225
USDA, 59

Vance, Rupert, 5, 77
Vanderbilt Agrarians, 49
Vanderbilt University, 224
Verner, Elizabeth O'Neill, 189
Vicksburg, Miss., 57, 72
Victoria, Tex., 78
Vinson, B. Finley, 207
Violence, 9, 38–41, 42, 91, 150, 229; gang, 64; domestic, 103
Virginia, 71, 72, 73, 75; banks, 19; suburban sprawl, 56; health conditions, 81; homelessness, 90; immigration, 95; and New Urbanism, 121; segregation, 146, 147
Virginia Beach, Va., 78, 79
Virginia Commonwealth University, 237
Virginia Company, 70
Virginia Union University, 237
Virgin Islands, 47
Volkswagen, 195
Voting Rights Act of 1965, 33, 186, 229

Wachovia, 20, 68, 162, 192
Wake Forest University, 234
Wallace, George, 147
Walls, Carlotta, 209
Wal-Mart, 12
Walt Disney World, 28, 141
Warren County, N.C., 51
Washington, Booker T., 145, 177
Washington, D.C., 51, 55, 57, 58, 70, 79, 81, 90, 146, 148
Washington, George, 191, 199
Waterfront development, **169–72**

Wells Fargo, 20, 162, 192
West Palm Beach, Fla., 78, 79
West Tampa, Fla., 243, 244
West Virginia, 72, 80
White Citizens' Council, 147
White flight, 49, 93, 127, 134, 140, 156, **173–75**, 208, 217, 226
White League, 125
Whitelegg, Drew, 180
White supremacy, 143, 213
Whittier Mill, Ga., 68
Wiese, Andrew, 157
William Jefferson Clinton Presidential Library, 208
Williams, Hank, 6, 223
Williamsburg, Va., 31, 84, 187, **199–200**
Wilmington, Del., 128
Wilmington, N.C., 71, 171–72
Wilson, William Julius, 166–67
Winchester, James, 215
Winston-Salem, N.C., 33, 72, 233
Wisconsin, 47
With Heritage So Rich, 86
Wofford College, 243
Wolfe, Tom, 100
Women: and environmental justice, 51–52; homelessness, 90, 91; immigration, 94; and COGIC, 196
Women, Infants, and Children, 61, 104
Woodward, C. Vann., 4, 156
Wooldridge, Alexander, 182
Works Progress Administration, 126
World War I, 222
World War II, 178, 185, 190, 201, 218, 220, 222, 232, 243
Wright, Moses "Preacher," 197
Wright Brothers, 222

Ybor City, Fla., 243, 244
Yorktown, Va., 171

Zephyrs, 231
Zoning, 32–33, 36, 99